Putting Content Online: A Practical Guide for Libraries

CHANDOS
INFORMATION PROFESSIONAL SERIES

Series Editor: Ruth Rikowski
(email: Rikowskigr@aol.com)

Chandos' new series of books are aimed at the busy information professional. They have been specially commissioned to provide the reader with an authoritative view of current thinking. They are designed to provide easy-to-read and (most importantly) practical coverage of topics that are of interest to librarians and other information professionals. If you would like a full listing of current and forthcoming titles, please visit our web site **www.chandospublishing.com** or contact Hannah Grace-Williams on email info@chandospublishing.com or telephone number +44 (0) 1865 884447.

New authors: we are always pleased to receive ideas for new titles; if you would like to write a book for Chandos, please contact Dr Glyn Jones on email gjones@chandospublishing.com or telephone number +44 (0) 1865 884447.

Bulk orders: some organisations buy a number of copies of our books. If you are interested in doing this, we would be pleased to discuss a discount. Please contact Hannah Grace-Williams on email info@chandospublishing.com or telephone number +44 (0) 1865 884447.

Putting Content Online: A Practical Guide for Libraries

MARK JORDAN

Chandos Publishing

Oxford · England

Chandos Publishing (Oxford) Limited
Chandos House
5 & 6 Steadys Lane
Stanton Harcourt
Oxford OX29 5RL
UK
Tel: +44 (0) 1865 884447 Fax: +44 (0) 1865 884448
Email: info@chandospublishing.com
www.chandospublishing.com

First published in Great Britain in 2006

ISBN:
1 84334 176 X (paperback)
1 84334 177 8 (hardback)
978 1 84334 176 5 (paperback)
978 1 84334 177 2 (hardback)

© Mark Jordan, 2006

Typeset by Domex e-Data Pvt. Ltd.
Printed in the UK and USA.

Printed in the UK by 4edge Limited - www.4edge.co.uk

Contents

Acknowledgements

I would like to thank Lynn Copeland (University Librarian and Dean of Library Services) and Brian Owen (Associate University Librarian for Processing and Systems) at Simon Fraser University for granting me a study leave to complete this book during an extremely busy period at the Library, and for getting me involved in lots of interesting projects. I would also like to thank my colleagues in Library Systems for taking on extra work caused by my absence.

David Kisly (Target Library and Information Services) and Gwen Bird (Simon Fraser University) read drafts of each chapter as I completed them and offered frank and insightful comments. Nina Saklikar (Simon Fraser University) read the entire manuscript and supplied a number of characteristically sensible suggestions. Despite these three people's contributions I claim credit for all remaining errors and omissions.

I would also like to thank my students in 'Developing Digital Collections' at the University of British Columbia's School of Library, Archival and Information Studies for challenging me to explain many of the topics covered in the following pages. Acknowledgements are due also to the following people for sharing with me their expertise, advice and encouragement: Ian Song, Elaine Fairey, Peter Van Garderen, Joe Tennis and Kim Lawson.

Lastly, thanks to Michele for her support and for tolerating my obsessive working habits.

List of figures

List of tables

About the author

Mark Jordan is Head of Library Systems at Simon Fraser University in Burnaby, British Columbia, Canada. His areas of expertise include digitisation, data integration and managing the development of open-source library software. He has published articles on electronic journal management, systems librarianship, metadata and open-source development tools and has presented at numerous Canadian library and information technology conferences.

Mark is also an Adjunct faculty member at the University of British Columbia's School of Library, Archival and Information Studies, and is the maintainer of Digitizationblog *(http://digitizationblog.interoperating .info)*.

The author may be contacted by email: mjordan@sfu.ca

Introduction

In the autumn of 2005, a series of announcements drew attention away from the media coverage Google Print had been receiving for almost a year. In the first announcement, the European Commission unveiled plans to initiate a 'concerted drive' to encourage member nations to digitise their cultural heritage and make it freely available to the world.[1] In the second, made a few days later, The Open Content Alliance, including partners such as Yahoo!, Adobe Systems, O'Reilly Media, Hewlett-Packard, the UK National Archives, the European Archive (presumably referring to the countries participating in the European Commission's plans, later renamed the European Library[2]), the Internet Archive, the University of California and the University of Toronto, announced that it would build 'a permanent archive of multilingual digitized text and multimedia content'.[3] In late October, Microsoft joined the Open Content Alliance. In mid-November, the Canadian Association of Research Libraries announced the Open Canada digitisation initiative.[4] Less than a week later, the Library of Congress announced that Google had contributed $3 million to help create the World Digital Library.[5]

These announcements occurred within a span of roughly two months. Together they represent an unprecedented level of enthusiasm for the digitisation and dissemination of printed material held by libraries. Google Book Search (as it was later renamed), the Open Content Alliance and earlier massive digitisation programmes such as the Million Book Project[6] will no doubt make substantial parts of national and major research library collections available online. However, the amount of resources required to deliver on these promises will be immense. It is not surprising that these announcements all describe large-scale co-operative efforts made up of many libraries and corporate partners.

Small and medium-size libraries also have the ability, if not always the means, to put content online without participating in these large-scale, mass digitisation projects. Many have developed at least one digital collection, typically of material that is unique, of local significance or of particular interest to the library's users. Some libraries have even succeeded in incorporating digital collection building into their mainstream services and are able to justify those ongoing activities in terms of their institutional mission and goals. Despite the breadth and depth of the content that research and national libraries have to offer, the material that smaller institutions decide to digitise contributes diversity and richness to the sometimes unbelievable array of what can be found on the web.

This book's intended audiences

Putting Content Online: A Practical Guide for Libraries is aimed at library staff who are contemplating developing a collection of digital documents, and at library staff who are already doing this type of work but who require guidance on dealing with specific aspects of their projects. Readers from archives and museums will also find this book useful but most of it, particularly the sections on metadata and search and display issues, is written from the perspective of libraries, and a large proportion of the examples used throughout the book are from libraries. However, chapters such as those on intellectual property, project management and operations, workflow, and preservation should be applicable to the production and delivery of digital content in a wide variety of organisations.

Putting Content Online is also suitable for use as a text in library and information studies courses on digitisation and digital libraries. The book is not intended to be academic: information science, software engineering and other disciplines are drawn on where relevant but I do not survey these fields exhaustively or claim to add to their bodies of knowledge. Nonetheless, instructors looking for a practice-orientated text may find this one useful; in fact, it is based to a certain extent on a course I teach at the University of British Columbia's School of Library, Archival and Information Studies.

In general, this book is intended to help libraries make informed decisions about creating online content and organising it into collections. Some readers may work at libraries that are considering creating their first collection of digital content. Other readers will already have experience in this area, and this book may provide them with new ways of approaching familiar problems. I hope this book will provide practical guidance in the planning, execution and delivery of collections in both of these cases.

The big(ger) picture

This book differs from others on the same topic by providing a broad view of all of the activities involved in creating digital content of all types and presenting it online to users. The other major English books on this topic – Stuart D. Lee's *Digital Imaging: A Practical Handbook*,[7] Anne R. Kenney and Oya Y. Rieger's *Moving Theory into Practice: Digital*,[8] and Maxine K. Sitts' *Handbook for Digital Projects: A Management Tool for Preservation and Access*[9] – focus primarily on the creation of digital images, whether they are of photos or of book pages. This focus is to be expected: still images are by far the most common type of digital resource that libraries produce, and a large proportion of textual resources put online by libraries are digitised and presented as a series of page images. Alternative ways of presenting text are becoming increasingly common, as are other types of resources. Therefore, *Putting Content Online* deals not only with images but equally with textual documents, sound and video, and data sets. It also discusses aspects of digital collection building in detail that have not received extensive coverage in the works listed above, such as content management systems, workflow modelling and metadata. Lee's book comes closest to this one in terms of its combination of scope and focus, but this book builds on Lee's and expands coverage of these topics considerably.

A number of organisations maintain best-practice guides intended to assist in the planning of digital collections. The US National Information Standards Organization's (NISO) *Framework of Guidance for Building Good Digital Collections*,[10] the National Initiative for a Networked Cultural Heritage's *Guide to Good Practice in the Digital Representation and Management of Cultural Heritage Materials*[11] and Arts and Humanities Data Service's *Creating and Documenting Electronic Texts: A Guide to Good Practice*[12] include information on creating and presenting content other than digital images, but they do not offer the amount of detail that the books cited above do. *Putting Content Online* strives to offer the advantages both of earlier books and of the best-practice guides. Its distinguishing features are:

- It identifies four types of digital resources – still images, textual documents, moving image and audio, and raw data files – and presents information about them in a balanced way, without giving 'digital imaging' priority. These types (plus a fifth type, complex objects, which contain more than one of the other four types) are intended to provide a broad vocabulary for generalising about digital resources and collections, and, as stated above, to acknowledge that digital collections developed by libraries are becoming increasingly diverse.

- It is intended to be practical. Although other books on this topic do describe some of the practical, applied aspects of digitisation projects, this book focuses on them and explains complex processes, warns of potential challenges and provides (what is hoped to be) useful advice for solving realistic problems.

- It is intended to be comprehensive: currently, there are very few inclusive treatments of the range of techniques and strategies for digitising and organising all types of material. Although *Putting Content Online* does not claim to describe every possible way of developing a digital collection, its goal is to cover every significant aspect of doing so in at least some detail.

- It intentionally avoids the technical aspects of digital imaging in detail because this information is available from a wide variety of sources (which will be referred to in Chapters 5 and 9). Also, this book does not provide basic introductions to XML (extensible mark-up language), the protocols typically used on the World Wide Web, or relational databases as this information is unnecessary in a book on digital library content and collections.

- In its final chapter, this book provides a fully developed case study that illustrates the topics covered up to that point.

Overall, the intent of *Putting Content Online* is to present the details of how libraries can create content and deliver it to users using standardised techniques and tools, and to describe how the various aspects of this activity relate to each other. In other words, it attempts not only to present a useful level of detail but also to put that detail within a larger context. Like library cataloguing, creating digital collections and presenting them effectively to users requires a sense of both minute detail and the big picture. Frequent cross-references to specific chapters attempt to connect some of the dots.

A word on terminology

Because this book discusses a number of technical topics, it contains a considerable amount of jargon. Every attempt has been made to introduce and explain this technical language clearly. Peppered throughout the book are terms that will be familiar to many readers but that should be defined here in order to avoid confusion later. Even the title *Putting Content Online* contains two of these words.

Content: The 'full text' of whatever you are putting on the Internet, whether it is text, images, sound, video or raw numerical data. This book does not cover the creation of general websites containing information about a library and its services, online services such as virtual reference and online bibliography management, or databases that contain only metadata describing documents. Particularly in Chapter 2, 'content' is also used to refer to the source material (whether printed books, video tape or born-digital images) that is under consideration for development into an online collection.

Collection: In the next section, I will be discussing the nature of digital collections in detail, but put simply, 'collection' is used in this book to mean any discrete group of digital resources or documents that are organised systematically. Collections usually contain not only resources but also metadata describing those resources and aiding in their use.

Online: 'Online' is generally synonymous with 'on the World Wide Web,' but as most readers will recognise, the World Wide Web is much broader than that part of the Internet that we experience through a web browser like Microsoft Internet Explorer or Mozzila Firefox. Although this book does not deal specifically with creation and delivery of content to mobile phones, personal digital assistants, wireless video game consoles and similar devices, it recognises that they can be used to access and deliver certain types of content as well as web browsers on a personal computer, as demonstrated by the University of Virginia Library Etext Center's collection of e-books.[13]

Resource, document, item, object: These terms are all used to mean the same thing: a discrete document in a collection, such as a single photograph, book, sound recording or data set. Although a document can comprise multiple digital files, 'object' is used in some places to mean a single digital file but that usage should be clear from the context.

Digitisation project, conversion project: This book covers the creation of digital content and collections based on both analog resources (such as printed photographs and books, audio and video tapes) and born-digital resources (such as digital photos and video, and documents that were created using word processors). 'Digitisation' is used to describe the processes required to make analog content digital, and 'conversion' is used to describe the processes involved in migrating born-digital content from its original format to other formats. This distinction varies from the common use of the phrase 'digital conversion project', which generally means the same as digitisation, but the distinction is made here because in a number of ways the two processes involve different tasks and require different resources.

Standard: As a noun, 'standard' is used loosely to describe a documented specification of any type that is commonly deployed, not necessarily a specification ratified by the International Standards Organization or any other recognised body such as the World Wide Web Consortium. As an adjective, 'standard' is used to mean 'commonly deployed'.

More on digital collections

Even though 'collection' does not appear in this book's title, the idea of a group of documents organised according to specific principles permeates nearly every chapter. Brick and mortar libraries, and virtual libraries that provide access to digital content they license from commercial vendors, view the information they organise as their 'collections', and the same attributes that define those collections apply to information generated by libraries using the set of techniques and processes described in the following pages.

Occasionally, a library will digitise a single book, image, sound recording or some other type of document, upload it up on a website, create a standard bibliographic description to put in the catalogue, and link to the digital document from that record (or, if the catalogue already contained a description of the original version, simply link to the digital version from that description). However, it is much more common for a library to assemble a *group* of digital documents into a collection and to organise the collection such that the aggregation of documents takes on an identity of its own. Because libraries for the most part tend to put documents online in groups and not in isolation, it will be useful to refer to digital 'collections' when discussing how we select documents for digitisation, how we describe them, how we find and display them, and how we create or prepare them for putting up on the Web.

A more thorough definition than the one supplied in the previous section, and one that is relevant to the scope and subject of this book, is provided in the NISO *A Framework of Guidance for Building Good Digital Collections*:

> A digital collection consists of digital objects that are selected and organized to facilitate their access and use. Good digital collections include metadata used to describe and manage them. Metadata

may be provided for the collection as a whole, for individual items within the collection, or both. In addition to objects and metadata, a digital collection will include at least one interface that gives access to it. This interface often includes a way to search for objects, a way to browse through meaningful categories of objects, and methods for retrieving, rendering, and using objects. As such, the whole is greater than the sum of the parts. Digital collections are generally created by organizations or groups of cooperating organisations, often as part of a project.

The *Framework* identifies seven principles that apply to 'good' digital collections (good meaning generally appropriate for the user groups the collection is aimed at). Briefly summarized, those principles are:

- a digital collection must have an explicit collection development policy;
- a digital collection should be described so users can discover its scope, restrictions on access and other characteristics easily;
- a digital collection should be sustainable over time;
- a digital collection should be usable by as wide a variety of people as possible;
- a digital collection should respect intellectual property rights;
- a digital collection has mechanisms to record information demonstrating how the collection is being used;
- a digital collection fits into larger initiatives.

These principles are essentially a reworking of the attributes of any type of collection managed by a library, regardless of what is in the collection or what form it takes. They serve equally well as defining characteristics and as evaluative criteria. In Chapter 8, Project Management, I will revisit the NISO principles and discuss them as the second of these two purposes.

Libraries are not the only cultural institution creating online content and collections – archives, museums and art galleries also do it. A distinguishing feature of digital collections created by libraries is that in general libraries avoid organising digital (and print) collections in ways that impose specific interpretations on the resources in the collection. As Clifford Lynch puts it, for libraries: 'The focus is on creating large amounts of digital content and providing some fairly simple access tools, rather than upon sophisticated systems for ongoing use or apparatus providing interpretation.'[14] It is common for libraries to create supporting material that assists in interpretation, such as teaching and learning guides for K-12 audiences, but apart from biases introduced by standard methods of organisation and description, collections created by libraries do not generally impose the same types of interpretive apparatus as do the 'virtual exhibits' frequently created by archives, museums and art galleries, which place content into a narrative, chronological, or thematic structure. Examples of collections and virtual exhibits have been created by all four types of institutions, but as a whole, libraries create more collections than virtual exhibits.

Examples of collections that libraries are putting online include:

- *Important or unique print collections*: Libraries of various types and sizes hold important or unique print collections and make digital versions of these available online. Often the online collections are subsets of the print collections.

- *Local historical documents*: Collections of local photographs, genealogical information, newspapers and government documents are a subtype of unique print collections. Libraries that collect local material are in an ideal position to develop digital collections, particularly if the material is old enough to be in the public domain and if it is unique.

- *Personal archives of writers, politicians and other public figures*: Another subtype of the first (and often an instance of the second), many libraries engage in collecting personal papers and manuscript collections.

- *Content associated with presentations, panel discussions and other events taking place at local venues*: Public libraries in particular are taking a role in making this type of material available. Libraries are often involved in efforts to increase access to Internet connectivity in their jurisdictions, and providing resources necessary to organise and maintain collections of locally produced content is a common extension of those broader activities.

- *'Archival' versions of electronic journals, electronic books and other material originally licensed from vendors*: Many commercial content providers are now including clauses in their product licences granting libraries perpetual access to online content that they stop subscribing to. Often this perpetual access is achieved by handing the library a set of CD-ROMs containing the content, leaving the library responsible for making it available to end users.

- *Material produced by local researchers*: Institutional repositories (IRs) are collections of articles, books and book chapters, conference presentations, technical reports, and other material of scholarly value that is produced by researchers at a university, technical institute or similar institution. Libraries typically host these collections and provide services such as metadata creation and quality control, technical and preservation support, advice on publishers' open access policies, and advocacy.

- *Electronic theses and dissertations (ETDs)*: Many universities are providing online access to the full text of theses and dissertations. ETDs are sometimes deposited in institutional repositories or take the form of separate collections.

- *Scholarly publishing by libraries*: In addition to institutional repositories, some libraries actively participate in the scholarly publication process by hosting electronic journals and collections of research documents on behalf of local faculty or departments. This type of collection is much like an institutional repository in that the library's role is to support faculty in various ways, but the same services can be offered, in particular revolving around metadata.

- *Textual documents, images, sounds, and other material intended to support teaching and learning*: Academic libraries frequently make collections of images and sound files, often licensed from commercial vendors, available to support teaching and other activities. In countries where copyright law permits, journal articles and other course readings are scanned and made available to students for the duration of the course; in countries where this activity is considered illegal, libraries often assist in the distribution of course material that is created locally, such as notes produced by the instructor or course lectures recorded on a notebook computer. Students onsite and at a distance benefit from the increased access provided by libraries that provide these types of service.

Some of these examples are more relevant to specific types of libraries – collections of local historical documents are commonly developed by public libraries, while collections of theses and dissertations are more likely to be developed by university libraries. They are listed in order to indicate the diversity of material that libraries are developing into online collections. I will revisit some of these examples throughout the book to illustrate the NISO principles and other aspects of digital collection planning and production.

Libraries as publishers

Libraries that create and organise content and distribute it online are acting as publishers. They do not fulfil all the functions that publishers traditionally perform, but they do add value of various kinds to the content. First, collections can take on an identity of their own that is more than the aggregate of the items in the collection. Second, descriptive metadata included in the collection increases the content's value by making it easier to find and to evaluate than if it were isolated. Third, items are presented in ways that allow them to be used effectively by their intended audiences.

These functions will become more important as technology and users evolve. Library services in general need to adapt to users' activities, and if libraries produce content in addition to providing services, the nature and delivery of that content will need to evolve constantly. For instance, audio files that were intended to be played on a personal computer can now be playable on iPods. Subject keywords can now be supplemented with user-contributed 'tags'. Even slow changes such as the gradual increase in the size of computer monitors (and decrease in their cost) over the last few years have influenced the optimal dimensions of images created and delivered as part of library collections, as I discuss in Chapter 6. The added value of creating an identity for locally created collections of all types will become particularly important as time goes on, because as the Web grows in size, local identities can easily become lost and obscured.

Some current trends

No introduction would be complete without looking past the book it introduces. This list of trends is brief, but its intent is to suggest some of the directions in which the creation, dissemination, and management of digital content and collections are moving.

Mass digitisation

The opening paragraph in this chapter listed a number of 'massive' or 'mass' digitisation efforts. In the past, libraries have led large-scale digitisation initiatives (such as Carnegie Mellon University Libraries' involvement in the Million Book Project), but Google's desire to leverage its search engine technology has motivated Yahoo!, Microsoft, Adobe and a number of other commercial interests to become prominent partners in putting content held in cultural institutions online, in most cases accessible to everyone free of charge.

The technology involved in digitisation is also evolving to keep up with the enthusiasm: several companies have developed fully automated hardware that can digitise bound books at rates of up to 3000 pages per hour,[15] many times faster than conventional scanners, which require a human operator to turn the book pages.

Emphasis on standards and software for digital libraries

Libraries have always relied on standards for enabling data interchange and for codifying rules of description. The mainstays of library standardisation, AACR2 and MARC, are heavily biased toward printed documents, which is not surprising given that they matured before digital documents were commonplace. The latest generation of standards specifically addresses issues with describing, identifying and preserving digital documents, and the role that modern network technologies play in the discovery and use of digital documents. I will cover these new standards and specifications in detail in Chapter 4, but at this point I will list Dublin Core, METS, MODS, OAI-PMH and PREMIS as such standards. Even the latest version of AACR2 has a new name that reflects the change in environment: Resource Description and Access (RDA).

Software used in digital libraries is also undergoing a major period of growth, in large part fuelled by the existence and development of standards mentioned above. Proprietary and open-source digital library platforms such as CONTENTdm, Fedora, Greenstone, DSpace and ePrints are constantly being improved, and traditional integrated library system vendors are marketing products that focus on the new generation of standards and on locally developed collections, in some cases basing their products on open-source applications. Tools used in the creation of content, such as library-orientated modules for common programming languages, preservation-orientated utilities such as JHOVE, and robust metadata management systems are also available. However, effective and widely available applications to perform rights and digital assets management are noticeably lacking.

Emergence of a library digitisation community

Specialised blogs on topics directly relevant to digital library content and collection development are starting to appear (and are listed in the next section), and a wiki devoted to digitisation has also been launched. A number of relevant journals exist (also listed below), but there is an opportunity in this area for the establishment of refereed and informal journals focusing specifically on digital content and collection building in libraries and other cultural institutions.

Open access

A dramatic shift in journal publishers' policies toward open access is resulting in the widespread archiving of content on researchers' personal websites and in institutional and disciplinary archives. The SHERPA Project maintains a current directory[16] of open-access journal publishers that at the time of writing indicated that 75% of the 127 publishers in their list supported some sort of archiving activity. National-level policies such as those of the National Institutes of Health[17] in the US and the Wellcome Trust[18] in the UK are likely to increase the amount of freely accessible scholarly research. Libraries are embracing the opportunity to assist in the dissemination of this content through the creation of institutional repositories and other venues for disseminating open-access content.

Recombinant digital content

To borrow from Ranganathan's first law of library science, 'Digital resources are for use'. They are also for reuse. The NISO *Framework* states that 'Objects, metadata, and collections must now be viewed not only within the context of the projects that created them but as building blocks that others can reuse, repackage, and build services upon.' Some digital library content management systems allow users to save resources and to use them in contexts that differ from the ones they are initially presented in. To a certain extent, systems such as CONTENTdm and MDID allow for personalisation and repackaging of resources into different forms such as PowerPoint.

The use of hardware devices such as Apple's iPod and other media players encourages the legal reuse of music, photos and, increasingly, video. This trend will have an impact on the ways libraries provide access to digital collections, particularly if these collections are made available under new licensing schemes such the Creative Commons[19] licences and the BBC's Creative Archive[20] licence. Libraries should take advantage of this trend. As Paul Miller says in his article 'Web 2.0: building the new library,' (Web 2.0 is the current term used to describe the rapid changes in Web culture and technology): 'We are seeing the emergence of Web-based services that pull data from a wide range of back-end systems to deliver value to users, when, where and in the form that they require it ... Web 2.0 is about remix.'[21]

Long-term curation and preservation

Over the last few years, digital preservation has matured from a set of problem statements into an active and practical field of research. Standards and tools are being developed and implemented, and large-scale national initiatives such as the Digital Curation Centre (DDC)[22] in the UK and the National Digital Information Infrastructure and Preservation Program (NDIIPP)[23] in the US are focusing attention on practical, feasible preservation strategies. I will cover digital preservation in Chapter 11.

Keeping current

Many of the topics covered in this book are evolving rapidly. Readers are encouraged to track collections, initiatives, tools, standards and events relevant to digital collection building and its constituent activities by using resources such as those listed here. This list is not comprehensive, and new current awareness tools continue to appear. All of the journals and newsletters mentioned here provide e-mail announcements of new issues.

Journals

- *Ariadne Magazine (http://www.ariadne.ac.uk/)* is a quarterly electronic journal whose goal is 'to report on information service developments and information networking issues worldwide, keeping the busy practitioner abreast of current digital library initiatives'. It has a UK bias but also includes articles and columns with international coverage.

- *D-Lib Magazine (http://www.dlib.org/)* focuses 'on digital library research and development, including but not limited to new technologies, applications, and contextual social and economic issues.' *D-Lib* is an electronic journal published 11 times a year.

- *Journal of Digital Information (http://jodi.tamu.edu/)* is a peer-reviewed online journal covering topics such as digital libraries, information discovery and usability of digital information. *JoDi* is published quarterly.

- *International Journal on Digital Libraries (http://www.dljournal.org/)* is a refereed journal emphasising technical issues in digital information production, management and use. Quarterly.

Newsletters

- *Current Cites (http://lists.webjunction.org/currentcites/)* is a monthly review that 'monitors information technology literature in both print and digital forms'. The editorial team monitors over 50 publications (listed on the website) and also solicits books and other material for review.

- *RLG DigiNews (http://www.rlg.org/preserv/diginews/)* is a 'bimonthly electronic newsletter that focuses on digitization and digital preservation'. In addition to articles and several regular columns, *RLG DigiNews* provides events and announcements sections.

Blogs, wikis and public e-mail lists

- *DAVA: Digital Audiovisual Archiving (http://av-archive.blogspot. com/)* is 'focused on the digital transformation and preservation of audiovisual material'.

- *Digitization 101 (http://hurstassociates.blogspot.com/)* covers 'issues, topics, and lessons learned surrounding the creation, management, marketing and preservation of digital assets'.

- *Digitizationblog (http://digitizationblog.interoperating.info/)* 'focuses on digitization and related activities (such as electonic publishing) in libraries, archives, and museums, and is intended to be a source of news relevant to people who manage and implement digitization projects'. Maintained by the author of this book.

- *Digiwik (http://digiwik.org/)* is 'designed to be a repository of digitization information for use by individuals, museums, libraries, researchers, and any other entities with digitization needs'.

- *File Formats Blog (http://fileformats.blogspot.com/)* provides 'news and comments about technical issues relating to file formats, file validation, and archival software'.

- *Imagelib (http://listserv.arizona.edu/cgi-bin/wa?A0=imagelib&D=1&H=0&O=T&T=1)* is an e-mail list covering technical aspects of image-orientated digitisation in libraries, archives and museums. Members frequently announce new collections or initiatives.

- Legal blogs such as *LibraryLaw Blog* (American, *http://blog.librarylaw.com/*) and *Digital Copyright Canada* (Canadian, *http://www.digital-copyright.ca/blog*). There currently appear to be no UK equivalents but the two mentioned here do report on copyright issues in the UK; the Patent Office's Intellectual Property site provides a news section (*http://www.intellectual-property.gov.uk/news/*) that is also useful.

- *Open Access News (http://www.earlham.edu/~peters/fos/fosblog. html)* is one of the best single sources on news on policies, publications, tools and events dealing with open access.

- *Metadata Librarians' List (http://metadatalibrarians.monarchos.com/)* is 'intended for Metadata Librarians, Digital Librarians, Metadata Architects, Information Architects, and other professionals working in cultural heritage institutions and the information sciences'. It covers applications of a number of metadata standards used in digital collection building.

Conventions used in this book

I have used notes at the end of each chapter to identify cited material and to provide examples. Books and articles are cited using a standard citation style but references to web pages usually contain only the URL. Also, in a number of cases I have included screen captures from websites and software applications, which should reduce the need to read this book while sitting next to a computer.

An unavoidable risk when writing about technology is that references to product names, computer hardware specifications, current standards and other similar details can appear quaintly outdated very rapidly. This will no doubt happen in the present case. On a related topic and following the example of most other cautious writers, I would like to state that any collection or product named in this book is the property of its owner and that mentioning an online collection or product or using it as an example is not an endorsement.

Notes

1. *http://europa.eu.int/rapid/pressReleasesAction.do?reference=IP/05/ 1202&format=HTML&aged=0&language=en&guiLanguage=en*
2. *http://www.theeuropeanlibrary.org/portal/*
3. *http://www.opencontentalliance.org/*
4. *http://www.carl-abrc.ca/new/pdf/OCDI_communique-e.pdf*
5. *http://www.loc.gov/today/pr/2005/05-250.html*
6. *http://www.library.cmu.edu/Libraries/MBP_FAQ.html*
7. Lee, S.D. (2001) *Digital Imaging: A Practical Handbook*. London: Library Association Publishing.
8. Kenney, A.R. and Rieger, O.Y. (eds) (2000) *Moving Theory into Practice: Digital Imaging for Libraries and Archives*. Mountain View, CA: Research Libraries Group.
9. Sitts, M.K. (ed.) *Handbook for Digital Projects: A Management Tool for Preservation and Access*. Andover, MA: Northeast Document Conservation Center.
10. NISO Framework Advisory Group. (2004) *A Framework of Guidance for Building Good Digital Collections*, 2nd edition. Bethesda, MD: NISO. Available at *http://www.niso.org/framework/Framework2.html*
11. The Humanities Advanced Technology and Information Institute and the National Initiative for a Networked Cultural Heritage. (2002) *The NINCH Guide to Good Practice in the Digital Representation and Management of Cultural Heritage Material*. Available at *http://www.nyu.edu/its/ humanities/ ninchguide/*
12. Morrison, A., Popham, M. and Wikander, K. (no date) *Creating and Documenting Electronic Texts: A Guide to Good Practice*. Available at *http://ota.ahds.ac.uk/documents/creating/*
13. *http://etext.lib.virginia.edu/ebooks/*
14. Lynch, C. (2002) 'Digital collections, digital libraries and the digitization of cultural heritage information', *First Monday* 7:5. Available at *http://www. firstmonday.dk/issues/issue7_5/lynch/*
15. *http://www.4digitalbooks.com/*
16. *http://www.sherpa.ac.uk/romeo.php*
17. *http://publicaccess.nih.gov/*
18. *http://www.wellcome.ac.uk/doc_wtd018855.html*
19. *http://creativecommons.org/*
20. *http://www.bbc.co.uk/calc/news/rules.shtml*
21. Miller, P. (2005) 'Web 2.0: building the new library', *Ariadne* 45. Available at *http://www.ariadne.ac.uk/issue45/miller/*
22. *http://www.dcc.ac.uk/*

Preliminary tasks

Like any potentially large, complex project, developing a digital collection requires careful and thorough planning. The phases typically involved in developing digital collections are:

1. Define goals and scope of the collection (this chapter)
2. Evaluate and select source material (this chapter)
3. Clear permission to use the source material (Chapter 3)
4. Define project objectives and milestones (Chapter 8)
5. Determine technical specifications (Chapters 4–7)
6. Develop workflows (Chapter 10)
7. Develop budget (Chapter 8)
8. Execute the project (Chapters 8 and 9)
9. Evaluate the project (Chapter 8)
10. Evaluate the collection (Chapter 8)

Chapter 8, Project management, provides details on a number of these phases, but this brief outline serves as a context for discussion of the first two phases, defining goals and scope for the collection and evaluating the source material. Preservation of digital content has its own chapter in this book, but is not included in the outline above because preservation activities are broader than any single collection and should apply to all the digital content of ongoing value that libraries manage.

Rationales for digitising

As context for defining collection goals, it is useful to look at common rationales for digitising analog materials. Rationales offer general reasons why libraries digitise, can serve as the basis for the goals a library may set for a particular collection, and can help establish specific criteria that can be applied to individual documents to determine if they should be digitised. They may also prove useful in justifying the development of a digital collection within a library's overall priorities.

Paula de Stefano calls these rationales 'motivations' and 'catalytic factors',[1] and discusses them in relation to various categories of methods for selecting items for digitisation – specifically, selection to enhance access, selection based on content and selection for preservation. de Stefano cites a large number of sources that list specific criteria for selecting material for digitisation (which I will cover below), but these three categories provide a useful framework for discussing the major reasons why libraries decide to build digital collections.

Enhancing access

de Stefano identifies two aspects of enhanced access that digitisation provides: increased access and new forms of access. Digitising material makes it available to users who are not at the same physical location as the source material. In addition, digital resources are available to multiple users at one time. Also, institutions that have a mandate to serve users over a large geographical area can fulfil their mandates effectively by making resources available online. Increased access is only one benefit: the other half of enhanced access is completely new forms of access, such as using software to reveal hidden content in documents that have been damaged, allowing texts to be searched, and facilitating new types of comparative analysis through encoding text using mark-up languages such as XML. One type of enhanced access not mentioned by de Stefano is that required by users with visual and other disabilities. Digitised texts can be read out loud to these users by software.

The effects of increasing access to digital resources of all types, not just library resources, have come to be known as 'the long tail'. Popularized by Chris Anderson in an article in the October 2004 issue of *Wired Magazine*,[2] the long tail describes trends in the consumption of media such as films, music and books which suggest that making material (or even descriptions of the material) available online will have a dramatic effect on the number of times the material is used. Specifically, 'the long tail' describes the amount of use that obscure resources receive in relation to the total amount of use that new, current or well-publicised material receives. In many cases the total amount of use of the obscure or older resources is higher than the total amount of use of new resources, although that aggregated higher use is spread out over many more individual resources.

The long tail is not mentioned here as a rationale or justification for digitising obscure material, but it does illustrate that increasing access to material has a generalised and quantifiable effect on how often the material is used (at least material whose consumption has a real monetary value such as the films, music and books described in Anderson's article). Simply put, increasing access to material increases use of the material. Library managers have noticed this effect in many contexts, some as obvious as what happens when a rack of paperbacks is moved out from behind a sign to somewhere more visible. Because of the often extremely high cost of digitisation, libraries need to develop rational criteria for selecting material to put online, but recognition that the long tail applies to digitised library resources does offer some validity to the assumption that 'if we build it, they will come'.

Content-driven rationales

The second category de Stefano identifies is based on the intellectual content of the material. In her view this motivation to digitise is particularly relevant if the material is of high interest to current researchers. This motivation is also important for justifying collaboration with other institutions that hold related material in order to create 'virtual collections', and she cites the William Blake Archive,[3] which contains digitised content from 23 different libraries, museums and archives as an example of this type of collaboration. Other virtual collections of related material contributed from multiple physical collections include the State of Colorado's Collaborative Digitisation Program[4] and the Internet Library of Early Journals.[5]

Another aspect of digitising material based on its intellectual content is achieving critical mass, which is the amount of material that needs to be available online so that using the material for research, teaching and other purposes is considered worthwhile. In other words, if there is not enough online content relevant to users' interests, those users may not consider using online resources useful. de Stefano points out that while using comprehensiveness as a justification to digitise (or as a specific selection criterion) implies large investments in the resources required to develop critical mass, comprehensiveness has traditionally been used as a key principle in collection policies for print materials. Her discussion of critical mass can be characterized as 'build it bigger and they will come.'

Preservation

de Stefano cites digitisation as an appropriate preservation strategy when doing so reduces the handling of fragile originals. In this regard digitisation performs the same functions that preservation photocopying and microfilming do. However, she warns that preservation of the digital versions of the material is much more problematic than preservation of microfilm.

Digitising as a preservation strategy has only recently gained acceptance, but it is still secondary to increasing access. Abby Smith's *Why Digitise?*,[6] written in 1999, clearly states that 'digitisation is not preservation – at least not yet' but by 2004 digital preservation had matured to the point at which the Association of Research Libraries (ARL) released a statement recognising digitisation as a valid 'preservation reformatting' method.[7] The ARL statement is cautious at the same time as it is optimistic, and acknowledges that although in the short term digitisation as a preservation strategy has proven to be viable, its long-term viability is still uncertain, and that the library community and others have to remain active in resolving numerous outstanding issues. The statement also acknowledges that the increasing amount of born-digital content is a key factor in legitimising the shift in attitude.

Other rationales

The motivations for digitisation codified by de Stefano focus on library collections and help explain why a library would undertake the work necessary to put digital collections (or at least selected portions of them) online. Another set of justifications that focus on the *institution* are presented by Stuart Lee.[8] These rationales are:

- 'Reducing costs and burden on existing resources': For example, a digitised version of a text on a course reading list may reduce photocopy costs.

- 'Generating income': Lee mentions charging for access to resources digitised by libraries, but also the fact that important collections can raise the profile of the library, which can result in increased opportunities and potential income for subsequent projects.

- 'Increasing awareness': Putting material online can increase awareness of a collection or subject, and can also be an opportunity to demonstrate institutional commitment to material that has been 'sidelined' in the past.

- 'Institutional support': In Lee's words: 'In a devolved environment, such as a dispersed library system or an educational establishment, it is essential that the digitization project can demonstrate clear local support (from the librarian or curator in charge of the items, or from academics who may use it in their teaching) as well as following the institution's IT strategy.' In other words, digitisation is an excellent opportunity to demonstrate that a library can plan, develop and sustain a large-scale project and can collaborate with other units within the institution.

- 'Ancillary effects': The two examples that Lee provides deal with building infrastructure for future or additional initiatives: raising the skill level of local staff and developing substantial hardware and software resources.

Lee refers to this group of 'advantages' of digitising as 'institutional strategies' and regards them as part of the 'political baggage' that surrounds digitisation projects, stating that: 'Recognition of institutional and commercial strategies at both national and local level is extremely important if the project is to succeed and prosper.'[9] Some of Lee's advantages are circular ('generating income' and 'ancillary effects' for example) in that they justify present activity by suggesting that the activity may prove to be beneficial in the future. For libraries that have long-term plans to participate in digital collection building, these motivations are valid. When applying for grants and for qualifying in some partnerships, libraries are often required to demonstrate that they have a history of successful participation in similar projects or to provide financial contributions to projects in the form of hardware infrastructure.

Applicability of rationales

The rationales presented here apply to any library that is considering creating a digital collection, whether they are large research libraries digitising rare first editions or small public libraries interested in putting up modest but unique collections of local content. All of the types of collections supplied as examples in the first chapter can be justified by one or more of these rationales. 'Justified' in this case means giving the activity of digitising content and making it available to users the same validity as other activities and services libraries undertake. Digital collection building must compete with other priorities, and I hope the information above will prove useful in making the case for a digital collection or digitisation project. Rationales also provide a context for defining collection goals, a topic I will cover in the next section.

So far I have only mentioned 'digitising' and have neglected born-digital resources. As we saw in the previous chapter, not all digital resources organised into collections by libraries need to be converted from analog to digital formats – many are already digital. The rationales most applicable to born-digital collections are those dealing with increased and improved access, and with preservation. Digital content is by nature accessible in that it can easily be distributed over the Web, via e-mail or in compact physical media such as CD-ROMs. But being in digital format does not necessarily mean it can be found by users who may be interested in it. By assembling groups of related born-digital resources into coherent collections, libraries help make them findable, and by adding metadata to the items in the collections, libraries add value to the items that would be absent if those items were not part of a collection. An additional rationale that can be applied to some born-digital content, such as electronic theses and dissertations, is that by organising it into collections, libraries make it part of larger, co-operative 'virtual collections' similar to those I described earlier.

Although digitising analog material is usually the most expensive aspect of building a digital collection (creating suitable metadata is sometimes more expensive than digitisation, however), assembling collections of born-digital resources requires substantial effort, and throughout the chapters that follow many of the processes that apply to digitised resources will also apply to those that are acquired by the library already in digital form.

Defining collection goals, scope, and objectives

The first task in developing a digital collection is to define the collection's goals and scope. Once these two parameters have been clearly articulated, objectives for the work necessary to produce the collection can be defined. This section will cover collection goals and scope, and Chapter 8, Project management, will cover project objectives.

Defining the collection's goals involves articulating the reasons for digitising the material, identifying primary and secondary audiences for the digital collection, and determining how the material will be organised and presented. A collection's goals are tied closely to the content because it is impossible to define goals without referring (implicitly at least) to the body of material. At the same time, capabilities of the technology that will be used to create the digital content limit (or depending on your perspective, expand) the possible ways that the content can be presented to the end user. As Paul Conway points out, there is a relationship among the characteristics of the material in the collection, the technology used to create and deliver the content, and the uses the collection will be put to.[10] A useful statement of goals should reflect all three of these facets.

What form should a collection's goals take? In their simplest form, all they need to do (other than indicate the collection's title) is describe the collection's content, but ideally the goals should also identify the collection's intended audiences. Additional information can include a brief description of the form the digital content takes, broad access restrictions and a brief indication of the role that metadata plays in the collection. Goals should be specific and clear, but not overly detailed. Collection goals are *not* a work plan – detailed analyses of the tasks necessary to create the collection, the resources required to complete those tasks and the amount of time the tasks will take all need to be left for a later stage in the collection planning process. Before these concrete details can be known, a considerable number of questions must be explored. A glance back at the list of phases involved in developing most collections listed at the start of this chapter reminds us that defining project objectives and milestones is the fourth phase; defining goals is only the first.

The expression of a collection's goals will evolve as the various aspects of the collection are developed. For example, a preliminary statement of goals could look like this:

> The Southeastern Regional News Collection contains selected issues of the *County Herald* and *Crighton Daily* newspapers published between 1900 and 1920.

With audience added:

> The Southeastern Regional News Collection contains selected issues of the County Herald and Crighton Daily newspapers published between 1900 and 1920. The collection will be of interest to local

historians, to genealogists and to the students seeking primary source material from the early part of the 20th century.

With other information added, after it has been finalized:

> The Southeastern Regional News Collection contains selected issues of the *County Herald* and *Crighton Daily* newspapers published between 1900 and 1920. The collection, which will be freely available to everyone over the World Wide Web, will be of interest to local historians, to genealogists and to students seeking primary source material from the early part of the 20th century. Access to the major articles in each issue will be aided by the addition of subject keywords. Each newspaper issue will be presented as a single Adobe Acrobat file for easy printing.

These statements of the collection's goals could be phrased in different ways for different purposes. For example, the way they are expressed in publicity or in information aimed at potential supporters may be different from the way they are phrased in internal planning documents.

Content

Evaluating and selecting the content for digital collections is covered in detail below, but it is important that all expressions of the collection's goals include a brief description of the content. Early in the planning process, references to content may be fairly broad ('selected issues of the *County Herald* and *Crighton Daily* newspapers published between 1900 and 1920') but as copyright status, technical specifications and other aspects of the collection are worked out, the way the content is described will probably change to reflect limitations (or expansions) of the content described in early versions of the goals.

Audience(s)

Too often, libraries do not explicitly identify the intended audiences for a collection clearly, which can make defining the other aspects of the overall goals difficult. Even if the stated audience is 'general users', at least *some* users have been identified, although the more specific collection planners are able to identify likely audiences, the more they can tailor the collection to those audiences.

The UK Joint Information Systems Committee (JISC) Technical Advisory Service for Images (TASI) considers a collection's audience to be so important that it places development of a user needs survey as the initial step in the selection process.[11] The purpose of the user needs survey is to 'establish who your potential users are, what their expectations and needs are, and how the images are likely to be used', and includes collecting information on who is likely to use the digital collection, the appeal of the collection to audiences wider than those currently using the source material, the purposes that the digitised collection will be used for, and whether digitising the collection is likely to increase use of the original source material.

TASI does not offer specific strategies for implementing user needs surveys, but it does recommend conducting periodic surveys 'if the user community changes significantly'. Initial surveys can be implemented using standard techniques such as printed questionnaires at service points regulating access to the original source material, general library user surveys, web-based surveys attached to other digital collections and focus groups. A natural place for the follow-up surveys is the collection's website, although that is not the only form they can take.

Another approach to determining audience needs is to establish an advisory committee consisting of representatives from known user groups. Advisory committees also legitimise the collection in the eyes of potential funders and partner libraries, and can assist in establishing metadata requirements, functional requirements for search and display systems, and quality control standards. As we will see below, collaborating with formalised committees of experts and potential users can be a productive approach to selecting material for inclusion in digital collections as well.

Access, functionality, and metadata

Access restrictions on the collection can usually be decided early in the planning process. Copyright clearance may complicate this decision, but a library generally knows early on if it will be making the content accessible to everyone, or accessible only to its own users. A mixed model is possible where some items are open and some restricted, and this might be a solution for collections where the rights to make all items universally accessible cannot be obtained.

It will be impossible for early versions of a collection's stated goals to include specifics about functionality and metadata, as coming to a decision on these technical aspects of the collection requires considerable thought and planning. Chapters 4–7 introduce the various technical aspects of planning and implementing a collection.

Scope

Scope describes the amount of material that will be in the collection, and can be expressed in terms of numbers of items, geographical coverage, temporal coverage or any other aspect of the collection that is appropriate. A collection's scope is often mentioned as part of the content description, as in the example above.

It is important to define the scope of a project early in the planning process because the amount of material in the collection will have a direct impact on the project's goals and therefore on costs. However, the scope will probably change from what was originally planned due to unforeseen or initially unknown factors such as copyright status, production cost, co-operation of partners, and other variables that are not always easy to control throughout collection development and content production. The most realistic strategy for defining a collection's scope is to identify the amount of content that would ideally be included in the collection, and monitor the factors that influence how much content actually makes it into the collection. Few collections end up with the same scope they had early in their planning stages. Even the most careful and experienced project managers have been caught off guard by overly optimistic appraisals of the content's copyright status, the efficiency of the hardware used to digitise the content and the amount of work that can be accomplished with available funds.

Evaluating and selecting source material

This section summarises a variety of specific approaches to selecting material for digitisation. Because the sources summarised here are quite detailed, you should refer to the sources themselves when planning your own collections.

Criteria for research collections

In *Selecting Research Collections for Digitisation*, Dan Hazen, Jeffrey Horrell and Jan Merrill-Oldham[12] provide 'a model of the decision-making process required of research libraries when they embark on digital conversion projects' that 'place[s] the questions of what and how to digitise into the larger framework of collection building by focusing, first, on the nature of the collections and their use, and, second, on the realities of the institutional context in which these decisions are made.' Their criteria apply not only to the source material but also to the digitised collections based on the source material (referred to as the 'digital product').

The following categories are used to group an extensive series of questions that are applied to items under consideration for digitisation.

- *Copyright*: Put simply, if the work is in the public domain or if the library has cleared the necessary permissions, the item can be digitised. Otherwise, it cannot.

- *The intellectual nature of the source materials*: The same types of assessments of overall quality that go into selecting print materials apply when selecting materials to add to a digital collection. In addition, material whose intellectual value will be enhanced by digitisation (for example, by allowing its full text to be searched) should get higher priority than material whose value will not.

- *Current and potential users*: Material that is judged to be underused is a good candidate for digitisation, if it is known to be of widespread interest. Material in poor physical condition, or material that is of very high monetary value, should be considered for digitisation so that access to the original can be reduced for preservation and safety purposes. Material that is widely dispersed geographically can benefit from digitisation (a variation on the 'virtual collection building' rationale described earlier).

- *Actual and anticipated nature of use*: The material should be at least as easy to use in digital form as it is in its original form, and ideally should allow new types of use when digitised. Investigation into how the material is used by researchers in its original form should guide how it is digitised and made available.

- *The format and nature of the digital product*: Considerations include the ability of the material to withstand the digitisation process, the requirement for the entire collection of material to be digitised versus only a sample, and the types of navigational features that can be built into the digital collection (and between collections).

- *Describing, delivering, and retaining the digital product*: This category includes questions about the findability of the digital collection, access to the collection, integrity of the digitised files, and long-term safeguarding and preservation of the digitised files.

- *Relationships to other digital efforts*: Items in this category include knowing if the candidate material has already been digitised by someone else, and the likelihood that the collection can become part of a co-operative effort to bring together related material that would otherwise remain disbursed.

- *Costs and benefits*: Questions include who will benefit most from the digitised collection, could an acceptable product be created at lower cost, how will long-term costs associated with the collection be addressed, and what is the likelihood that external funding can be raised?

Hazen, Horrell and Merrill-Oldham's approach is comprehensive and straightforward. To structure the long list of questions, the authors provide a 'Decision-making matrix', which is essentially a flowchart that incorporates a number of the questions defined under the sections summarized above.

A systematic approach to selection

Although all the approaches to selection described here are systematic to some degree, Diane Vogt-O'Connor[13] provides what might be characterised as a *highly* systematic approach that combines structured stages in the selection process, role-based committees and prioritisation based on computed scores.

Vogt-O'Connor breaks down the selection process into three stages: nomination, evaluation and prioritization. During nomination, a broad variety of stakeholders recommend which groups of materials to select for digitisation and which ones not to select (or 'deselect'), and provide their reasons for each nomination. Stakeholders include collection creators, donors, researchers, managers and others. Vogt-O'Connor uses the term 'material' and the phrase 'groups of material,' although the techniques she presents can also be applied at the item level if that is appropriate to the collection being evaluated, and if time and funds are available to inspect every item in the collection.

During evaluation, a selection committee (comprising discipline specialists, education specialists, digitisation specialists, librarians, researchers experienced in working with other online collections, conservationists and lawyers) compares the groups of materials that were nominated for selection and deselection and sets aside material that appears in both lists for further evaluation. Material that had been initially deselected can be selected at a later time if the reason for deselection changes, such as copyright status.

If less material is nominated than is identified in the scope of the collection or project, statistical sampling is used to select additional material that was not initially nominated. Prioritisation comes into play when too much material is nominated. During prioritisation, groups of material are prioritised by value, risk and use:

- *Value*: Vogt-O'Connor identifies six different types of 'value' that may be scored. In the interests of brevity I will only describe one type here, informational value. Material of high informational value contains information significantly relevant to the collection focus, moderate-value material is relevant to the collection focus and low-value material provides little information relevant to the collection focus.

- *Risk*: The three types of risk are legal, social and preservation risk. Material of high legal and social risk will be weeded out during the normal course of the nomination and evaluation processes. Therefore, preservation risk should be addressed explicitly during prioritisation. High-risk material is chemically unstable (such as certain types of film), and moderate-risk material is suffering physical damage or gradually losing informational value due to deterioration. In general, the higher the preservation risk, the higher the priority to digitise.

- *Use*: Scores for use must be determined by local reference statistics and other countable measures. One strategy is to base scores on median usage values calculated from the number of uses annually per group of items. Material that is used often should be digitised.

Numerical scores (e.g. 6 for high, 3 for moderate, 1 for low) are assigned to each of value, risk and use. Scores are then tabulated and groups of material ranked. Vogt-O'Connor points out that this method of scoring can be modified to the institution's mission and overall collection policies. For example, an institution may emphasise value or use and not risk if doing so reflects that institution's collection policies. She supplies examples of evaluating and ranking collections, nomination forms for selection and deselection, and a checklist for evaluation.

Advantages of this highly systematic approach are that it accommodates a wide variety of opinions and perspectives and that it is objective. Also, the three-stage approach decreases the likelihood that problematic items make their way into the collection. However, owing to its highly structured approach to selecting material for inclusion in a digital collection, this approach may be overkill for small or homogeneous collections.

A matrix approach to selection

Stuart Lee[14] builds on the work of Hazen, Horrell, Merrill-Oldham and others who have used a matrix (or more accurately a flowchart) to represent and guide the numerous decisions that need to be made during selection. Lee's matrix employs checklists at various points to represent multifaceted aspects of the selection process, such as responses to the questions: 'What demands will be met, in terms of increasing access, if the collection is digitised?' and 'What demands will be met, in terms of preservation, if the collection is digitised?'

The start point of Lee's matrix is the initial request to digitise a set of items. If the material has already been digitised by someone else, no further action is taken. Material that has not already been digitised moves through the flowchart to decisions on intellectual property rights, increased access, preservation and institutional strategies (described earlier in this chapter). Lee provides a full working example in which he evaluates a collection of books owned by Charles Dickens.

Lee makes it clear that the matrix should be considered a general guide and not an inflexible requirement, and that institutions should modify it to reflect their own priorities before using it as an evaluative tool: 'For example, a public library or publishing house would probably rank several of the sections under "increasing access" much higher than a copyright or legal deposit library (which is more concerned with the preservation of the item).'[15]

Less systematic approaches to selection

The approaches to selecting material for inclusion in digital collections presented so far are tailored to conventional collections typical of those found in major research libraries or other libraries that hold significant research collections. These approaches can be used effectively for a wide variety of collections, but some libraries may not choose to take an approach as systematic as these, particularly if the collection they are planning contains material considered to lack widespread research value, or if the collection contains non-traditional material that may be considered by many to be of peripheral interest to mainstream researchers. Examples of these types of material include (in the former case) locally significant material whose national or international relevance may not be obvious, or (in the latter case) unusual material such as comic books, postcards or postage stamps. These libraries are faced with the problem of using selection criteria designed for collections that have little in common with the ones they are intending to digitise. In addition, for some libraries, justifying the development of a digital collection using the institutional strategies that Lee identifies may be more important than justifying the collection based on perceived intellectual value.

Even in these cases, however, some criteria need to be defined in order to choose which items are to be digitised, unless it is established from the beginning that the entire collection is to be digitised. A set of criteria that may be useful for selecting material in these situations is Columbia University Library's 'Selection Criteria for Digital Imaging.'[16] Their criteria are comprehensive – the list includes sections on copyright status, preservation concerns and technical feasibility – but the section 'Collection Development Criteria' is conspicuously brief, breaking down the criteria into three categories: value, demand and non-duplication:

Value

Many factors contribute, but certainly they include intellectual content, historic, and physical value:

- rareness or uniqueness
- artifactual or associational value
- importance for the understanding of the relevant subject area
- broad or deep coverage of the relevant subject area
- useful and accurate content
- information on subjects or groups that are otherwise poorly documented
- enhancement of historic strengths of the institution
- potential for enduring value in digital form

Demand

To justify the effort and expense, there should be a reasonable expectation that the product will have immediate utility for members of the Columbia community and/or other appropriate audiences:

- support for current high priority activities
- importance for the functioning of the institution
- an active, current audience for the materials

- advocacy for the project from the Columbia community
- realistic expectation of attracting new users even if current use is low
- requests from potential partners in collaborative or consortial efforts

Non-Duplication

- There is no identical or similar digital product that can reasonably meet the expressed needs.

Although it could be argued that this list is simply a distillation of the other approaches presented here (and in some cases that is the case), the brevity and generality of this section of the Columbia list makes it more applicable to a wider variety of material than detailed and structured criteria, and is included here as an simpler alternative to the other three approaches.

Another set of cases where the structured approaches summarised earlier, and even the much more succinct and flexible set of criteria in the Columbia list, may not apply is collections of born-digital resources, where the content is judged to be of significance but has never been part of a traditional research collection. Examples of this type of collection are institutional repositories and collections of material intended to support classroom teaching. Because these collections tend to be fairly specialized or are created with specific purposes in mind, criteria for inclusion should be developed locally or by using other libraries' experience as a guide. The guidelines published by the Australian National University,[17] for example, may be useful to libraries establishing an institutional repository.

Copyright status is, of course, the single criterion that must be applied to any material that libraries assemble into collections and make accessible to users, and should be a significant component in any approach to selecting content. The next chapter is entirely devoted to that aspect of digital collection building.

Cultural sensitivity and privacy issues

Respect for cultural sensitivity and individual privacy should be considered when selecting material for inclusion in digital collections. A number of well-developed guides on cultural sensitivity are available.

For example, the Alaska Native Knowledge Network provides a comprehensive list of guidelines that 'address issues of concern in the documentation, representation and utilization of traditional cultural knowledge as they relate to the role of various participants, including Elders, authors, curriculum developers, classroom teachers, publishers and researchers.'[18] Charles Darwin University provides a useful document titled 'Aboriginal and Torres Strait Islander Protocols for Libraries, Archives And Information Services'[19] that covers intellectual property issues, subject heading and classification guidelines, and discussion of sacred and offensive materials. These two guides are specific to the cultural groups they describe but they serve as models for the treatment of materials from other groups as well.

Preserving respect for individual and family privacy can be an issue, particularly when dealing with archival, manuscript and photographic material. Libraries that include items in their digital collections which may violate individuals' privacy, or the privacy of named or depicted people's living descendants, should exercise caution. Each library will have a different comfort level with the potential for controversy created by distributing material that could be perceived as violating privacy.

Collection policies

The development of collection policies is related to evaluating and selecting source material. These policies may be a rephrasing of the selection criteria, or can be identical to the selection criteria, as is suggested in the NISO principles discussed in the Chapter 1. In addition to making selection criteria transparent to users, collection policies relate digital collection development to the mission and goals of the library, attract and inform potential donors or collaborators, and serve as the basis for responses to complaints about items in the collection that some users may find questionable or offensive.

Example digital collection policies include those from the International Children's Digital Library,[20] the State Library of New South Wales[21] and the New Jersey Digital Highway.[22]

Summary: preliminary tasks

This chapter provides the most common rationales put forth for creating digital collections. These rationales are similar to those that applied to print or commercially licensed digital collections – increasing access to information, developing resources that will be useful to the library's user community, and ensuring ongoing access and management of the collections. Within this context, libraries need to undertake the more focused activity of defining a particular digital collection, its goals and its scope, and in turn the activity of defining and articulating clear criteria for selecting the content that will make up the collection. Once this set of preliminary tasks has been completed, copyright issues need to be addressed.

Notes

1. de Stafano, P. (2000) 'Selection for digital conversion', in *Moving Theory into Practice: Digital Imaging for Libraries and Archives*. Edited by Anne R. Kenney and Oya Y. Rieger. Mountain View, CA: Research Libraries Group, p. 11.
2. Anderson, C. (2004) The Long Tail. *Wired Magazine* 12:10, 170–7. Available at *http://www.wired.com/wired/archive/12.10/tail.html*
3. *http://www.blakearchive.org/*
4. *http://www.cdpheritage.org/*
5. *http://www.ukoln.ac.uk/services/elib/projects/early/*
6. Smith, A. (1999) *Why Digitise?* Washington, DC: Council on Library and Information Resources. Available at *http://www.clir.org/pubs/reports/pub80-smith/pub80.html*
7. *http://www.arl.org/preserv/digit_final.html*
8. Lee, S.D. (2001) *Digital Imaging: A Practical Handbook*. London: Library Association Publishing, pp. 26–8.
9. ibid., p. 26.
10. Conway, P. (2000) 'Overview: rationale for digitisation and preservation', in *Handbook for Digital Projects: A Management Tool for Preservation and Access*. Edited by Maxine K. Sitts. Andover, MA: Northeast Document Conservation Center, p. 9.
11. *http://www.tasi.ac.uk/advice/creating/selecpro.html*
12. Hazen, D., Horrell, J. and Merrill-Oldham, J. (1998) *Selecting Research Collections for Digitisation*. Washington, DC: Council on Library and Information Resources. Available at *http://www.clir.org/pubs/reports/hazen/pub74.html*
13. Vogt-O'Connor, D. (2000) 'Selection of materials for scanning', in *Handbook for Digital Projects: A Management Tool for Preservation and Access*. Edited by Maxine K. Sitts. Andover, MA: Northeast Document Conservation Center, pp. 35–63. Available at *http://www.nedcc.org/digital/iv.htm*
14. Lee, *op. cit.*, pp. 17–33.
15. *ibid.*, p. 33.

16. *http://www.columbia.edu/cu/libraries/digital/criteria.html*
17. *http://sts.anu.edu.au/demetrius/standards/*
18. *http://www.ankn.uaf.edu/publications/knowledge.html*
19. *http://www.cdu.edu.au/library/protocol.html*
20. *http://www.icdlbooks.org/policies/collection.html*
21. *http://www.sl.nsw.gov.au/online/dig_selection.pdf*
22. *http://www.njdigitalhighway.org/documents/njdh-coll-dev-policy.pdf*

3

Copyright and digital library collections

As indicated in my discussion of selection criteria, material that has not had its copyright status clarified should not be included in a digital collection. All other criteria for what could potentially be a successful collection may be met, but if the library has not thoroughly addressed intellectual property issues, the collection should not be launched. Strictly speaking, if the library ignores intellectual property issues they may be engaging in illegal activity.

However, fear of breaking the law should not prevent libraries from building digital collections, as there are a number of ways to digitise and distribute material legally. This chapter introduces the aspects of intellectual property that libraries should be aware of when planning digital collections and also describes strategies for effectively managing intellectual property issues. Information and opinions presented here are subject to the well-known standard disclaimer: before acting on anything presented here, consult with whoever in your institution is responsible for legal matters. Even lawyers are careful about distinguishing between legal advice and legal information. The intent in the pages that follow is to introduce a number of issues, not to advise on any particular issue, and the information presented here should not be used as a substitute for the advice of a lawyer.

Copyright is the aspect of intellectual property that defines the rights of content producers and content consumers. Other aspects of intellectual property, such as patents and trademarks, are generally not applicable because libraries' focus is on 'literary and artistic works' as they are defined in most national and international laws: written works (literary and otherwise), graphical works (including photographs), artistic works in other media, audio recordings, and film, video and television.

National copyright law and digital collections

Each nation has its own copyright laws, so the specific ways in which copyright laws impact a library's ability to create digital collections will vary from country to country. In addition, copyright laws change frequently, and interpretation of copyright laws by courts in each country make generalising about copyright difficult. For the most part, the location of the library, and not the location of origin or publication of the work, determines the jurisdiction. To illustrate how aspects of copyright relevant to libraries differ across three countries (UK, US and Canada), I will compare three aspects of copyright law that are relevant to libraries creating digital collections:

- *Term:* The amount of time a work is protected by copyright. Within a single nation's laws, a number of factors determine the duration of copyright protection. In Table 3.1, the number of years indicated is for a published literary work by an individual author (such as a book) and for an unpublished literary work by an individual author (such as a personal letter).

- *Fair dealing and fair use*: 'Fair dealing' defines the specific uses a copyrighted work can be put to without explicit permission from the copyright owner, and is defined in the copyright laws of the UK, Canada and other countries. 'Fair use' is the US equivalent, but it is less specific than fair dealing.

- *Orphan works*: Works whose copyright status is difficult or impossible to determine because the creator is either not known or cannot be found.

Some of the differences in these aspects of national copyright law are summarised in the following table.

The wide variety among term, fair dealing/use and regulations governing orphan works illustrates why it is important that libraries seek the advice of legal professionals when assessing copyright issues. In general, a work cannot be digitised or distributed legally unless permission is received by the copyright holder, or use of the work meets a small set of conditions, which I will cover in the next section.

Table 3.1 Summary comparison of term, fair dealing/use, and orphan works in UK, US and Canadian copyright law

	UK	US	Canada
Term for published works	70 years after death of the author	70 years after death of the author	50 years after death of the author
Term for unpublished works	Until at least 2039[1]	Same as for published works[2]	If the author died prior to 1948, the work is in the public domain; if author died between 1849 and 1998, the work will enter the public domain in 2049; if the author died after 1998, the work will enter the public domain 50 years after death[3]
Fair dealing/fair use	Fair dealing is limited to activities including research and private study, criticism; certain educational uses and public performances of sound recordings[4]	Fair use covers reproduction of a work for the purposes of criticism, comment, news reporting, teaching, scholarship, and research,[5] but determining whether an activity falls under fair use is determined by a set of 'factors' or criteria	Fair dealing is limited to activities including research and private study, criticism[6]
Orphan works	Copyright is not infringed if 'it is not possible by reasonable inquiry to ascertain the identity of the author' and it is reasonable to assume that copyright has expired[7]	No special exceptions; policy currently under review[8]	Licence may be obtained from federal government[9]

What libraries can put online

The conditions described here are either legal exceptions to regular creators' rights within most nations' laws, or they override copyright regulations because they are covered under contract law. Copyright laws give creators the right to control distribution of their works (hence the name 'copyright') while also giving users certain rights. The first two conditions describe users' rights, and the last two conditions describe creators' rights to control the distribution of their works.

Fair dealing and fair use

It is difficult to argue that fair dealing as defined in UK and Canadian law allows digitising material and distributing it to end users, because the uses identified by fair dealing are relatively explicit: research, private study and criticism. One notable exception that is allowable (under the laws of many countries[10]) is digitising copyrighted material without the copyright holder's permission in order to make it accessible to users with certain types of disabilities.

In the US, however, fair use is often cited as allowing the distribution of copyrighted material. US copyright legislation defines four factors to be considered in determining whether or not a particular use is covered by fair use:

- the purpose and character of the use, including whether such use is of commercial nature or is for non-profit educational purposes;
- the nature of the copyrighted work;
- amount and substantiality of the portion used in relation to the copyrighted work as a whole; and
- the effect of the use upon the potential market for or value of the copyrighted work.[11]

Interpretation of these factors broadens the scope of fair use far beyond the narrow scope of fair dealing in the UK and Canada, while at the same time blurring the distinction between what types of use are legal and what types are illegal. In cases where the distinction is not clear, the courts can decide whether or not a particular case falls within fair use. For example, Google's defence of scanning books protected by copyright is that doing so is allowable under fair use,[12] but the Association of American Publishers has sued Google[13] on the grounds that Google's actions do not fall within fair dealing. As Mary Minnow, lawyer and author of *Library Digitization Projects and Copyright* puts it:

> The only way we'll know whether it's okay to digitise works and put them on the web using a FAIR USE argument is if a library does so, gets sued and wins. Or loses. And the Appeals process concludes one way or the other. At least we'd know. Even then, unless the court is expansive in its narrative, the decision could apply only to the circumstances in a particular case.[14]

In situations where digitising or making available copyrighted material is not clearly allowed, libraries should consult with legal professionals experienced in copyright law to ensure that their actions are defensible under fair dealing or fair use as defined in their national copyright laws.

Material in the public domain

Copyrights usually last for a specific number of years (the 'term' defined in Table 3.1). Once the term is up, the copyright expires and the work goes into the public domain, which means that no one owns the copyright and the work can be used by anyone. The specific terms that apply in a given country are indicated in the copyright legislation, and they can vary within a single country depending on the type of work. In some countries, certain works are in the public domain as soon as they are created. In the US, government documents and most works created by federal government employees fall into this category.

Libraries are free to digitise material that is in the public domain without receiving permission from the original copyright holder. However, sometimes determining whether the copyright of a given work has expired is difficult because for most works, the term is defined to be a certain number of years after the death of the author. Therefore, to determine how long copyright lasts on a work, libraries have to perform research to determine when the author died, or based on the publication date of an item, feel reasonably certain that the required amount of time has passed. For example, if a 50-year term applies to a given work, and it is known that the work was published in 1850, it is fairly safe to assume in 2000 that the author died before 1950.

In general, once a work enters the public domain it remains in the public domain, but there are exceptions. Changes in copyright laws that extend the copyright term can restore copyright after it has expired. In European Union countries, a 2001 directive harmonising copyright laws resulted in the published works of authors who died between 1 January 1926 and 31 December 1945 to revert into copyright on 1 January 1996, when the extended copyright term starts to apply.[15] Sections 104A and 109(a) of the US copyright law restore copyright to certain types of foreign works that had moved into the public domain.[16]

As mentioned in the previous paragraph, copyright laws are sometimes changed so that terms are extended. This extension is happening in many countries. A representative example of how a series of cumulative copyright extensions can postpone movement into the public domain can be found in US copyright law. The length of time copyright lasts in the US has been extended 11 times since 1962;[17] in the last 30 years, copyright term has nearly tripled.[18]

Material covered by a written agreement

If a work is protected under copyright, libraries must receive permission from the copyright holder to digitise the work (unless fair dealing or fair use apply). This permission usually takes the form of a written statement of some sort. I will discuss specific aspects of permission agreements in 'Managing permissions' below.

Some libraries create collections containing material that is licensed from vendors. Unlike content that the vendor hosts and makes available to libraries over the Web, some vendors only supply the content, and the library is responsible for mounting it on the Web (or otherwise distributing it), for ensuring that access is restricted to authorised users, and in some cases, for creating descriptive and other types of metadata. Still images, audio files, raw scientific and statistical data, and the full text of journals and books are common types of content available in this way. In these cases, the library signs a licence agreement with the vendor allowing the library to use the content in specific ways such as making the material available to remote users, so the library does not have to receive permission from the creator of every individual item in the collection.

Material distributed with an explicit licence

Although creators have always been able to add statements to their work such as 'This book is in the public domain', in the last few years a number of formal licences have evolved that allow creators to indicate specifically which rights they reserve and which rights they grant to users. Without an explicit licence, users must contact copyright holders and receive permission before using works in ways not covered by fair dealing or fair use. Authors who attach explicit licences to their work are simply indicating that users may legally use their works in certain ways without receiving written permission.

The most common explicit licences are those provided by Creative Commons.[19] Creative Commons is a set of licences, localized to be consistent with the laws of nearly 30 countries, that creators can include with their works to tell users how they can use those works. Using tools provided on the Creative Commons website, creators can choose whether the licence they attach to their works allows commercial use of the work, modification of the work, and if modifications are allowed, whether users must share the modified version under the same licence that was attached to the original version. The creator still retains copyright, and uses allowed under fair dealing and fair use continue to apply.[20] Creative Commons also supplies special licences for use of work in developing nations, a 'sampling' licence that applies to use of music, photos and movies, and several other specialized licences.

Creative Commons licences are relevant to digital library collections in two ways. First, all Creative Commons licences allow the redistribution of works, so a library's ability to distribute works released under a Creative Commons licence is perfectly legal and never in question. Second, Creative Commons licences are explicit – they clearly define what users can and cannot do with the work. This allows libraries to avoid the need to develop separate policies defining how works can be used, and allows libraries and authors to avoid engaging in complicated and potentially costly negotiations about what the library can distribute. Currently, few digital collections hosted by libraries contain large numbers of works released under Creative Commons licences. However, this type of licence is starting to appear in institutional repositories, and tools for choosing Creative Commons licences are integrated into the DSpace institutional repository platform.

Standardized explicit licences other than Creative Commons exist. The most common is the GNU Free Documentation Licence,[21] which is most commonly used in documentation accompanying open-source software.

Works made available through publishers' Open Access policies often have Creative Commons or other types of explicit licences attached to them. Open Access itself is not an explicit licence. The basic tenet of Open Access is that scholarship should be freely available to everyone.

As Peter Suber puts it, Open Access 'focuses on literature that authors give to the world without expectation of payment.'[22] The SHERPA/ROMEO list,[23] which is the most comprehensive source of information describing journal publishers' Open Access policies, indicates that (at the time of writing) 75% of publishers in the list allow article authors to distribute their work before or after it has been published by the journal. These articles are often linked from authors' websites, or are placed in collections such as disciplinary archives or institutional repositories.

Managing permissions

Managing permissions to digitise and distribute material is an essential component of developing a digital collection. Every item that a library intends to make available to users must have its copyright status clarified, and if necessary, the rights holder must give permission to use the item. An outline of the steps required to perform this task follows. Specific jurisdictional requirements are not included, and as suggested above, each library's administration (and legal staff) must approve the processes that will minimise the risk to the library:

1. Determine the copyright status of the item. Generally, the two statuses will be (a) the item is in the public domain or (b) the item is covered by copyright.

2. If the item is covered by copyright, determine whether fair dealing or fair use allows the library to include the item in an online collection.

3. If fair dealing or fair use do not apply, determine who the rights holder is and contact him or her to seek permission to include the item in an online collection.

4. If the copyright owner grants permission, the item can be included in an online collection.

As we have already seen, even completing the first of these steps can be complicated. Exactly how a library determines whether an item is in the public domain depends on how national copyright laws define the copyright term, and in some countries the term depends on who created the work, whether it was published or unpublished, and the medium of the work (written, painting, musical work, and so on). The activities required to complete steps 2 and 3 can also be challenging. Whereas fair dealing tends to be fairly narrow, American fair use is quite broad, but in either case, if a library decides that its activities are covered under the relevant exceptions as described in national copyright laws, the library must be prepared to justify its decision. The third step, contacting the rights holders to seek permission, can pose huge logistical challenges. For example, determining who the rights holder is can depend on whether the work was written under terms of regular employment (in most countries, the employer owns the copyright) or under contract. Once the copyright holder (or the copyright holder's heirs, if applicable) has been contacted, clearing the required permissions can be challenging and require substantial effort, time and money.

All of these activities must be considered when estimating costs and timelines for a particular project. In some cases, the copyright status of the source material will be clear. A collection of books that is old enough to be in the public domain will not require item-level analysis to determine copyright status. Also, large groups of material by the same creator can often be cleared with a single permission request. At the other extreme, digitising a set of newspapers that are recent enough still to be covered under copyright may require contacting the author of every article and the owner of every advertisement. In this situation, the required permissions may never be obtained because it may not be possible to identify and contact all necessary parties. Estimates of the time and resources required to perform the necessary tasks will depend on the nature of the collection (as exemplified above), and in order to undertake an assessment of the source material, planners must understand jurisdictional copyright laws and their applicability to the material.

Record-keeping requirements for permissions must be thorough and accurate. This type of documentation is a form of administrative metadata (which I discuss in the next chapter), and may include information such as the following:

- activities relating to determining who the rights holder is;
- activities relating to contacting the rights holder;
- response from the rights holder;
- fees, if any, that are paid as part of the agreement to use the work;
- duration of the agreement to use the work;
- details about who may access the digital version of work;
- details about whether the digital work may be converted into other formats as part of technological migration or preservation activities.

Some of these types of information describe the work involved in seeking permission whereas others describe the conditions of the agreement to include the work in a digital collection. The specific information that a library collects and manages will be determined by local workflow and legal requirements.

Any type of organisation that uses content whose copyright it does not own – including libraries, educational institutions, publishers – must define acceptable levels of risk associated with managing permissions to use other creators' content. Apart from libraries' obligations to respect the rights of content creators, legal considerations such as potential penalties should determine the amount of attention paid to clearing permissions. Library managers and administrators, the people in their parent institutions who they report to, and the people responsible for legal affairs in the parent institution will all have to be comfortable with the processes put in place to secure permission to include copyrighted content in their library's digital collections.

Two plausible scenarios illustrate the importance of determining acceptable levels of risk. First, in cases where the date of the creator's death determines when their work moves into the public domain, there is some risk involved in assuming (and not thoroughly researching) that the required amount of time has passed to place the work in the public domain. Few would question the copyright status of a book published in 1830, but what about a book published in 1930? Another situation is cases where permission to digitise and redistribute a work has been received. However, even though the creator has signed a letter indicating that he or she is the copyright owner and has the right to grant the permission, it is possible that the person who granted permission is not the legal copyright owner (for example, the author of a book assumed he or she owned copyright to the photos in the book but they were taken by someone else). As stated above, libraries are not the only types of institutions facing these complex questions, but the questions are directly relevant to the creation and maintenance of digital libraries' collections.

Additional issues

Two other intellectual property issues that impact library digital collection are Technological Protection Measures (TPMs) and copyfraud.

TPMs (also known as Digital Rights Management technologies, or DRM) restrict how digital media and content can be used. A common example is the region codes embedded in commercial DVDs that work in conjunction with players to prohibit the use of DVDs in countries they were not sold in. This type of TPM renders DVDs purchased in Europe useless in players sold in North America (as long as the player respects region codes, which most brand-name players do). Another example of TPMs is the features of some commercially downloadable music formats, such as Apple's FairPlay and Microsoft's Windows Media DRM, which restrict the number of devices that the music will play on.

TPMs are relevant to library digital collections in a number of ways. First, as part of their agreements with libraries, rights holders may request that libraries use TPMs in the files that they make available to end users. Such a request is reasonable because the copyright holders have the right to restrict how their works are used. However, creating and managing files that contain TPMs can impose administrative overheads for the library. For example, if the copyright owner requests that users not be able to print his or her work, Adobe PDF could be a suitable file format because it contains DRM mechanisms that allow documents to be viewed but not copied or printed. Printing can be re-enabled if the user (authorised by the owner, of course) enters a password. If this password is not recorded somewhere, it will be impossible, or at least fairly difficult, to print the document. For a large collection of such documents, maintaining and controlling the passwords could require considerable resources. Second, TPMs may prevent end users from using works in ways that are covered by fair dealing or fair use. Copyright law allows specific types of use under fair dealing or fair use, but in many cases TPMs interfere with those uses (such as the user's right under Canadian copyright law to make a copy of a music CD for personal use). Some libraries may have philosophical issues with distributing content protected in this way. Finally, if TPMs are required on master copies of files (as opposed to being required on the copies created for distribution to end users), standard digital preservation activities such as file format migration may not be possible, which means that the master files will have a very limited practical lifespan. In addition, countries that are changing their copyright laws to meet WIPO (World Intellectual Property Organization) compliance are required to make circumvention of TPMs illegal. This would mean that libraries would be prohibited by law from migrating files containing DRM technology even if it were technically possible to do so.

The second intellectual property issue that impacts library digital collections is copyfraud. Copyfraud is falsely claiming copyright ownership of works in the public domain. The term 'copyfraud' comes from an article published in 2005 by Jason Mazzone,[24] in which he argues that libraries, archives, museums, publishers and other organisations are guilty of copyfraud when they claim they own copyright on copies of a public-domain work. Mazzone's article describes copyfraud within the context of US copyright law, but he points out that: 'As a result of the Berne Convention, there are some basic similarities throughout much of the world.[25]

Mazzone states that institutions are free to impose conditions on the use of copies of public domain works that they create for users, but these conditions are part of the contract between the institution and the party the copies are made for,[26] and they have nothing to do with copyright. His analysis of copyfraud therefore invalidates statements that claim that the digital representations of public-domain works are protected under copyright. In fact, he cites the Library of Congress as an example of an institution that clearly explains that it does not own copyright on specific collections simply because it holds those collections in physical form or because it has put digital copies on the Web. A useful antecedent to Mazzone's article is available on the LibraryLaw blog,[27] which debates the legitimacy of claiming copyright on digitised versions of public-domain texts.

Summary: making decisions about intellectual property

The issues presented here are intended to suggest the complexity of copyright laws as they pertain to the creation and maintenance of digital collections by libraries. It is extremely important that collection planners understand the copyright status of material they are considering for digitisation or inclusion in an online collection. Libraries should ensure that they have consulted with legal professionals if they are uncertain or uncomfortable with the risk inevitably involved when using works protected by copyright without the owner's permission. They should also be prepared to commit the resources necessary to ensure that all works intended for inclusion in digital collections have been authorised for that use.

Further reading

Harris, L.E. (2002) *Licensing Digital Content: A Practical Guide for Librarians*. Chicago and London: American Library Association.
Harris' book is intended to provide guidance to libraries that are licensing content (databases, full text, CD-ROMs, etc.), but its treatment of intellectual property law (mainly US but also UK and Canadian), legal

language, licence boilerplate and negotiation techniques will be useful to libraries creating digital collections as well.

Lessig, L. (2004) *Free Culture.* New York: Penguin.
Lessig's book, which is available at *http://www.free-culture.cc/remixes/* under a Creative Commons licence in a number of formats, documents the shift from a 'free culture', where copyright laws balanced the rights of creators and users, to a 'permissions culture', where copyright laws favour the rights of creators and stifle creativity by restricting fair use. This shift corresponds to changes in US copyright law, such as term extensions and the removal of the requirement to register copyrights. Lessig is the founder of Creative Commons.

Minnow, M. *Library Digitization Projects and Copyright.* Available at *http://www.llrx.com/features/digitisation.htm*
This website provides detailed information on determining whether published and unpublished works have passed into the public domain under US copyright law, and uses numerous examples, such as unpublished letters, baseball cards and newspaper issues to illustrate the technical information it presents. The author is also the maintainer of the LibraryLaw Blog (*http://blog.librarylaw.com/librarylaw/*).

Noel, W. (1999) *Copyright Guide for Canadian Libraries.* Ottawa: Canadian Library Association.
Noel's *Guide* clarifies Canadian copyright law as it pertains to all aspects of library operation. Although it has little to say specifically about digitising works for inclusion in online collections, it provides a useful overview of when various types of works move into the public domain in Canada. The *Guide* contains the compete text of the Canadian copyright Act and some additional copyright regulations.

Ockerbloom, J.M. *How Can I Tell Whether a Book Can Go Online?* Available at *http://onlinebooks.library.upenn.edu/okbooks.html*
This website contains information on determining if a book is in the public domain, on researching copyright status, and on topics such as reprints, copyright jurisdiction and special exemptions for libraries. Even though it focuses on US copyright, it contains some information that will be of use to libraries in other countries as well. Ockerbloom's site also contains numerous links to other useful resources dealing with copyright.

Technical Advisory Service for Images. *Copyright.* Available at *http://www.tasi.ac.uk/advice/managing/copyright.html*

The Technical Advisory Service for Images (TASI) offers practical information and advice on UK copyright law as it applies to digitising images. The website also contains detailed sections on clearing permission and writing license agreements. An accompanying site, 'Coping with Copyright' (*http://www.tasi.ac.uk/advice/managing/copyright2.html*), provides a comprehensive list of questions regarding copyright that should be raised early in the planning stages of a digitisation project.

Troll Covey, D. (2005) *Acquiring Copyright Permission to Digitize and Provide Open Access to Books.* Washington, DC: Digital Library Federation and Council on Library and Information Resources. Available at *http://purl.oclc.org/dlf/trollcovey0509*

Covey's book presents the results of three projects at Carnegie Mellon University that involved requesting permission to digitise books and make them available on the Web, a 'Random Sample Feasibility Study,' the 'Fine and Rare Book Study' and the 'Million Book Project Study.' The results of the three studies (respectively) were that 27, 43 and 23% of publishers Carnegie Mellon was able to contact granted permission to scan their material and make it available to end users. Her analysis also breaks down the studies' results by restrictions imposed by publishers, publisher type, publication type, year of publication and transaction costs. She also includes a section on lessons learned for each of the three studies.

Notes

1. *http://www.intellectual-property.gov.uk/faq/copyright/unpublished.htm*
2. *http://www.copyright.cornell.edu/training/copyrightterm.pdf*
3. Noel, W. (2002) 'Copyright Protection in Unpublished Works: Final Report'. Unpublished report, p. 2. Available at *http://www.cla.ca/resources/23april2002.pdf*
4. *http://www.intellectual-property.gov.uk/faq/copyright/exceptions.htm*
5. *http://www.copyright.gov/fls/fl102.html*
6. *http://laws.justice.gc.ca/en/c-42/39417.html*
7. *http://www.patent.gov.uk/copy/legislation/legislation.pdf*
8. *http://www.copyright.gov/orphan/*
9. *http://www.cb-cda.gc.ca/unlocatable/index-e.html*
10. *http://www.ifla.org/IV/ifla70/papers/177e-Lung.htm*
11. *http://www.copyright.gov/fls/fl102.html*
12. *http://googleblog.blogspot.com/2005/10/point-of-google-print.html*

13. *http://www.publishers.org/press/releases.cfm?PressReleaseArticleID=293*
14. *http://www.llrx.com/features/digitisation4.htm#Salamis*
15. *http://tyler.hrc.utexas.edu/uk.cfm*
16. *http://www.eldred.cc/eablog/000117.html*
17. Lessig, L. (2004) *Free Culture*. New York: Penguin, p. 134.
18. *ibid.*, p. 135.
19. *http://creativecommons.org*
20. *http://creativecommons.org/about/licenses/fullrights*
21. *http://www.gnu.org/copyleft/fdl.html*
22. *http://www.earlham.edu/~peters/fos/overview.htm*
23. *http://www.sherpa.ac.uk/romeo.php*
24. Mazzone, J. (2005) 'Copyfraud' (August 21). Brooklyn Law School, Legal Studies Paper No. 40. *http://ssrn.com/abstract=787244*
25. *ibid.*, p. 4.
26. *ibid.*, p. 34.
27. Hirtle, P.B. (2004) 'The Public Domain, Digitization, and Copyright'. Entry on LibraryLaw Blog, July 30. Available at *ttp://blog.librarylaw.com/librarylaw/2004/07/the_public_doma.html*

4

Metadata for digital collections

Metadata is structured information that describes or is otherwise associated with individual items in collections. This definition is intentionally broad and takes into account structured information other than that typically recognised by traditional library cataloguing, such as information describing a digital object's structure, and the history of how its constituent files have been migrated to new formats. This definition of metadata is not opposed to traditional library cataloguing, but recognises that libraries have generally focused on recording only certain types of information when describing printed books, serials and other formats. Describing the basic attributes of an item (its title, author, origin and so on) and describing what the item is 'about' are tasks that libraries have been doing for a long time, and these tasks are as important for digital collections as they are for print collections. However, digital documents differ in many ways from printed documents and appropriate use of a number of types of metadata is necessary for their management.

This chapter describes the types of metadata that you may create to accompany the content you are putting up on the web. Knowing the types of metadata and how they work together will assist you in a number of ways, such as in making decisions about the importance of metadata in your digital collections, in allocating the human and technological resources required to create and manage metadata, and in assessing the capabilities of systems used to create, store, make accessible and maintain digital content. This chapter also introduces the major metadata standards that you are likely to encounter; introduces topics associated with the creation and deployment of metadata, including application profiles, interoperability and persistent identifiers; and concludes by outlining some of the factors that should influence the decisions you make about the metadata you will be creating for your digital content.

Types of metadata

The types of metadata presented here all perform different functions:

- Descriptive metadata describes basic attributes of a resource such as its title, author, date of creation, publisher, its relationships to other resources, etc., that someone might use to find the resource.

- Administrative metadata describes details about a resource that are necessary for its administration or management.

- Structural metadata describes the relationships of a resource's component parts.

- Preservation metadata describes information pertaining to the history of a resource and the digital files that it consists of.

Defining these types helps us to clarify the roles played by the various types of metadata we record regarding digital resources, such as metadata's function within the systems we use to access those resources, and its functions surrounding the current and future management of those resources.

Descriptive metadata

As stated above, descriptive metadata records those attributes of a resource that someone might use to find that resource. These attributes are equivalent to the elements identified by the International Standard Bibliographic Descriptions, which define an element as: 'A word or phrase, or a group of characters, representing a distinct unit of bibliographic information and forming part of an area of the bibliographic description.'[1] The Dublin Core Metadata Initiative (DCMI) uses the term 'properties'; a property is a 'specific aspect, characteristic, attribute, or relation used to describe resources'.[2] Examples that fall under both definitions include a book's title, author, publication details, and so on.

A group of attributes describing a single resource is commonly known as a descriptive record. A descriptive record provides several functions, including assisting users in discovering resources, evaluating resources and grouping related resources together. An additional and important function that descriptive metadata serves is that it can be tailored to the resource discovery needs of a specific audience; for example, metadata intended to best suit the needs of primary school teachers may differ significantly from metadata describing the same resources but intended for adult education instructors. Finally, descriptive metadata from a variety of sources can be collected together to create 'virtual' collections. An excellent example of this type of aggregation is RePEc (Research Papers in Economics), which brings together the descriptive metadata of over 40 major and a large number of minor collections of material in the discipline of economics.[3]

A basic issue we must confront when planning a collection of digital content of any kind is whether the benefits of creating descriptive metadata for that content outweigh the potential costs and effort of creating it. Our choices can be represented as a continuum: at one end, we simply upload the content onto a web server and let search engines provide access to individual documents or parts of the collection. At the other end, we create detailed, complex and expensive descriptions of each item in our collection.

The first option, although appealing to many people as it totally eliminates the need for conventional descriptive metadata, is less than desirable for a number of reasons. Current general web search engines, while useful for finding textual documents on the open web, only look for text strings in documents and therefore are not equipped to deal with queries that contain terms having multiple meanings (or 'polysemic' terms). An often-cited example of this type of term is the English word 'mercury', which can be the name of a Roman deity, the name of an American carmaker, the name of a metal, the surname of a British singer and the name of a planet. The inability of general web search engines to handle polysemic terms can be compensated for by combining them with other terms, but this type of search only works if the additional terms exist within the same text as the polysemic term. General web search engines do not allow retrieval through the use of synonyms, broader topics or narrower topics (i.e. they do not incorporate any type of thesauri or syndetic structure). Another reason that general web search engines are not desirable as all-purpose resource discovery tools is that non-textual content, such as still images, audio and video, is typically not indexed by general search engines other than words that happen to be in the filenames or URLs of the image, audio or video files.

Most librarians do not need to be convinced that web search engines are not the best tool for every job. The opposite end of our continuum, creating detailed and complex descriptions of our items, may not be the best approach for most libraries either, for the simple reason that creating detailed, rich bibliographic descriptions is very time consuming and therefore very expensive. Ideally, we would strike a compromise between the first and second approaches. The challenge is to determine the appropriate amount of descriptive metadata to create. I will discuss the functional requirements of metadata later in this chapter, but the decision can be influenced by a number of factors including the nature of the material, the assumed nature of the intended audiences, the amount of staff and financial resources available, and the library's intent to commit to similar projects in the future.

Another issue surrounding descriptive metadata that planners of digital collections need to consider is defining exactly what the metadata describes, the original work or the digitized reproduction. The DCMI has articulated this problem as the 'One-to-One Principle' but it is relevant to any metadata. Put simply, there should be a 1 to 1 relationship between the description and the resource. As the DCMI puts it:

> In general Dublin Core metadata describes one manifestation or version of a resource, rather than assuming that manifestations stand in for one another. For instance, a jpeg image of the Mona Lisa has much in common with the original painting, but it is not the same as the painting. As such the digital image should be described as itself, most likely with the creator of the digital image included as a Creator or Contributor, rather than just the painter of the original Mona Lisa. The relationship between the metadata for the original and the reproduction is part of the metadata description, and assists the user in determining whether he or she needs to go to the Louvre for the original, or whether his/her need can be met by a reproduction.[4]

This principle is significant because descriptions of digitised versions of printed works will require elements that are not applicable to the print originals. For instance, the digital image representing a painting will have its own dimensions (and a file size), rights management information, and as the DCMI document cited above points out, its own creator (the person who took the digital photo of the painting). It will also contain information about its relationship to the original painting (using in MARC a 530 field, or in Dublin Core a Relation element, for example). In practice, however, it is not uncommon to include information describing the original version, such as the physical dimensions of the original, in the description of the digitised version with no indication that the information does not apply to the digitised version. Violation of the one-to-one principle can confuse end users (for example, if elements containing dimensions, location, availability, etc., do not unambiguously describe the digital representation of the resource or the resource itself), and can make management of the metadata problematic (for example, when the digital representation of the resource changes for some reason). However, the realities of metadata creation for many libraries mean that little attention is paid to respecting this principle, and collection planners will have to weigh the costs of respecting it against the benefits.

Descriptive metadata standards typically do not address rules of description – they only stipulate what elements should make up a description (i.e. the structure of the descriptions), not how the content of those elements should be derived. Most libraries base their cataloguing on AACR2 rules of description, and even though those rules are book-orientated, they are also applicable to metadata describing resources in digital collections, in particular those rules that apply to manuscripts. An important aspect of planning the metadata for a collection is to determine which cataloguing rules should apply. In addition to AACR2, other descriptive cataloguing rules of potential use include ISAD(G) (General International Standard Archival Description),[5] APPM (Archives, Personal Papers, and Manuscripts)[6] and GIHC (Graphic Materials: Rules for Describing Original Items and Historical Collections).[7] The Western States Metadata Best Practices guidelines[9] provide a useful example of the variety of cataloguing rules that can be used, and also serve as an example of good documentation for the generation of descriptive metadata.

The major descriptive metadata standards used by libraries for digital collection include MARC, Dublin Core, and MODS. We will discuss these in detail later in this chapter.

Administrative metadata

Administrative metadata facilitates the management of items or documents in a digital collection or in a repository containing a number of collections. The standards defining the elements that comprise administrative metadata for locally created content are not as mature as standards for descriptive metadata. The Digital Library Federation has developed a standard for managing collections licensed by libraries through its Electronic Resource Management Initiative[9] but its standard is not directly applicable to the management of digital collections created by libraries.

One articulation of administrative metadata is provided as part of METS (Metadata Encoding and Transmission Standard), developed by the Library of Congress. METS is an XML format for encoding descriptive, administrative and structural metadata pertaining to a resource in one file. METS breaks administrative metadata down into technical, intellectual property, source and digital provenance functions, but does not provide specific elements for each of these functions. Instead, for each of these functions it provides a 'wrapper' element for including metadata defined by other standards. For example, the technical metadata section of a METS file may contain specific elements from the NISO Z39.87 (Technical Metadata for Digital Still Images) standard,[10] or the intellectual property rights metadata section might contain elements from the eXtensible rights Markup Language.[11] The types of administrative metadata defined by METS are:

- *Technical metadata*: Information describing the files constituting a resource in terms of their creation, format and use characteristics.

- *Intellectual property rights metadata*: Information describing copyright and licensing of the digital resource.

- *Source metadata*: Information describing the print or analog original that the digital resource is based on.

- *Digital provenance metadata*: Information describing any master/derivative relationships between files that make up the digital resource, file migration history and other information relevant to preserving the digital resource.

Unfortunately, unlike standards for descriptive metadata, widely accepted standards enumerating specific elements for administrative metadata do not yet exist, so many libraries may choose not to implement METS, or at least the administrative metadata sections in METS. The Library of Congress provides the element set from a 1998 pilot project,[12] and the Making of America 2 project also provides an element set from around the same time.[13] The University of Virginia Library is currently developing an element set that contains administrative elements,[14] and a number of other libraries have published the element sets they use for their own collections. The University of South Carolina is one such library, and although its element set[15] is useful for describing projects, it does not apply to individual resources.

Given the lack of standardised administrative metadata elements, the best source for elements libraries can use is the standards for preservation metadata. For instance, the PREMIS Data Dictionary offers the following groups of elements:

- *Object*: Describes the files that make up the resource. Object metadata includes the unique identifier of the object, characteristics such as size, format; the creating application (for example, Adobe Photoshop CS2 for Windows XP), storage locations.

- *Events*: Describes actions (such as scanning, reformatting, moving and so on) that involve one or more Objects. Events metadata includes event type, event date and time, event outcome, and references to objects and agents.

- *Agents*: Describes people, organisations and software associated with events. Agent metadata includes identifiers, names, etc.

- *Rights*: Permission statements, details on the granting agreement and so on.

As PREMIS is focused on preservation and not general administration, not all of its elements will apply to general administration of digital resources; for example, its rights metadata only deals with rights to perform preservation activities such as migration to new formats, not to record transactions that a library has made in licensing copies of the resource to other parties for re-use and publication and other specific purposes. Widely applicable administrative metadata is still an evolving topic and PREMIS is used here only as an example of what *types* of elements should be included in such an element set.

The lack of a suitable element set should not be a rationalisation for avoiding the creation and management of administrative metadata. Libraries should record administrative metadata even if they need to create their own element set. Planned carefully, much of this metadata can be mapped to standards as they develop. At a minimum, libraries that are creating digital content should record the following administrative metadata:

- Unique identifier for resource, including an indication of collection or project.

- Copyright status of the resource, including any restrictions on its use and all re-uses of the resource by parties other than the creating library (re-publication in print or online, inclusion in other works, etc.).

- Date of digitisation (print) or initial processing (born digital).

- Date of various major steps in document production (creation of derivative files, optical character recognition, XML markup).

- Date the resource passed final quality control.

- Date the master files making up the resource were archived, and location of the files.

- Date the resource was made available to users.
- Problems discovered through normal quality control checks on the files and metadata generated during project operations, including the actions taken to resolve the problems (covered in detail in Chapter 9).

The name and if applicable contact information of people involved with any of these activities (the 'agents' in PREMIS' jargon) should also be recorded. Strategies for managing this administrative metadata vary – much of it can be included in the master list used during the production of the digital resources, but situations in which more than one agent has performed the same task can complicate the metadata management process, such as when a long book has taken more than one staff shift to scan. Again, spreadsheets and desktop database applications are suitable tools, as long as all the information pertaining to each resource can be retrieved efficiently.

Structural metadata

Structural metadata provides two functions: (1) to record information necessary to 'reconstruct' a resource from its constituent files and (2) to describe the structure of a resource to facilitate access to that resource.

The first function is necessary because the process of digitising documents often involves creating a number of files, and unless care is taken to describe the relationship of one file to another, it will not be possible to assemble the document into its original form. This issue applies to born-digital documents as well, because even documents created in word processing software, for example, may contain embedded images and other types of information that exist as separate files. This function of structural metadata is particularly important over time, as the files that make up a resource are moved to new storage media and are migrated to new file formats. A popular example for illustrating the necessity for robust structural metadata is that if you drop a book, you can pick it up and still flip through it from cover to cover, but if you lose track of the digital files that capture each page, you may never be able to view all the pages in their correct order.

The information required to do this cannot be generated from directory and filenames reliably. First, even though filenames sort predictably, it is common for errors to occur during the digitisation process, such as the accidental skipping of pages, which are therefore not named in sequence. Second, given the short maximum lengths of directory and filenames (as low as 255 characters on some popular operating systems), it is difficult to represent relationships between files if those relationships are more complex than a simple sequence, such as the files that make up an archived website. Despite these problems, filenames can serve as a useful form of structural metadata if properly assigned. For instance, filenames of resources consisting of multiple files that can be assembled into a linear sequence of pages, such as books and magazines, and non-textual resources consisting of discrete segments, such as multipart audio recordings, can effectively encode the proper sequence of the files. A simple example of such filenames is 001.tif, 002.tif, 003.tif, etc, where the last digit before the file extension identifies the first file, second file and third file corresponding to the first, second and third pages of a book. I will look at file naming conventions in more detail in Chapter 9.

The second function of structural metadata facilitates easy and flexible access to the resource, or more specifically, to particular locations within the resource. Using the book as an example again, a printed book's table of contents allows easy navigation to chapters of potential interest. In an online book, it may be desirable to replicate that navigation by providing hypertext links from the table of contents directly to the beginning of each chapter. This function of structural metadata does not apply to all types of resources or to all digital collections, but it can enhance access in a number of ways. Another example of this type of structural metadata is time indexes in a sound or video file that allow users to enter the file at a specific point other than the start of the file. Although not as important for preservation purposes as the first function of structural metadata, the information necessary to enable this type of access describes the structure of a resource.

METS offers a much richer framework for both the first function and the second function (structural map section) in more detail than it does for administrative metadata. METS' file element has a SEQ attribute that is used to define the order in which files follow to make up the described resource, as in the simplified example in Figure 4.1. This structural metadata can be created and maintained in a spreadsheet and then converted to METS XML when (or if) required (Table 4.1). Similarly, METS' structMap element can be used to encode information required to accomplish the second function of structural metadata (Table 4.2):

Figure 4.1	Simple METS fileSec metadata represented in XML

```
<fileSec>
  <fileGrp ID='BOOK0001'>
    <file ID='FILE001' SEQ='1'>
      <FLocat LOCTYPE='URL'>file:book0001/001.tif
        </FLocat>
    </file>
    <file ID='FILE002' SEQ='2'>
      <FLocat LOCTYPE='URL'>file:book0001/002.tif
        </FLocat>
    </file>
    <file ID='FILE003' SEQ='3'>
      <FLocat LOCTYPE='URL'>file:book0001/003.tif
        </FLocat>
  </file>
  </fileGrp>
</fileSec>
```

Table 4.1	The same METS fileSec metadata represented in a spreadsheet

fileGrp	fileID	SEQ	FLocat
BOOK0001	FILE001	1	001.tif
BOOK0001	FILE002	2	002.tif
BOOK0001	FILE002	3	003.tif

Table 4.2	Simple METS structMap metadata represented in a spreadsheet, showing the books and chapters in H. G. Wells' *War of the Worlds*

Div ID	Order	Label
Div1	1	Book I: The Coming of the Martians
Div1.1	2	Chapter 1: The Eve of the War
Div1.2	3	Chapter 2: The Falling-Star
Div1.3	4	Chapter 3: On Horsell Common
Div2	19	Book II: The Earth Under the Martians
Div2.1	20	Chapter 1: Under Foot
Div2.2	21	Chapter 2: What We Saw from the Ruined House
Div2.3	22	Chapter 3: The Days of Imprisonment

Preservation metadata

Preservation metadata is information required 'to manage and preserve digital materials over time and which will assist in ensuring contextual, historical, and technical information are preserved along with the digital object.'[16]

In their *Preservation Management of Digital Materials: A Handbook*, Maggie Jones and Neal Beagrie identify a number of differences between print and digital resources that make preservation metadata important. A selection of these differences includes:

- *Technology*: Unlike print materials, digital resources cannot be used without computer technology, and because technology changes so rapidly, documenting the technical requirements of digital resources is necessary to ensure it can be used as technology evolves.

- *Change*: The continual evolution of file formats requires periodic migration from one format to another (for example, from a word processor format to Acrobat PDF), and documenting these migrations may assist in the future use of the resource.

- *Rights management*: Normal use of digital resources and management of digital resources requires that they be copied; if sufficient information on the user's legal right to copy the resource is not available over time, the resource may not be used or managed.

- *Future re-use*: The re-use of digital materials in the future will not be possible unless sufficient information about the material is recorded to enable that re-use. For example, a book that was scanned to mount on the web for improved access may be used in the future to create a printed copy; if the location of the high-resolution versions of the scanned pages is not known, printed copies created from the low-resolution files created for mounting on the web will be of unsatisfactory quality.[17]

Many of these issues apply to non-digital resources as well; for example, audio tape cannot be used without a specific type of technology, and printed books have been reformatted into microfilm for decades. However, digital technology changes much faster than these analog technologies.

The major preservation metadata standards are PREMIS and the New Zealand National Library Preservation Metadata Schema. I will look at both of these later in this chapter.

How the types of metadata relate to each other

In some cases, the distinctions between the various types of metadata blur. What is the difference between administrative and preservation metadata? Some specifications (e.g. PREMIS) consider administrative metadata to be a part of preservation metadata whereas others (e.g. METS) consider preservation metadata to be part of administrative metadata. The standard types are based on functional differences in the way metadata can be used; therefore, the same metadata element can be classified as multiple types if it performs multiple functions. The information contained in an element named 'rights' can be used by one person to evaluate if that resource meets his or her information needs and can be used by a different user to determine who licence fees are paid to.

Theoretically, the various types of metadata about a given resource could be created, stored and maintained independent of each other. The advantage of managing metadata in this manner is that the tools, workflow and access restrictions pertinent to each type of metadata can also be distributed as appropriate for each type. As long as all of the metadata describing a resource can be accessed when needed and assembled in meaningful ways for searching and display, where it is created and managed is not important. Libraries already take advantage of this type of distributed metadata management environment. For instance, this is the way libraries manage the information about a given book in their collections – the bibliographic record is managed by the cataloging staff, and inventory information for each physical copy of the book is managed by the circulation staff. When an end user looks at the OPAC record for the book, the two kinds of relevant information are pulled together dynamically for display. The book's description is managed separately from information about its availability.

However appealing this model is, in practice most metadata for digital collections is managed and stored in a more centralised fashion. It is common to find metadata in digital collections that stores all information about a resource generated by a library in the course of making it available online in one 'record', exposing end users to types of metadata that they probably do not have to be exposed to, such as internal, administrative information documenting who scanned an image, when was it scanned and its system-level serial number. Although putting all of the metadata associated with a resource in the public record may simplify management of that metadata, doing so usually confuses end users and clutters record displays.

Selected major standards

This section identifies several important metadata standards that are relevant to digital collections produced by libraries. Before looking at some specific standards, we should consider two topics: functional requirements and application profiles.

Functional requirements for metadata

From a user's point of view, descriptive metadata assists in finding resources and in helping the user decide if a discovered resource meets his or her needs. Libraries must keep a number of factors in mind to ensure that the metadata they create to describe resources in their collections meets these goals effectively. All too often libraries choose a metadata schema without questioning whether it is the best one for a particular resource, collection, user group or intended use.

The International Association of Library Associations and Institutions' *Functional Requirements for Bibliographic Records*[18] (also known as FRBR) has focused attention on the tasks that users typically perform when using bibliographic descriptions. FRBR adopts a 'user-focused approach to analyzing data requirements insofar as it endeavours to define in a systematic way what it is that the user expects to find information about in a bibliographic record and how that information is used.'[19] The decision to select a descriptive metadata structure for a given digital collection should be based on careful consideration of the following factors, which, while not specifically mentioned in the FRBR report, are relevant to a user-centred approach to descriptive metadata:

- *The nature of the intended audience(s) for your collection*: Are they likely to be specialist or general users? If specialist, to what extent should you use terminology they will be familiar with? Is it possible to create metadata that satisfies both general and specialized users?

- *The nature of the material you are putting in your digital collection*: What are the most effective access points for this material? What level of granularity will most likely benefit your users. For example, is a description of a digitised book sufficient, or are your users likely to want to search for individual chapters, sections or illustrations within the book?

- *The 'level' of description (to borrow a term from AACR2)*: How many elements should make up a description? Is creator, title and date sufficient, or are other fields necessary as access points and as information that might be of interest to users?

- *The size of your collection*: The larger the collection, the more important metadata becomes for effective use of the collection.

- *How important is interoperability with services outside of your collection*: Will your metadata be shared with centralised search services, or searched along with metadata from other collections as can be done using federated search technologies?

- *The resources your library has for creation and long-term maintenance of the metadata*: How much effort do you want to invest in creating descriptive metadata? Given the nature of the material and your intended users, what elements will provide the greatest benefit at the lowest cost?

Typical user tasks can be defined in terms of 'use cases', which are structured descriptions of scenarios that are likely to occur when people are using your collection. Use cases are described in the next chapter in the context of defining functional requirements for planning the search and display functional requirements for a collection. The methods described there can be applied to defining use cases for determining desired elements for descriptive and structural metadata as well. However, use cases that are less structured than those described in the next chapter are also effective. An example of a less-structured use case intended to assist in determining the functional requirements for descriptive metadata for a collection of electronic theses could take the following form:

> A graduate student wants to see whether anyone else has written a thesis recently on the subject he is considering for his thesis, consumer attitudes to hybrid gasoline-electric vehicles.

This is a fairly plausible scenario, one that a librarian might encounter at a reference desk or in an e-mail from a graduate student. To apply a use case analysis to this scenario, we determine how a user might best go about finding relevant works and itemise any descriptive metadata elements that would likely assist in the search. We know that (1) the user is only interested in theses (as he is not looking for information on consumer attitudes to hybrid vehicles, but rather if anyone has written a thesis on that topic), (2) the user is interested in recent theses and (3) we know the relevant subject area (consumer attitudes to hybrid vehicles). Drawing these requirements out of the scenario allows us to identify the elements in a descriptive record that would assist in finding relevant records: (1) an element that identified the work as a thesis (in other words, an element that describes the work's form, genre or type; (2) an element that indicated the work's date of publication; and (3) one or more elements that describe the work's subject(s). This type of analysis, based on a set of use cases that covers a wide variety of plausible types of queries that a given audience for a given collection would be interested in, will allow us to identify a comprehensive set of element types for inclusion in the descriptive metadata for that collection. The number of use cases that should be considered is determined by the factors listed above. Members of the intended audience are the best source of realistic use cases, so information on how the source material is already used (in analog form) is extremely valuable when creating use cases for analysis.

Application profiles

Creating a metadata schema of your own is a time-consuming, complex and resource-intensive endeavour. It is always better to use an existing schema such as the ones I will describe later in this chapter, not only to save your library the effort of creating its own metadata schema but also to promote consistency with other digital collections.

An alternative to creating your own schema or using an existing one is to develop an application profile for your collection. Application profiles are 'schemas which consist of data elements drawn from one or more namespaces, combined together by implementors, and optimised for a particular local application.'[20] Using application profiles (or APs as they are abbreviated), it is possible to borrow metadata elements from a variety of standards or schemas (the namespaces mentioned in the quotation) and to combine them to create descriptions that are most applicable and effective for a given collection of material or a given use of that material. To rephrase the above definition, application profiles define and document which metadata elements you are using, where you borrowed them from and how you are using them.

The idea that we can create our own metadata structures using components borrowed from others means that we do not have to be bound by existing metadata element sets if those element sets are not applicable to the material we are describing. It also means that if existing metadata structures are not appropriate to our material or users, we do not have to create our own element set from the ground up – an activity that would require more resources than most libraries are willing to invest.

Application profiles supply mechanisms for 'mixing and matching' diverse elements such that they are combined in systematic, standardised ways. Guidelines for constructing Dublin Core-based application profiles have been formalised by the European Committee for Standardization[21] to provide specifications for the overall structure application profiles, for the definitions of the components that make up application profiles, and for best practices in combining diverse elements and element refinements.

Even though implementers are free to develop their own application profiles, the DCMI has created a Library Application Profile[22] that many implementers will find is both comprehensive and flexible enough for their needs. Most of the elements in this profile are taken from the DCMI Metadata Terms element set, but the dateCaptured, edition and location elements are borrowed from MODS (which is described below), and several elements are original to the AP, such as DOI (referring to the standard Digital Object Identifier), ISBN, ISSN and SICI (referring to the standard Serial Item and Contributor Identifier). In addition to defining an element set for use in library applications, the Library Application Profile documents a large number of element refinements, encoding schemes and usage guidelines for specific elements.

One last point about application profiles: you will eventually encounter references to 'machine-readable' schemas for application profiles. One of the long-term goals of application profiles is to provide mechanisms enabling software to process structured metadata consistent with the vision of the Semantic Web, typically by expressing metadata in RDF (Resource Description Framework) structures. Even though this use of application profiles is emerging as a primary focus for the DDCMI and is motivating an active research community (as demonstrated by the annual Dublin Core conferences), application profiles continue to be the best way to document the metadata structures we are employing in our digital collections so that *humans* can apply and use metadata effectively.

MARC

MARC is the standard format in which libraries exchange bibliographic records and other types of associated information. Integrated Library Systems (ILSs) can import and export bibliographic records in this format, and it is the format understood by software for manipulating catalogue records purchased from commercial services and obtained from other libraries.

The following is an example of a brief MARC record describing this photograph of a bridge in Vancouver, British Columbia (Figure 4.2):

Figure 4.2 A view of Vancouver's Lions Gate Bridge

Figure 4.3 is a simple MARC record, formatted in conventional field–indicator–subfield layout, that describes the photograph:

Figure 4.3 A simple description encoded in MARC

```
100     1     _aJordan, Mark
245     00    _aA view of Vancouver's Lions Gate Bridge
              _h[picture]
260           _aUnpublished
              _c2005
342     00    _g-123.139
              _h49.3154
522           _aPhoto taken from Ambleside Park West
              Vancouver, looking east toward
              Vancouver Harbour.
651     0     _aLions Gate Bridge
              _xVancouver, B.C.
651     0     _aVancouver, B.C.
```

This example is not intended to illustrate proper use of AACR2 or any other rules of description, but rather to show that the standard record structure that most librarians are familiar with can be used to encode metadata describing a type of resource typically found in digital collections. However, encoding metadata in MARC only makes sense if the collection being described will be accessible via a system that supports MARC, in most cases an integrated library system. Many libraries choose not to make locally created collections available in their catalogues but rather to make them accessible through other types of database or content management software (some examples of which will be covered in Chapter7).

Dublin Core

The Dublin Core element set 'is a standard for cross-domain information resource description'[23] that can be applied to any type of resource. There are 15 Dublin Core elements ranging from Creator (which can include the roles of author, artist, photographer, composer, etc.) to Rights (which includes information about copyright and legal uses of the resource being described). The DCMI is responsible for maintaining the element set, for co-ordinating a number of working groups, and for promoting collaboration with other agencies such as the Library of Congress.

Dublin Core metadata can be either unqualified or qualified. Unqualified Dublin Core uses only the 15 standard elements to describe resources (in simple element/value pairs) whereas qualified Dublin Core specifies additional information about the values using either *refinements* or *encoding schemes*. Refinements make the Dublin Core element more specific, and encoding schemes 'aid in the interpretation of an element value'[24] by identifying controlled vocabularies or standard notations for expressing dates, addresses and other types of data.

Tables 4.3 and 4.4. illustrate the use of Dublin Core in both its unqualified and qualified forms, showing simple element/value pairs:

Table 4.3 A simple description encoded in unqualified Dublin Core

Element	Value
Title	A view of Vancouver's Lions Gate Bridge
Creator	Jordan, Mark
Date	July 24, 2005
Subject	Lions Gate Bridge (Vancouver, B.C.)
Subject	Vancouver (B.C.)

Table 4.3 A simple description encoded in unqualified Dublin Core (*Cont'd*)

Description	Photo taken from Ambleside Park West Vancouver, looking east toward Vancouver Harbour
Type	Image
Coverage	Latitude 49.3154 Longitude −123.139

Here is the same description, this time using qualified Dublin Core elements:

Table 4.4 A simple description encoded in qualified Dublin Core

Element	Qualifier	Value
Title		A view of Vancouver's Lions Gate Bridge
Creator		Jordan, Mark
Date	Created [DCMI]	2005-07-24
Subject	LCSH	Lions Gate Bridge (Vancouver, B.C.)
Subject	LCSH	Vancouver (B.C.)
Description		Photo taken from Ambleside Park West Vancouver, looking east toward Vancouver Harbour
Type	DCMI	Image
Coverage	Spatial [DCMI]	Latitude 49.3154 Longitude −123.139

In the second column, 'Created' and 'Spatial' are element refinements (coming from the DCMI Metadata Terms set[25]), and 'LCSH' is an encoding scheme, indicating that the subjects come from the Library of Congress Subject headings vocabulary.

These examples of Dublin Core could have been expressed in XML[26] or HTML[27] instead of in a simple table; the Dublin Core element set does not prescribe a particular syntax for its expression. The intent here is to present the same values ('A view of Vancouver's Lions Gate Bridge', '2005-07-2', etc.) used in the MARC example but structured using Dublin Core elements.

The Dublin Core element set is often criticised for being too simple, particularly when compared with the perceived 'richness' of MARC. This complaint stems from a misunderstanding of the roles of unqualified and qualified Dublin Core. Critics of Dublin Core seem to forget that the elements can be qualified to the extent necessary for a given application, and that qualified Dublin Core can be as rich as MARC or any other metadata format. Application profiles are the conventional mechanism for documenting qualifications. Unqualified Dublin Core, although in most cases too simple to serve as a native metadata structure, plays an important role in the 'Dumb-Down Principle',[28] the ability to provide a common set of elements that other, richer metadata formats can be translated into for a wide variety of purposes. Although 'dumbing down' has been misinterpreted to be a negative aspect of Dublin Core, the phrase describes a significant feature, not a limitation. As we will see later in this chapter, standardised mappings, or tables of equivalent elements, exist to translate MARC, MODS and other metadata formats to (and from) Dublin Core for the purposes of aggregating and federated searching.

MODS

MODS (the Metadata Object Description Schema) is a metadata standard that 'includes a subset of MARC fields and uses language-based tags rather than numeric ones, in some cases regrouping elements from the MARC 21 bibliographic format.'[29] MODS is maintained by the Library of Congress and is thoroughly documented, including detailed information on how MODS elements map to MARC fields, Dublin Core elements and other well-known metadata formats. A full XML schema for MODS has also been developed, which promotes automated validation of MODS records and high levels of interoperability with other schemas, such as Open Archives Initiative Protocol for Metadata Harvesting and METS, both of which are discussed below. There is also a documented version of MODS called MODS Lite that only contains elements that correspond to the 15 Dublin Core elements. The official MODS website contains links to a number of software tools and utilities for working with MODS, including stylesheets for batch converting other MARC, Dublin Core and other records to and from MODS.

Perhaps MODS' most attractive feature is that it is both richer than unqualified Dublin Core and simpler than MARC. Also, it is more flexible than MARC in some ways; for example, there are no required elements (but each MODS record must have at least one element, unlike Dublin Core), and all elements are repeatable, and, as Karen Coyle has pointed out, the concepts of 'main entry' and 'added entry' do not exist in MODS.[30]

Collections that use MODS include the New Jersey Digital Highway[31] and the Election 2002 Web Archive,[32] although end users do not and probably should not know what XML schema is being used to structure

Figure 4.4   A simple MODS description

```
<?xml version='1.0' encoding='UTF-8' ?>

<mods xmlns:xlink='http://www.w3.org/1999/xlink'
version='3.0'
xmlns:xsi='http://www.w3.org/2001/XMLSchema-instance'
xmlns='http://www.loc.gov/mods/v3'
xsi:schemaLocation='http://www.loc.gov/mods/v3
http://www.loc.gov/standards/mods/v3/mods-3-0.xsd'>

  <titleInfo>
    <title>A view of Vancouver's Lions Gate
Bridge</title>
  </titleInfo>

  <name type='personal'>
     <namePart>Jordan, Mark</namePart>
     <role>
       <roleTerm type='text'>photographer</roleTerm>
     </role>
</name>

  <typeOfResource>picture</typeOfResource>

  <originInfo>
    <publisher>Unpublished</publisher>
    <dateIssued>2005</dateIssued>
  </originInfo>

<note>Photo taken from Ambleside Park West Vancouver,
looking east toward Vancouver Harbour</note>

<subject authority='lcsh'>
  <topic>Lions Gate Bridge</topic>
  <geographic>Vancouver (B.C.)</geographic>
</subject>
```

Figure 4.4	A simple MODS description (*Cont'd*)

```
<subject authority='lcsh'>
  <geographic>Vancouver (B.C.)</geographic>
</subject>

<recordInfo>
  <recordCreationDate encoding='marc'>050730
  </recordCreationDate>
    <recordChangeDate
encoding='iso8601'>20050830080228.8
    </recordChangeDate>
  </recordInfo>
</mods>
```

a collection's metadata. Both collections provide documentation on their metadata that is orientated to librarians and other potential implementers.[33] A list of examples describing other types of material is available on the MODS website.[34]

Figure 4.4 shows a MODS record for describing the photo of the Lions Gate Bridge (represented in XML).

METS

METS (the Metadata Encoding & Transmission Standard) is 'a standard for encoding descriptive, administrative and structural metadata regarding objects within a digital library, expressed using the XML schema language.'[35] METS is not a descriptive metadata standard but instead acts as a 'container' for other types of metadata pertaining to a single resource. A METS file can include the following sections:

- *METS header*: This section contains information about the METS file itself, including its creator, the date it was last modified, etc.

- *Descriptive metadata*: A METS file can point to a record describing the resource using a URL, PURL (persistent URL) and other addressing schemes; alternatively, a METS document can contain a descriptive metadata record, or it can both point to and contain such records. Valid types of descriptive records include MARC, MODS, Encoded Archival Description and Dublin Core, to name a few common types.

- *Administrative metadata*: Technical, intellectual property, source and digital provenance (described earlier in this chapter).

- *File section*: Lists all the files that make up the resource. Can contain separate <fileGRP> elements grouping similar files together, such as thumbnails, high-resolution TIFF files, etc. It is also possible to embed the actual files that make up the resource in this section of a METS file by converting them to a textual representation that can be reconstructed using a standard algorithm.

- *Structural map*: Defines a hierarchical structure that facilitates navigating through the described resource. Also provides mechanisms for pointing to other METS files, such as those describing another resource that the current one is part of. Elements in the structural map section point to files listed in the file section. The structural map is the only required section in a METS file.

- *Structural links*: Most relevant to the description of websites, this section defines any hypertext links between files described in the structural map.

- *Behaviour*: METS has the ability to associate 'executable behaviours' with the other elements included in the METS file. These behaviours can be described in terms of input and output to abstract algorithms or specific software applications.

The METS Implementation Registry[36] lists collections that use METS, including the California Digital Library's Content Management System/Digital Object Repository, the Chinese Ministry of Education's Chinese Digital Museum Project and the National Library of Wales' Digital Mirror set of collections.

Because METS provides a structured method for describing a comprehensive set of metadata elements about a resource, it is being adopted by a number of digital preservation initiatives. As pointed out on the METS homepage, METS can be used within the OAIS (Open Archival Information Systems) Framework, which I will describe in Chapter 11. Work is underway to make METS files produced by the DSpace Institutional Repository platform comply with the OAIS framework, for example.[37]

PREMIS and the New Zealand National Library Preservation Metadata Framework

The PREMIS Data Dictionary for Preservation Metadata: Final Report of the PREMIS Working Group, which I have already discussed in the context of administrative and structural metadata, is a joint effort between the Online Computer Library Center (OCLC) and the Research Libraries Group (RLG). Maintenance activities are hosted by the Library of Congress.[38] In addition to defining a preservation metadata element set, the *Data Dictionary* illustrates the application of the element set to a range of resources and their constituent objects, including a Microsoft Word document, an electronic thesis comprising an Adobe Acrobat PDF and an MP3 audio file, a newspaper created in QuarkXPress, a website, a digital signature and a digital photograph. The Report also discusses issues in implementing a preservation metadata records keeping system, such as requirements for PREMIS compliance, implementation of the data model, metadata storage, automated metadata generation, and issues related to the preservation of metadata associated with websites and HTML pages.

An alternative to PREMIS is the National Library of New Zealand's Metadata Standards Framework – Preservation Metadata.[39] The NZNL framework is intended to 'serve as an implementation template while at the same time remaining consistent with standards being developed internationally around preservation metadata.' The NZNL framework defines fewer elements than PREMIS (72 versus 122), and is in general much simpler. However, the NZNL element set only describes the 'preservation master' – i.e. the single copy of the preserved resource – and not multiple representations of a resource, as PREMIS does (although PREMIS acknowledges that a repository may elect not to preserve more than one representation of a resource[40]).

Format-specific metadata schemas

The metadata formats above are general in the sense that they can be applied successfully to any type of resource. Many metadata standards exist that focus on particular kinds of resources. The brief list presented here is not intended to be comprehensive but only to illustrate some of these standards.

MPEG-7[41] is emerging as the leading general metadata standard for describing audio and video resources. MPEG-7 defines a comprehensive XML schema for descriptive, structural and technical metadata, and allows extensions to be created so that it can adapt to new applications easily. One of the most important aspects of MPEG-7 is that it provides mechanisms for describing segments of video and audio within resources based on time indexes.

NISO Z39.87 (Data Dictionary – Technical Metadata for Digital Still Images),[42] mentioned earlier in relation to METS, documents technical aspects of raster image (images consisting of rectangular grids of pixels, such as images in TIFF, JPEG2000 and DejaVu formats). Elements in this specification include those describing format, compression, file size, colour profile and image capture technologies such as scanners and digital cameras. NISO Z39.87 does not include provenance, rights management and other types of metadata that are covered by PREMIS and other more comprehensive standards.

Metadata specifications for raw data sets include DDI (Data Documentation Initiative) for social science data and CSDGM (Content Standard for Digital Geospatial Metadata) for geospatial data. DDI[43] describes not only the files containing the raw data but also the study that produced the data, the survey variables that were used to generate the data and any other supporting documentation for the data. The CSDGM is intended to 'provide a common set of terminology and definitions for the documentation of digital geospatial data'[44] such as GIS (Geographic Information Systems), remote sensing and biogeographical data. It defines metadata elements and provides guidelines on determining element values, and also provides a number of case studies.

Collection description

Although most discussions of metadata for digital collections focus on descriptions of individual items within a collection, in some cases it is useful to describe an entire collection of digital documents. The most obvious example of this type of description is an entry in a directory of collections. The DCMI Collection Description Working Group[45] is developing an application profile, vocabularies and supporting documentation for collection-level descriptions.

This type of description is important because it facilitates the creation of human-readable and machine-interoperable directories and registries of collections, which in turn lead to more effective resource discovery. As the Working Group's website cited above puts it:

> The creation of collection descriptions allows the owners or curators of collections to disclose information about their existence and availability to interested parties. Although collection descriptions may take the form of unstructured textual documents, for example a set of Web pages describing a collection, there are significant advantages in describing collections using structured, open and standardised formats. Such machine-readable descriptions enable:

- users to discover and locate collections of interest,
- users to perform searches across multiple collections in a controlled way,
- software to perform such tasks on behalf of users, based on known user preferences.

There are additional advantages where item level catalogues do not exist for collections, as a collection description may provide some indication to the remote user of content and coverage.

An entire issue of *D-Lib Magazine* (September 2000) is devoted to collection-level descriptions,[46] and NISO is currently developing a standard for collection description, Z39.91.[47]

Subject access and authority control

I have not yet discussed subject access to resources in digital collections. However, most libraries will want to provide some sort of subject access to their content. All of the techniques used in providing subject access to print collections can be applied successfully to digital collections, and in general the processes involved are the same as those used for subject cataloguing of print materials. Unfortunately, this means that classifying your digital resources, adding controlled subject headings or descriptors, and providing summary notes are expensive activities that will increase the costs of metadata creation considerably.

Assigning subject headings to books and to items in a digital collection differs in three significant ways. First, the subject headings most commonly used in English-speaking libraries – namely the Library of Congress Subject Headings – are not necessarily the most suitable vocabulary for some types of digital resources. Finding appropriate vocabularies can be challenging. Two lists of alternative subject vocabularies are the TASI (Technical Advisory Service for Images) list[48] and Michael Middleton's list of controlled vocabularies.[49] Second, it is likely that many of the authors or creators of resources that are being added to local digital collections will not have authority records for their names in standard sources, meaning that libraries will end up creating and maintaining authority records for these names outside of traditional name authority sources. Finally, the mechanisms for incorporating subject vocabularies and name authority records into digital library metadata creation tools is, in general, not as sophisticated as the analogous tools incorporated into standard integrated library systems. These three factors may complicate metadata creation and maintenance and should be considered early in the process of planning for digital collection building workflows.

A trend that is currently receiving considerable attention is folksonomies, or user-contributed subject descriptors. This approach should probably not replace conventional subject access, but it is worth exploring because it has the potential to enrich traditional subject access while allowing users to become engaged with library collections in new ways. Library-orientated tools for managing bibliographies are emerging, such as Connotea[50] and CiteULike,[51] but little has been published on the use of folksonomies in library collections of any type. It is interesting to note that the topic is receiving some attention in the museum sector.[52]

Persistent identifiers

Each resource in a collection must have an identifier. This identifier must be unique, persistent (in other words, it should not change over time) and it must have a public form (i.e. it must be something that can be used outside the context of the content management system or file system that stores the resource). These qualities of identifiers are important so that users can be led to the resource (in other words, so each resource can have its own unique address) but also so that various components of a resource, including master files and different types of metadata, can be associated reliably with the resource.

I have already discussed filenames and how they can encode simple structural metadata. Filenames (more precisely, file paths including directory structures) serve as unique identifiers for the individual files on a computer's file system, but because many resources consist of multiple files, filenames are not suitable as resource identifiers. Furthermore, files can change location during normal maintenance over time, and although the changes in location should be documented as part of administrative and preservation metadata, the fact that the filenames can change makes them unsuitable for persistent identifiers. This is not to say that filenames cannot be derived from identifiers; rather, identifiers should not be derived from filenames.

Identifiers can either be assigned automatically as a byproduct of entering metadata about a resource into software that generates its own internal unique identifiers, or be assigned manually. In the first case, applications such as relational databases assign a unique serial number to a resource as part of their internal record creation processes. In relational databases, this number is called the 'primary key' for the resource's record. This key is guaranteed to be unique within the database. It can also be used outside of the system that created it as part of a resource's unique identifier. Because these keys are generated by a specific instance of the database, care must be taken when migrating from the application that assigned the identifier to another application (e.g. from one relational database management system to another) so that the keys remain the same for each record. Identifiers assigned in this way do not encode any information other than the order in which they were created by the database.

Manually assigned identifiers have the advantage over automatically assigned identifiers in that they allow certain types of information to be encoded into the identifier. This information may include one or more codes indicating specific collections or projects, and it may also include a serial number that is either manually incremented or based on an existing unique identifier already in use by the library, such as an accession number used for the version of the resource in the library's print collection. For example, in a project digitising the following titles by Daniel Defoe, a library might assign the following identifiers (Table 4.5):

Table 4.5   **Sample persistent identifiers**

dfoe0001	The Complete English Tradesman
dfoe0002	Dickory Cronke
dfoe0003	An Essay Upon Projects
dfoe0004	The Fortunes and Misfortunes of the Famous Moll Flanders
dfoe0005	From London to Land's End
dfoe0006	The Further Adventures of Robinson Crusoe

The first four characters of the identifier indicate the collection and the last four indicate the serial number within that collection.

Codes that are used to represent institutions, projects or collections should be chosen such that they do not have to be revised because their scope changes in the future. For example, the choice of 'dfoe' in our example is suitable for a collection that will only contain items by that author or otherwise fall within that specific collection, but is not suitable for a collection that also includes works by Defoe's contemporaries or that might in the future be expanded to include works other than those by Defoe. Also, it is important that certain types of information *not* be used as part of persistent identifiers, including publication dates, ISBNs and ISSNs, or codes for physical locations, as these can change over time or are otherwise insufficiently reliable to be considered persistent.

A hybrid approach to creating resource identifiers, combining the advantages of automatic and manual identifier assignment, is to use software to add 'coded' components of the identifier to the unique primary keys generated by a database to form unique resource identifiers. This type of concatenation can be programmed into spreadsheets or database applications used to manage administrative metadata.

The public version of a resource's identifier can take many forms, but the most typical form is that of a URL (Uniform Resource Locator). URLs point to specific addresses on the Internet, most commonly to addresses accessible via the Hypertext Transfer Protocol and prefixed with the characters 'http'. The problem with URLs is that because they reflect domain, server, directory and file names, they change too frequently to be considered reliable persistent addresses. To overcome this problem, a number of mechanisms have been developed. The most common of these are the Handle system, PURLs, and DOIs. The Handle System[53] provides tools and protocols for maintaining stable identifiers for resources that point to current URLs for those resources. Handles are implemented in the DSpace institutional repository software. PURLs[54] are similar to handles in that they act as stable identifiers that reroute, or 'resolve', to a resource's current URL. Both of these systems are based on simple data structures that associate a resource's stable address with the actual current address. Handles and PURLs both require that the URLs associated with the stable addresses be maintained manually, however. DOIs[55] are another type of identifier used mainly by journal publishers to assign unique identifiers to individual articles. Libraries have not adopted DOIs as persistent names for resources in their digital collections, probably because there are direct costs associated with registering DOIs. Other persistent naming schemes that are worth investigating include the info URI scheme[56] and ARK (Archival Resource Key).[57] The Library of Congress maintains a useful overview of naming schemes that provides links to further information.[58] A publicly available example of a file naming and persistent identifier guideline is available from the National Library of Australia.[59]

A common approach to creating URLs within digital collections is to include resources' unique identifiers in the URLs. Using this technique, a resource's URL can change as long as the embedded identifier can still be associated reliably with the resource. The migration from old URLs to new ones can be managed using the ability of standard web servers to 'rewrite' URLs so that obsolete ones are automatically mapped to new ones, parsing out the resource identifier in the old address to create the new address as the old URL is requested.

To summarise, best practices for creating unique identifiers for resources are:

- Create unique identifiers for every discrete resource using sequentially assigned serial numbers, either assigned manually or by a database management system or other types of software.

- Assign codes indicating the collection, project, etc., associated with the resource, as long as those codes will not change over time.

- Do not base unique identifiers on potentially unreliable information such as ISBNs.

- Consider implementing a PURL or Handle server so that persistent network addresses can be assigned to resources. These resolving systems require considerable maintenance, however.

- Consider incorporating resource identifiers in URLs to aid in migrating from old URLs to new ones.

Interoperability

Digital resources do not exist in a vacuum. Users may want to search multiple collections of resources at the same time, libraries may want to distribute metadata describing their resources for a variety of reasons, and the same metadata can be used in different contexts for different purposes. Interoperability refers to the ability of metadata to fulfil these types of functions. The term is certainly not specific to metadata – it is an important concern in telecommunications and software engineering, for example, and in many other sectors. As it applies to metadata, interoperability describes a number of qualities including metadata's ability to be transformed or converted into different schemas while still remaining useful, its ability to be processed by a variety of different technologies and its ability to be combined with similar metadata effectively.

Libraries tend to use 'interoperability' to refer to metadata and to systems. I have already discussed an important aspect of the Dublin Core schema that facilitates interoperability between groups of metadata: the dumb down principle. Here I am using it to serve as an illustration of interoperability in metadata. If two rich metadata schemas both contain elements that can be dumbed down to the Dublin Core Creator element, a user can perform a search on the common Creator element effectively because the two sets of metadata are compatible, or interoperable. The search will be a 'simple' search in the sense that the user is no longer able to enjoy the richness of the respective schemas, but the advantages of being able to search a common element from multiple schemas may outweigh the loss of richness if the goal of this type of search is simple resource discovery.

Interoperability in metadata systems can be illustrated by two protocols used by libraries, the OAI-PMH (Open Archives Initiative Protocol for Metadata Harvesting)[60] and Z39.50 (Information Retrieval: Application Service Definition & Protocol Specification).[61] Although these two protocols serve different purposes (OAI-PMH defines how metadata can be harvested and Z39.50 supports searching and retrieval), they both define types of interoperability that are required to achieve specific tasks.

OAI-PMH defines mechanisms to allow metadata to be 'exposed' by digital collections ('repositories') so that software applications called 'harvesters' are able to request that metadata. The protocol defines six simple verbs (such as Identify, ListRecords, GetRecord) that harvesters can issue to repositories, and defines an XML syntax for packaging up the repository's responses. The purpose of exposing your metadata to harvesters is to allow it to be collected and used in services such as centralised searching, current awareness services, etc. OAI-PMH can expose metadata in any format but requires as a minimum that metadata be harvestable expressed in unqualifed Dublin Core. Applications such as DSpace, ePrints, Greenstone, Fedora, and CONTENTdm support OAI harvesting. The best known service built on metadata harvested using OAI-PMH is OAIster,[62] which makes nearly six million harvested records searchable at once.

Z39.50 provides a language, or set of commands, for searching metadata and for retrieving found records. The goal of Z39.50 is to allow any compliant client (known as the 'origin') to search any compliant server (known as the 'target') and for the server to return records in formats that the client can display, download and so on. Z39.50 is commonly deployed in integrated library systems to facilitate federated searching for interlibrary lending and other types of resource sharing. Although not as common in systems used for managing digital collections, Z39.50's ability to provide powerful, platform-independent search and retrieval capabilities makes it a important requirement for many libraries when they are selecting systems. Some implementations of Z39.50, such as SRU/W,[63] combine the sophistication of the protocol with newer, web-based technologies that will widen its applicability to digital collections.

To summarise my discussion of interoperability, the greater the extent to which metadata adheres to standards and accepted specifications, the more likely it will be successful at interacting with other metadata and with a wide variety of software applications. Attention paid to interoperability issues in the planning, creation and maintenance of metadata associated with digital resources will pay off in terms of re-usability, compatibility and usefulness in the future.

Native vs. derived metadata

Closely related to interoperability is the idea of native versus derived metadata. Metadata schemas such as MARC and MODS prescribe a syntax for structuring records – MARC according to the ISO 2709 standard and MODS according to a particular XML schema – but there is no reason that the metadata in MARC and MODS records has to be created and managed in these particular formats. The individual elements could be maintained in relational database tables, using software interfaces that 'know' nothing of MARC and MODS. When records are needed in these formats so that they can be shared, information in the relational database can be converted into valid MARC and MODS, as long as it is possible to identify which fields in the database tables correspond to the correct fields, indicators and subfields in MARC and the correct elements and attributes in MODS. As another example, descriptive metadata that is structured according to the Dublin Core element set could be created and stored in a spreadsheet, then converted to XML for OAI harvesting, converted to MARC for loading into an integrated library system and encoded in HTML META tags for inclusion in a web page.

These examples illustrate that it is possible to manipulate metadata so that its structure conforms to multiple formats. The process by which this manipulation is achieved is variously known as 'converting', 'transforming', 'mapping' or 'crosswalking' metadata from one format to another. Through these processes, it is possible to use metadata intended for one application in many others. The examples above use descriptive standards, but our discussion of structural metadata earlier in this chapter illustrates how values maintained in a spreadsheet could be converted into elements in a METS document. The overall idea is that metadata in one format can be converted into other formats using software utilities of various kinds.

However, this conversion is not always possible or desirable. Converting from a richer format (such as MARC) to a simpler format (such as unqualified Dublin Core) often results in a loss of data; unqualified Dublin Core cannot encode how many characters of a title should be ignored when sorting records alphabetically, as MARC field 245 and 440 second indicators do, for example. Going in the opposite direction, from simpler to richer, is only possible if the values in the simpler format meet the minimum requirements for corresponding elements in the richer format.

In addition, transformation between metadata formats is problematic if done inconsistently. This is particularly evident if the reason for transforming the metadata is to bring together records from a variety of sources so they can be searched, processed or otherwise used centrally. Effective mappings for transformations to and from common formats are available for general use. For example, the Library of Congress maintains a list of standard mappings between MARC and other formats.[64] Table 4.6 below illustrates how selected MARC fields map to MODS and unqualified Dublin Core.

Table 4.6   **Mappings between MARC, MODS and unqualified Dublin Core**

MARC fields and subfields	MODS elements	Unqualified Dublin Core elements
100, 700	<name> with type='personal'	Creator
245 afgk	<title> with no <titleInfo> type attribute	Title
260 $g	<dateCreated>	Date
500 $a	<note> with no 'type' or 'uri' attribute	Description
600, 610, 611, 630, 650, 651	<subject> with appropriate 'authority' attribute	Subject
760–787 $h	<extent>	Relation

A more general list of mappings, which includes formats other than MARC, is available from UKOLN.[65]

Sources of metadata

Unlike descriptive records for published items acquired by libraries, descriptive metadata for many resources that are digitised or otherwise processed for inclusion in digital collections generally cannot be obtained from external sources but must be created locally. Administrative, structural and preservation metadata must also be created for these resources – even if a catalogue record for a book is available from the library's catalogue or from another library, information about the files being generated by digitising it and their relationships to one another will not be. Workflows for generating all types of metadata are an important component of planning the operational aspects of developing digital collections and will vary widely depending on the type of resource being digitised or converted, the types of metadata being generated and the tools available for generating the metadata.

Several sources of descriptive metadata for digital collections that are external to the library do exist. For some types of resources, the authors or creators can be persuaded to become involved in necessary workflows. Author-generated metadata is commonly used in institutional repositories[66] and electronic theses and dissertation collections. Although author-generated metadata sometimes falls below librarians' expectations, in some situations it has proven to be useful and effective.[67] Another source of metadata external to libraries is content vendors. So far I have been assuming that digital collections are of material that is unique and that therefore it is impossible to purchase metadata from a vendor. However, some content vendors such as Saskia,[68] which licenses digital versions of art images to libraries for local mounting, supply descriptive metadata to accompany their content. In multi-institution projects, the work of generating the required metadata can be spread among several partners. For instance, some partners can create descriptive metadata, some (probably those where the creation of the files occurs) can create structural metadata and others can focus on preservation metadata. Finally, libraries have the option of hiring cataloguing service providers to create descriptive metadata.

Some types of metadata need not be created manually. A great deal of attention is currently being paid to automatic metadata generation techniques, particularly for administrative and preservation metadata such as format, file size, modification date and so on. JHOVE (the JSTOR/Harvard Object Validation Environment)[69] performs format-specific identification, validation and characterisation of digital objects. Identification is the process of determining a file's format (such as TIFF, XML, plain text); validation is the process of determining the level of compliance a file has with the format's formal specification; and characterisation is the process of determining the format-specific properties of a file (such as those described in NISO Z39.87). JHOVE can be used to generate formatVersion and other elements in the PREMIS preservation metadata element set.

Research on techniques for using software to generate abstracts of textual resources and on classifying resources is showing promise. A number of products capable of performing this type of metadata generation exist, both proprietary (such as Autonomy's IDOL Server[70] and Teragram's Dictionary Builder and Classifier[71]) and open source (Open Text Summarizer,[72] Classifier4j[73] and the INFOMINE iVia tools[74]). Automatic classification and summarisation tools are worth investigating as supplements to manually created metadata, but it will probably be some time before they can replace human-generated subject analysis.

Strategies for metadata creation and maintenance

Libraries are accustomed to creating bibliographic records using the tools provided by their integrated library system. As we have seen throughout this chapter, most types of metadata that digital resources require are quite different from the types that libraries normally create and manage. In general, integrated library systems focus on descriptive metadata, and their record creation and maintenance tools are closely bound to the structures of MARC records (although integrated library systems also provide tools for acquisitions, items, circulation and patrons). These tools are not designed to assist with the creation and management of structural, administrative and preservation metadata, unless the integrated library system vendor has integrated special tools for creating metadata for locally created digital resources.

Specific strategies for managing metadata of the various types associated with digital resources should be tied to other aspects of the production of the resources, such as clearing permission to digitise an item to loading it into a content management system for public access. A wide variety of tools and techniques can be used to create and manage metadata generated in a digitisation or conversion project. Some options that should be considered include:

- For descriptive metadata, use the integrated library system. If staff who are creating descriptive metadata are already familiar with cataloguing tools provided by your integrated library system, this metadata can be exported as MARC records that can then be transformed into Dublin Core or MODS, for example, for use in other systems.

- Creating metadata on paper worksheets and then adding it to a database is a viable option in some cases, such as when cataloguing rare materials that are stored in areas where a desktop workstation or notebook computer cannot be used.

- As we have seen earlier in this chapter, spreadsheets are suitable for managing some types of metadata. Metadata created using spreadsheets or desktop database managers such as Microsoft Access, FileMaker or OpenOffice Base can be transformed into other formats for bulk loading into other systems.

- Finally, digital library content management systems such as Greenstone, Fedora and CONTENTdm provide tools for creating and maintaining metadata, particularly descriptive metadata. The advantage of these tools is that the metadata is created in the format required by the content management system.

As suggested in the previous section, some file formats, including XML, Microsoft Office formats, Acrobat PDF, TIFF, MP3 and Ogg Vorbis, support embedded metadata; in other words, textual information can be included in the file itself. Best practice favours storing metadata separately from the files that make up a resource. It would be unwise to store the only copy of a resource's metadata in the resource itself as loss of the resource would also mean loss of all information about it. Metadata is automatically embedded in some of the formats mentioned above (such as Office and PDF), generated from sources such as the name of the current user logged into the computer used to create the document. Embedded metadata in other types of files might be useful in some situations; for example, digital audio players such as the Apple iPod use embedded metadata to allow access to files by performer, title and so on. Both of these types of embedded metadata can be extracted for use in search and retrieval and content management systems. The *Final Report of the AMeGA (Automatic Metadata Generation Applications Project)* contains the results of a 2004 survey in which the authors asked 217 metadata specialists about their use of the metadata generation functionality of six popular content creation software packages (such as Microsoft Word and Adobe Acrobat, both of which call this embedded metadata 'document properties'). The authors found that just over half (58%) of the respondents used this type of feature.[75]

Summary: making decisions about metadata

Metadata is more than information describing a resource's title, author and publication date. The creation and management of digital content requires corresponding administrative, structural and preservation metadata, and decisions on how to implement these various types of metadata will be determined by a number of factors including functional requirements for descriptive metadata, the applicability of existing standards and specifications, the options opened up by application profiles and available metadata creation tools. Standards for administrative and preservation metadata are still evolving, further complicating matters. Looking outward, libraries have to decide how important it is that the metadata they create can interoperate with similar metadata and how to deal with the inevitable problem of maintaining persistent addresses for resources. Adherence to standards (and, as we have seen, there are a lot to choose from) is both desirable and challenging, but libraries have a successful history of implementing standardised ways of structuring records and populating them consistently.

Further reading

Research Libraries Group (2005) *Descriptive Metadata Guidelines for RLG Cultural Materials*. Mountain View, CA: RLG. Available at *http://www.rlg.org/ en/pdfs/RLG_desc_metadata.pdf*
Documents the descriptive metadata used in RLG Cultural Materials (*http://culturalmaterials.rlg.org*), a commercially available collection of

digitised manuscripts and images produced by the Research Libraries Group. This publication serves as a useful example of thorough, detailed documentation that could be developed for any collection.

Hillmann, D. (2005) *Using Dublin Core*. Available at *http://dublincore. org/documents/usageguide/*
Intended as an 'entry point for users of Dublin Core'. Covers syntax and storage issues, controlled vocabularies and Dublin Core qualifiers. Also links to a useful bibliography on Dublin Core and a glossary by Mary S. Woodley that covers metadata terminology in general.

Lyons, S. (2005) 'Persistent identification of electronic documents and the future of footnotes' *Law Library Journal* 97:4, 681–94. Available at *http://www.aallnet.org/products/pub_llj_v97n04/2005-42.pdf*
This article surveys previous research on the extent of 'link rot' (links becoming dead through time) in citations found in scholarly journals and describes the various strategies for reducing the problem. Adds detail to the brief survey of persistent addressing schemes introduced in this chapter.

NISO (2004) *Understanding Metadata*. Bethesda, MD: NISO Press. Available at *http://www.niso.org/standards/resources/Understanding Metadata.pdf*
This 20-page booklet replaces the earlier but also very useful *Metadata Made Simpler*. Describes and provides examples of standard metadata schemes and element sets (some of which are not covered in this chapter) and contains a useful glossary.

Notes

1. *ISBD(G): General International Standard Bibliographic Description* (2004 Revision), p. 3. Available at *http://www.ifla.org/VII/s13/pubs/isbdg2004.pdf*
2. *http://www.dublincore.org/documents/abstract-model/*
3. *http://repec.org/*
4. Hillmann, D. *Using Dublin Core*, *http://dublincore.org/documents/ usageguide/*
5. *http://www.ica.org/biblio/cds/isad_g_2e.pdf*
6. Hensen, S.L. (1989) *Archives, Personal Papers, and Manuscripts: A Cataloging Manual for Archival Repositories, Historical Societies, and Manuscript Libraries*, 2nd edn. Chicago: Society of American Archivists.
7. Available in several versions at *http://www.loc.gov/rr/print/gml/ graphmat.html*

8. *http://www.cdpheritage.org/resource/metadata/wsdcmbp/*
9. *http://www.diglib.org/pubs/dlfermi0408/*
10. *http://www.niso.org/*. At the time of writing (October 2005), Z39.87 was still in balloting.
11. *http://www.xrml.org/*
12. *http://www.loc.gov/standards/metable.html*
13. *http://www.clir.org/pubs/reports/pub87/contents.html*
14. *http://www.lib.virginia.edu/digital/metadata/administrative.html*
15. *http://www.sc.edu/library/digital/dacmetadata.html#admin*
16. Jones, M. and Beagrie N. (2001) *Preservation Management of Digital Materials: A Handbook*. London: The British Library, p. 11.
17. *ibid.*, pp. 115–16.
18. *http://www.ifla.org/VII/s13/frbr/frbr.pdf*
19. FRBR, p. 3.
20. Heery, R. and Patel, M. (2000) 'Application profiles: mixing and matching metadata schemas', *Ariadne* 25. Available at *http://www.ariadne.ac.uk/issue25/app-profiles/intro.html*
21. *http://www.cenorm.be/cenorm/businessdomains/businessdomains/isss/cwa/cwa14855.asp*
22. *http://dublincore.org/documents/library-application-profile/index.shtml*
23. *http://dublincore.org/documents/dces/*
24. *http://dublincore.org/documents/usageguide/qualifiers.shtml*
25. *http://dublincore.org/documents/dcmi-terms/*
26. *http://dublincore.org/documents/dc-xml-guidelines/*
27. *http://dublincore.org/documents/dcq-html/*
28. *http://dublincore.org/documents/usageguide/*
29. *http://www.loc.gov/standards/mods/*
30. Coyle, K. (2005) 'Understanding metadata and its purpose', *Journal of Academic Librarianship* 31:2, 163.
31. *http://www.njdigitalhighway.org/*
32. *http://lcweb4.loc.gov/elect2002/*
33. *http://www.njdigitalhighway.org/documents/wms-guidelines.pdf*; *http://www.loc.gov/minerva/collect/elec2002/catalog.html*
34. *http://www.loc.gov/standards/mods/mods-home.html#examples*
35. *http://www.loc.gov/standards/mets/*
36. *http://sunsite.berkeley.edu/mets/registry/*
37. Tansley, R. *et al.* (2003) 'DSpace as an Open Archival Information System: Current Status and Future Directions', European Digital Library Conference, *http://www.ecdl2003.org/presentations/papers/session11b/Tansley/dspace-ecdl2003.ppt*; also Wolfe, R. and Reilly. W. *DSpace METS Document Profile for Submission Information Packages (SIP)*, *http://www.dspace.org/standards/METS/SIP/profilev0p9p1/metssipv0p9p1.pdf*
38. *http://www.loc.gov/standards/premis/*
39. *http://www.natlib.govt.nz/files/4initiatives_metaschema_revised.pdf*
40. PREMIS 1–4.
41. *http://mpeg7.nist.gov/*
42. *http://www.niso.org/standards/resources/Z39-87-200x-forballot.pdf*
43. *http://www.icpsr.umich.edu/DDI/*

44. *http://www.fgdc.gov/metadata/contstan.html*

45. *http://dublincore.org/groups/collections/*

46. *http://www.dlib.org/dlib/september00/09contents.html*

47. *http://www.niso.org/standards/standard_detail.cfm?std_id=815*

48. *http://www.tasi.ac.uk/resources/vocabs.html*

49. *http://sky.fit.qut.edu.au/~middletm/cont_voc.html#Thesauri*

50. *http://www.connotea.org/*

51. *http://www.citeulike.org/*

52. Bearman, D. and Trant, J. (2005) 'Social Terminology enhancement through vernacular engagement: exploring collaborative annotation to encourage interaction with museum collections', *D-Lib Magazine* 11:9. Available at *http://www.dlib.org/dlib/september05/bearman/09bearman.html*

53. *http://www.handle.net/*

54. *http://purl.net/*

55. *http://www.doi.org/*

56. *http://info-uri.info/registry/docs/misc/faq.html*

57. *http://www.cdlib.org/inside/diglib/ark/*

58. *http://www.loc.gov/standards/uri/*

59. *http://www.nla.gov.au/initiatives/persistence/PIappendix1.html*

60. *http://www.openarchives.org/*

61. *http://www.niso.org/z39.50/z3950.html*

62. *http://oaister.umdl.umich.edu/o/oaister/*

63. *http://www.loc.gov/z3950/agency/zing/srw/index.html*

64. *http://www.loc.gov/marc/marcdocz.html*

65. *http://www.ukoln.ac.uk/metadata/interoperability/*

66. Carr, L. and Harnad, S. (2005) *Keystroke Economy: A Study of the Time and Effort Involved in Self-Archiving.* Available at *http://eprints.ecs.soton.ac.uk/10688/*

67. Greenberg, J., *et al.* (2001) 'Author-generated Dublin Core metadata for web resources: a baseline study in an organization', *Journal of Digital Information*, 2:2. Available at *http://jodi.tamu.edu/Articles/v02/i02/ Greenberg/*

68. *http://www.saskia.com/*

69. *http://hul.harvard.edu/jhove/*

70. *http://www.autonomy.com/*

71. *http://www.teragram.com/*

72. *http://libots.sourceforge.net/*

73. *http://classifier4j.sourceforge.net/*; a web-accessible version that readers can try for themselves is available at *http://www.mackmo.com/summary/index.jsp*

74. *http://ivia.ucr.edu/*

75. Greenberg, J., Spurgin, K. and Crystal, A. (2005) *Final Report of the AMeGA (Automatic Metadata Generation Applications) Project*, p. 25. Available at *http://www.loc.gov/catdir/bibcontrol/lc_amega_final_report.pdf*

5

File formats

This chapter provides information on the most common file formats used for digital collections, and describes best practices for the creation and delivery of the files that make up digital resources. I will not go into great detail about some of the technical aspects of image formats, and I will also avoid similar detail when discussing formats for text, sound and video. Rather, this chapter will provide an overview of these aspects and refer to sources that supply more information.

I will also discuss factors to consider when selecting file formats for various types of digital collections. Most digital resources can be characterised as one of four simple types: still images, textual resources, moving images or sound, and raw data. A fifth type, complex objects, contains more than one of these four simple types. Defining these five types serves two purposes: first, to provide a vocabulary for describing the files that make up digital resources, and second, for describing *collections* of digital resources and how they are typically presented online (which is the subject of the next chapter, 'Search and display'). At the end of the section for each type is a brief summary of general best practices for selecting file formats for that type.

Finally, a guiding principle in this chapter is borrowed from NISO's *Framework of Guidance for Building Good Digital Collections*: 'A good digital object will be produced in a way that ensures it supports collection priorities, while maintaining qualities contributing to interoperability and reusability.'[1] Specific aspects of interoperability and re-usability (such as the recommended resolution of still images) change over time, but this principle articulates what should be the primary motivation for selecting specific file formats.

Master vs. derivative versions

The files that make up digital resources typically take two forms, a 'master' version and various 'derivative' versions. The master is the version that is stored for long-term management and preservation, while derivative versions are created by processing a copy of the master version to suit a particular application, use or environment. A typical scenario is to scan images and save them as TIFFs (the master versions), and then to create JPEG versions for delivery on the web (the derivatives). Creating a number of derivative versions of the same master is also common; many collections provide a small thumbnail version and one or more larger versions of each image file, depending on the functional requirements defined for the display of each resource to the end user. Another example of masters and derivatives is a textual document marked up in XML (master) but converted to HTML and PDF (derivatives) for mounting on the collection's content management system.

This distinction is important because the two types are optimised for their respective functions and the two functions are often incompatible with each other. Master versions tend to be created so that they contain the most information possible and using file formats that are as flexible as possible. They often have higher or more complex storage requirements than derivative versions; for example, masters tend to take up more disk space than derivative versions (as is the case with the TIFFs in the previous example). Derivative versions tend to have smaller file sizes as they are optimised for delivery over networks of varying speeds. If a derivative version is in a format suitable for end users, it is referred to as a 'delivery format'.

Open vs. proprietary formats

In the following discussion of file formats, the terms 'open' and 'proprietary' will be used frequently. 'Proprietary' is used here to describe file formats that are owned and controlled by an individual, a company or a group of companies or organisations that do not make specifications widely available. Generally, propriety formats are implemented in software owned by the controlling body (usually a company), and use in applications other than those developed and distributed by the controller requires payment of licensing fees. 'Open' describes file formats that can be used by anyone and that do not require payment of licensing fees. Related to the simple distinction of whether or not a format can be implemented in applications only with the controller's permission is the availability of documentation on the technical details of a file format (often known as the format's 'internals'). This second distinction has a number of implications, such as availability of software tools, the type of support options available to users, and perhaps most importantly, the likelihood that medium- or long-term digital preservation strategies apply to files in a given format.

A file format can be owned by a company and still be 'open'. Two examples are Adobe's PDF and TIFF formats. Adobe makes the specifications for these two formats freely available, and within the PDF specification, includes language explicitly defining how the specification and format can be used[2] (the TIFF specification was last updated in 1992, and presumably language similar to that found in the PDF documentation will be included in future editions of the TIFF specification). A number of recent open formats that are not owned by companies but rather by foundations or other types of organisations have licences that explicitly state that the format can be used by anyone, without formal agreements or payment of licensing fees. For example, the FLAC audio format is available under a licence that states that the format is 'fully open to the public to be used for any purpose' and is 'free for commercial or noncommercial use'[3] other than setting the format's technical specification and certifying conformance.

The National Digital Information Infrastructure and Preservation Program (NDIIPP), led by the Library of Congress, calls this aspect of file formats 'disclosure', which it defines as 'the degree to which complete specifications and tools for validating technical integrity exist and are accessible to those creating and sustaining digital content.'[4] The NDIIPP explanation also points out that the availability of documentation exists along a continuum:

> A spectrum of disclosure levels can be observed for digital formats. Non-proprietary, open standards are usually more fully documented and more likely to be supported by tools for validation than proprietary formats. However, what is most significant for this sustainability factor is not approval by a recognized standards body, but the existence of complete documentation, preferably subject to external expert evaluation.

For master versions, the more 'open' the format, the better. Simply put, the use of proprietary file formats does not promote long-term management, access or preservation of digital resources. Unless a format is documented publicly and is free from intellectual property restrictions, the only tools that will be available to manipulate files will be those that are produced by the company owning the patents on the format, or companies approved by the controller. If the company goes out of business, the software tools will probably be difficult or impossible to acquire in the future. Similarly, technical support for files in closed formats will be limited as documentation on how the format works will not be openly available and therefore the number of people who have detailed knowledge of the format will dwindle over time. Open file formats that are encrypted or otherwise protected by Technological Prevention Measures (see Chapter 3) are not suitable as master formats because many countries' laws make it illegal to circumvent these devices.

Proprietary file formats are suitable for derivative versions because, in theory, if the issues described above prevent the use of derivative files in obsolete formats, new derivative versions can be created from the open-format masters. However, if use of derivative file formats requires a browser plug-in that is only available from a single source (the controller of the format, for example), whatever advantages that format has over its more open competitors should be weighed against the potential short- and long-term availability of the required software.

Formats for still images

Most images used in digital collections are raster images (also knows as bitmap images), which means that the files consist of a rectangular grid of points of colour (known as pixels). A second type of digital image, vector graphics, do not consist of pixels, but are based on geometric shapes. Raster images are by far the more common in digital library collections as they are suitable for capturing digitised images or for born-digital photographs.

The most common file formats used for still images include:

- GIF (Graphics Interchange Format): GIF images are limited to 256 colours, so are best suited as a delivery format for line art, diagrams and other types of graphical materials that do not contain high numbers of colors.

- *JPEG (Joint Photographic Experts Group)*: Commonly considered a format, but JPEG is actually a compression algorithm. JPEG files are well suited as delivery formats for images containing scanned photographs, including pages from printed material; however, too much compression can lead to visible artefacting (visual side-effects of removal of information, generally manifested as smeared or blurry patches). JPEGs are supported natively by all graphical web browsers.

- *JPEG2000*: Intended to supersede JPEG, this format achieves high compression levels without the risk of artefacts. Supports both lossless (which retains all of the information in the image file) and lossy compression (which removes information from the image file), and also has robust metadata embedding features. Currently, support for JPEG2000 files is lacking in web browsers but a number of plug-ins are available. Support in image editing software is also poor at this point. Some components of the JPEG2000 compression mechanisms are protected under patents. JPEG2000 also supports assembling files together into video. The blog devoted to use of JPEG2000 in libraries and archives is a good resource for tracking development of this important format.[5]

- *PNG (Portable Network Graphics)*: For photographs, JPEG can produce smaller files with comparable quality; for text, line drawings and diagrams, PNG produces better image quality than JPEG files of comparable size. Web browsers natively support PNG files.

- *SVG (Scalable Vector Graphics)*: An open XML-based format for vector graphics. SVG is useful for describing diagrams and other non-photographic illustrations, but supports embedding raster graphics as well.

- *TIFF (Tagged Image File Format)*: The preferred format for master version still images created by digitising printed materials. As stated above, TIFF is owned by Adobe but because they make the specification available freely, TIFF has been implemented in many software applications.

Resolution, colour depth and compression

Raster images are described in terms of their resolution and colour depth. 'Resolution' has two meanings: (1) an image's density and (2) an image's dimensions. Image density (also known as 'pixel density') describes how many pixels exist in a given unit of measurement, such as an inch, or less commonly a centimetre. Image density is expressed in dots per inch (DPI) or pixels per inch (PPI), the former referring to the image if it were printed and the latter referring to the image in its digital form (although this distinction is rarely made in practice). Typical resolutions for still image files are 600 DPI for master images and 100 for derivative versions intended to be distributed over the web. As image density increases, so does the amount of detail that is captured in the image file. This extra detail is most obvious when the image is printed or when viewing software is used to zoom in on the image (much like looking at something through a magnifying glass). Because high-resolution images contain more detail than low-resolution images, it is possible to zoom in on them further before the detail becomes obscured or blurred.

High-resolution images can also be manipulated by image processing software more reliably than can low-resolution images, which is an important reason why master versions should have a high image density. The reason that derivative images meant for use on the web are converted to a relatively low density (usually around 100 DPI) is that as most computer monitors only support approximately 100 pixels per inch, there are no real advantages to putting denser images on the web, particularly considering that file size increases exponentially relative to image density (see Table 5.1). In addition, decreasing the resolution of an image does not appreciably reduce the amount of detail that can be perceived in the image, as long as the user does not zoom in on the image.

As stated above, 'resolution' is also used to describe the dimensions of an image. A low-resolution image might be 200 pixels wide and 280 pixels high (a common thumbnail resolution), whereas a high-resolution image might be 2000 pixels wide and 2800 pixels high. If an image that is larger than the source document is required (e.g. if the source

Table 5.1	Effects of resolution, dimensions, colour depth and compression on image file size

Attribute	Effect on file size
Resolution	At same colour depth and dimensions, doubling resolution quadruples size
Dimensions	At same density and colour depth, doubling length and width quadruples file size
Colour depth	At same density and dimensions, increasing from 8-bit to 24-bit colour triples size
Compression	Varies, but depending on type of file and compression algorithm used, reducing file size by 80% is common.

document if very small), it is preferable to use the scanner driver software to scan the image at a size greater than 100% than to use image manipulation software to enlarge the image later. Scanner drivers usually have a control that allows creation of an image that has physical dimensions greater than the document being scanned, at the scanning resolution. For example, a small postcard that measures 9 × 14 cm might be scanned at 200% of its original size, and when printed at the same resolution that it was scanned at (say 600 DPI in this example), the image would measure 18 × 28 cm and would produce the same effect as enlarging a photographic print of the postcard. This technique is frequently used when digitising small format items such as 35-mm negatives and postage stamps.

The second aspect of raster images is colour depth, or the amount of colour information that is encoded in each pixel. Colour depth is usually expressed in 'bits'; common values include 1-bit (in other words, black and white are the only two values) and 24-bit (which can encode 16,777,216 different colours). Greyscale images usually have a colour depth of 8 bits, which provides 256 shades of grey.

Another important aspect of raster images is whether or not they are compressed. Compression reduces file size by applying various algorithms, typically eliminating what the algorithm considers redundant information. Compression can either be lossless or lossy; as the names suggest, lossless compression retains all of the information that was present in the uncompressed image whereas lossy removes information in order to reduce file size. Common types of image file compression include LZW (often applied to TIFF and GIF files) and JPEG (which produces what are commonly known as JPEG files). One disadvantage of compressing image files is that lossy compression, particularly JPEG compression, introduces 'artefacts' into the image, which are visual side-effects of removal of information, generally manifested as smeared or blurry patches. Another risk is that the compression algorithm itself can be proprietary, so unless an open compression algorithm is used, even files saved in open formats can suffer the same problems that proprietary files can. LZW, although the most common image file compression algorithm, is considered by many to be proprietary, whereas the popular ZIP compression algorithm is open. The disadvantage of using ZIP for images is that few image manipulation applications can inflate (or decompress) files natively; the files must first be inflated using a separate program and then viewed or processed. LZW support is typically integrated into a wider range of software, and viewing files compressed with it generally does not require separate image inflation.

Image density, image dimensions, colour depth and compression all influence the size of image files. As Table 5.1 illustrates, file sizes can grow very high if resolution, dimensions and colour depth are increased; likewise, compression can reduce the size of image files substantially.

To illustrate these formulas, Table 5.2 shows average file sizes and total disk space requirements for 150 book pages scanned into 24-bit colour TIFFs, first with no compression applied, and then with LZW compression (the most common type applied to TIFFs) applied.

The compressed files use only about 25% as much space as the uncompressed files. The advantages of creating high-resolution files and storing them with no compression must be weighed against the benefits of requiring less disk space, whether that space is saved by storing lower resolution files or by compressing them.

Best practices for still image formats

For master formats, uncompressed TIFF is preferred, scanned at 24-bit colour. The resolution of TIFFs should be determined by the goals of the collection or project, but scanning at less than 300 DPI is not advisable for anything but short-lived files. Files created from unique, fragile or at-risk originals usually have resolutions of 600 DPI or more.

Delivery formats include JPEG for photographic images and PNG for text and line drawings. As computer monitors do not currently exceed 100 DPI, that is the optimal resolution for files intended for viewing onscreen. Files that are intended to be printed, however, should be of considerably higher resolution (300–600 DPI).

Table 5.2   Sample disk space requirements for image files

Resolution (DPI)	100	300	600
Average disk space for each image (no compression)	2.6 MB	23 MB	90 MB
Total disk space required (no compression)	390 MB	3.45 GB	13.5 GB
Average disk space for each image (with compression)	720 KB	5.6 MB	19.1 MB
Total disk space required (with compression)	108 MB	840 MB	2.9 GB

Formats for text

The most common approaches to presenting textual resources online are:

- present each text as a single file;
- present each text as a series of still image files, each representing a single page (known as the 'page image' approach);
- present each text as one or more HTML files.

These approaches can be implemented using a variety of derivative file formats. The master file formats for textual resources should be selected based on the nature of the original source material (e.g. analog or born-digital), the goals and functional requirements of the collection, the amount of resources available for the creation of the digital resources, and the preservation goals of the digitisation or conversion project.

The most common file formats used for textual resources include:

- image formats
- plain text
- XML
- PDF
- DjVu

Image formats

One of the most common ways of presenting digitised texts online is the 'page image' approach, in which each page of the source document is displayed as a scanned image. Navigation between pages is typically provided by HTML links to the next, previous, first and final pages. As the pages are simple images, selecting formats for the master and derivative versions of the page images is much the same as selecting formats for still images.

Plain text

Plain text (i.e. ASCII or Unicode characters only with no formatting other than line breaks, spaces and tabs) versions of digitised documents are used most often to provide full text searching for page images. Plain text is generally created in two ways, by being typed (known as 'keying' or 'rekeying') or by using Optical Character Recognition (OCR) software to convert page images into plain text. OCR can be very accurate, but it is rarely free of errors (inaccurately recognized characters or words) when applied to source images that are skewed, show dirt or other types of markings on the pages, or that have captured pages whose typefaces are not distinct. If the text resulting from OCR is used only to provide full text searching, many libraries do not correct mistaken characters or words because the labour involved in doing so would be prohibitive. Uncorrected text produced by OCR and used for this purpose is known as 'dirty OCR'. If very high accuracy is required, the source documents are typed, which is actually faster than proofreading and correcting occasional errors. Accuracy in the range of 99.99%, or one error per 10,000 characters, can be achieved by a technique known as 'double keying', in which two people type a copy of the same page and the resulting text files are compared using a software utility. Owing to the high labour costs of double keying, libraries generally do not perform this work onsite but send page images or printed hard copy of the source documents to vendors.

XML

Adding XML markup to plain text adds structure to and allows control of the appearance of the text. The advantages of encoding documents in XML include multiple presentation options, compatibility with specialised readers and element-specific querying. Multiple presentation options are possible thanks to XML's ability to separate the structure of a document from the way it is rendered by a web browser or other types of software. Technologies such as Cascading Style Sheets (CSS) or XSL Transformations (XSLT) allow the creation of multiple versions of HTML files that contain formatting defined in arbitrary style sheets. A common example of this type of multiple-format output is to use one set of CSS for on-screen reading and another set for printing the same document. XSL Formatting Objects (XSL-FO) is a technology similar to CSS that defines how XML is formatted in environments other than HTML, such as in Rich Text Format and Adobe PDF documents. Documents encoded in standardized XML document type definitions (DTDs) or schemas can also be transformed into other schemas appropriate for a given viewer. For example, documents encoded in DocBook can be converted into the DTB (Digital Talking Book) schema for use in specialized readers that read text to users who cannot see printed text. Element-specific querying allows end users to limit their searches to particular elements in an XML document; for example, if the text of a book is marked up such that each chapter is in its own <chapter> element, a user can limit searches to within chapters only. In other words, this feature of XML allows the equivalent of fielded searching within documents.

XML is the successor of SGML (the Standardized General Markup Language), which has been used extensively in digital library collections before the advent of XML. SGML DTDs are not as commonly used now because XML is generally simpler and is supported by more applications than SGML. However, an SGML DTD is available for TEI and DocBook (and HTML other than XHTML is actually based on SGML).

A number of XML DTDs are commonly deployed in digital library collections:

- *HTML*: Using HTML markup in the master versions of textual documents is not uncommon, but doing so is not advisable because adding HTML tags is only slightly less work than adding tags in a more general XML format such as TEI or DocBook, which would add considerably more flexibility and functionality to the resulting files. HTML can easily be produced from files encoded in XML, whereas highly structured XML files cannot easily be produced from HTML. XHTML[6] is an implementation of the HTML element set using XML syntax, but like other types of HTML is best used as a format for derivative versions and not master versions of documents.

- *The TEI (Text Encoding Initiative)* XML DTD is 'an international and interdisciplinary standard that facilitates libraries, museums, publishers, and individual scholars [to] represent a variety of literary and linguistic texts for online research, teaching, and preservation.'[7] TEI is widely deployed (the website lists 125 projects that use the standard) and is well suited to historical and literary texts of a variety of types and comes in full and simplified (Lite) versions.

- *DocBook*[8] is a popular DTD commonly used to encode technical documentation, but it is applicable to a wide variety of document types. DocBook is used to structure book content by a number of book publishers, including O'Reilly & Associates, and is used in some electronic theses collections, and collections of technical documents.

Other XML specifications that may be appropriate for some types of digital library collections include OpenDocument[9] for born-digital word processor, spreadsheet and presentation documents; OEBPS

(Open eBook Publication Structure)[10] for e-books; and the Daisy DTB (Digital Talking Book)[11] specification for text optimised for automated reading out loud. OpenDocument has the advantage of tight integration with the OpenOffice suite of applications, which has the ability to read a large number of other formats (including proprietary formats) and convert them to OpenDocument reliably. OEBPS and Daisy DTB are optimised for their respective target applications, and are therefore most applicable as derivative formats for delivery to end users.

If a document is encoded in an XML format other than XHTML, it must be converted to HTML in order to be formatted so that it is suitable for viewing in standard web browsers. This can be done either in a batch (i.e. the XML files are converted to HTML and these new files are placed on a web server for access) or dynamically (i.e. the XML files are converted into HTML only when they are requested by a web browser). In both cases, XSLT is typically used for the conversion.

As the list of established XML document types above illustrates, libraries can choose a DTD based on its applicability to the particular collection they are developing. Using XML formats that are already deployed widely is justifiable for a number of reasons: someone else had already developed a document model and the element set required to describe the model; existing document types are usually very well documented; and existing document types are likely to be compatible with a wide selection of editing, management and delivery tools. Like the decision to use a descriptive metadata schema, the decision to use a proven XML document type allows libraries to avoid the initial and ongoing work required to develop their own schemas. Creation (and necessary maintenance) of a new schema should only be done if there are extremely persuasive reasons why existing schemas are not applicable. Claiming that 'our material is special' without substantial support for that argument is not sufficient reason to go it alone.

PDF

Adobe Systems' PDF is the most popular format for presenting multipage textual documents in a single file. Its advantages are that it is very widely deployed, free readers for the major computer platforms are available and it allows documents to be printed easily. Even though the PDF format is the property of a single company, the specification is freely available. PDF files are usually created in three ways, either from within office applications using standard 'Save as' operations, by printing the documents to a special printer driver that creates the PDF file, or by converting a group of TIFF or JPEG page images into a single PDF file. The Adobe Acrobat software application contains OCR functionality, so collections of files created using that application can be searched using third-party indexing and search applications.

A subset of the full Adobe PDF specification, PDF-A (PDF Archival),[12] is currently in development as an International Organization for Standardization standard (ISO 19005-1). PDF-A prohibits the use of video, audio, JavaScript and digital rights management technologies in order that files compliant with this specification are as independent of particular computing platforms and devices as possible and so they meet general requirements for preservation file formats.

DjVu

LizardTech's DjVu[13] format allows the delivery of high-quality representations of textual documents in small files. It is in many ways a competitor to PDF but claims to provide smaller files and better readability than PDF. Like PDF, it requires the use of a browser plug-in. LizardTech makes the DjVu specification freely available (including a licensing statement[14]), and in addition to the company's fee browser plug-in, a number of open-source viewers exist, as does an open-source suite of utilities for creating DjVu files. DjVu is used by the Internet Archive and a number of university libraries to deliver textual documents over the web.

Best practices for text formats

Even though the formats for textual documents vary widely, the most common formats for master versions of texts are TIFF page images, created according to the same best practice guidelines as still images described above. If full text searching or other types of enhanced access or functionality are required, rekeying the text and encoding it in TEI or some other standard XML schema is common. Dirty OCR is suitable for some forms of full text searching, provided the potential presence of errors in the searchable text is acceptable.

Choice of file formats for delivery of text varies from JPEG or PNG versions of the page images, to singe-file formats such as PDF or DjVu, to HTML created from XML. Table 5.3 summarises the most common

Table 5.3 Summary of best practices for selecting file formats for text

	Analog		Born digital	
	Master	Derivative	Master	Derivative
Single file	TIFF	PDF	Original format, PDF	PDF
Page image	TIFF	JPEG	Original, PDF	JPEG
HTML	TIFF, XML	HTML	Original, XML	HTML

approaches to storing and presenting digitised and born-digital texts, indicating the most common types of file formats for each approach.

Formats for sound and video

There are a number of suitable formats for the delivery of sound and video to the end user, but selecting formats for master versions of sound and video files is not as straightforward as it is for still images or even textual documents because there is little consensus about which formats offer the best combination of long-term viability. Sound and video content is less common in digital library collections than still images and textual documents, so libraries do not have as much experience creating, processing, and preserving audio and video resources. Collections such as the Internet Archive are setting examples for others, however, and the amount of digital audio and video managed by libraries will only increase.

Just as we distinguished between raster images and vector graphics, sound formats can be classed as either MIDI (Musical Instrument Digital Interface) or waveform. Formats based on the MIDI specification are not common in digital library collections, as the other major type of sound file, waveform, is more effective at capturing sound digitised from analog sources. MIDI formats are similar to vector graphics in that they comprise sets of instructions for producing sounds, whereas waveform formats contain representations of the wave patterns similar to those found in natural sounds. The amount of information captured in these representations is known as a file's 'bit rate' (roughly analogous to image density) and is expressed in bits per second or kilobits per second (kbit/s). The higher the bit rate, the better the sound quality. Common bit rates for audio files are 8 kbit/s (roughly telephone-quality sound), 32 kbit/s (roughly AM radio quality) and 256 kbit/s (roughly audio CD quality).[15]

Digital video formats range from the formats used in the television and motion picture industries down to those commonly found on the World Wide Web. As with audio, the bit rate of digital video is important, but additional factors influencing quality include frame rate (the number of consecutive images, or frames, that are displayed in a second) and display resolution (the number of pixels that make up a digital video image). Video formats usually include either a standard audio format or some type of internal audio encoding mechanism. In addition, to a certain extent digital video formats are determined by the hardware that is used to create them; for instance, the video files produced by a professional-level DV (Digital Video) camera are quite different than those produced by a consumer-level MiniDV camera, and the files created by digitising VHS or other analog formats are quite different still. This dependence on hardware complicates converting from one digital format to another and limits options for the short- and long-term management of the files compared with image and text files.

To complicate matters further, most sound and video files consist of the content data and a 'codec', which acts as a container or wrapper around the content data that usually incorporates compression technologies of some type. Codecs are necessary given the high disk space and network bandwidth requirements of sound and video formats. For example, one hour of PCM uncompressed audio (the format used in audio CDs) takes up 600 MB, and one *minute* of uncompressed DV video at 640 × 480 resolution can consume nearly a gigabyte of disk space. Codecs complicate manipulation, conversion and long-term preservation tasks in various ways, not the least of which is that many of them use lossy compression techniques.

Common file formats and codecs used for audio include:

- *AIFF (Audio Interchange File Format)*: General-use sound format that can be uncompressed or compressed. Initially developed by Apple but the specification is freely available and free from patents, and the format is playable on common computer platforms. Can be used as either master or delivery format.

- *FLAC (Free Lossless Audio Cocec)*: An open-source, patent-free codec for lossless compression of PCM audio data.

- *MP3 (MPEG audio layer-3)*: Lossy compression codec used as delivery format for all types of sound. MP3 is widely supported on major computer platforms despite a number of patent issues.[16]

- *Ogg Vorbis*: File format and accompanying lossy compression codec. Ogg Vorbis is an open-source, patent-free technology that competes with MP3 as a delivery format.

- *PCM (Pulse Code Modulation)*: Uncompressed audio data format with open specifications. When encoded into the WAVE format, suitable as a master file format.

- *WAVE (Waveform Audio File Format)*: Similar to AIFF but developed by Microsoft and IBM. Used mainly as an encoding format for PCM data, and playable on all major computing platforms.

Common file formats and codecs used for video include:

- *AVI (Audio Video Interleaved)*: Format developed by Microsoft and IBM. Frequently compressed using the DivX codec. Suitable as a delivery format.

- *DivX*: Proprietary compression codec that is commonly used in AVI files distributed over the Internet.

- *DV (Digital Video)*: A group of related formats that can store uncompressed video data or that can be encoded in AVI or QuickTime files. Suitable as a master file format if uncompressed.

- *Flash*: Macromedia Flash files use vector graphics to create animations, although the format can support embedded raster graphics and a number of interactive features. Suitable as a delivery format, but requires the use of a plug-in.

- *MPEG (Moving Picture Experts Group)*: A group of lossy video and audio compression formats that are used in a wide variety of applications. Includes MPEG-1 (now largely obsolete other than as the basis for MP3 audio compression), MPEG-2 (used in digital television and DVDs) and MPEG-4 (used as the basis of a number of file formats including Windows Media Video and QuickTime).

- *QuickTime*: Proprietary format developed by Apple but supported on all major platforms. Suitable as a delivery format.

- *RealVideo*: A proprietary but widely used video compression codec that is suitable as a delivery format. Usually packaged with RealAudio data into a RealMedia file. Requires a browser plug-in.

- *WMV (Windows Media Video)*: Format developed by Microsoft. Suitable as a delivery format.

Best practices for sound and video formats

For master formats, DV and MPEG-2 files are currently the best choices for video, and WAV or AIFF for audio. Both video and audio should be encoded using as high a bit rate as possible. Masters should also be uncompressed if possible, and if compression codecs are used they should be lossless and open, not proprietary.

Delivery formats should be compressed to allow effective delivery over networks, and should be playable on as many computing platforms as possible.

Formats for data sets

Libraries are likely to have little control over what formats raw data sets are in, as this type of resource is usually created outside the library for use in specialised statistical or scientific data analysis software applications. In the next section I will discuss the differences between converting analog content to digital form and dealing with content that is born digital. Libraries typically have fewer options for master and derivative file formats when dealing with born-digital resources. Distributing data files in their original formats is not necessarily a bad thing – the formats that these files are created in are usually the same ones that end users will want as well, particularly if the formats are tied to specific statistical analysis software applications that are used heavily by researchers in the same or related disciplines as the creator's.

However, if these formats are proprietary, converting them into open formats for preservation is desirable if doing so is possible without jeopardising the integrity of the data. The only practical option in these cases is to convert proprietary formats to plain ASCII or Unicode text, and to document the file structures. Raw data sets tend to be fairly well documented by codebooks, experimental procedures and other information that is used during research. Associating these necessary components with the raw data can be accomplished with robust metadata (e.g. METS could be used to identify the various files and their relationships to each other).

Sector- or discipline-specific standardised file structures exist, but there is no general, open format for such a wide-ranging and at the same time highly specialised category as 'raw data sets'. However, an increasing amount of attention is being paid to the problems associated with making raw data accessible and preserving it, particularly in Britain and the US. Two influential reports, *Preserving the Whole: A Two-Track Approach to Rescuing Social Science Data and Metadata*[17] and *Long-Lived Digital Data Collections: Enabling Research and Education in the 21st Century*[18] define the problems and recommend strategies for the social science and physical science communities, respectively. The *Long-Lived Data Collections* report in particular is evidence that national-level granting agencies (in this case in the US) are becoming aware of the issues surrounding the precarious nature of digital data sets and are beginning to develop policies on the disposition of data created with their support, as long-term access to these data is an essential aspect of 'e-science' (the UK term) and 'cyberinfrastucture' (the US term). Discipline-specific organisations are also developing standards for the creation and long-term preservation of raw data; for example, the Inter-university Consortium for Political and Social Research (ICPSR), based at the University of Michigan, has published a detailed guide to data creation that contains information on data archiving,[19] and the UK Economic and Social Data Service supplies guidelines for the deposition of data sets into its archive.[20]

The most common file formats for raw data include:

- *Plain text*: Many statistical analysis software applications can export and import data files in delimited formats. Even though the file format is plain text, the data structures are often those used by specific statistical analysis software applications.
- *Microsoft Excel*: Similarly, a considerable amount of raw data, particularly in the social sciences, is distributed as Excel files.
- *International or national standards for sector-specific data*: Examples include the ISO geographical information series of standards.[21]

Best practices for raw data formats

Whenever possible, both the original formats and a plain text version should be preserved as master formats. It is vital that all associated data dictionaries, codebooks, data definition files and other textual documentation be converted to open formats such as plain text or PDF, and that, whenever possible, standardised metadata such as that developed by the Data Documentation Initiative[22] should be used to describe the raw data.

Formats for complex documents

Complex documents contain some combination of images, text, audio and video, such as XML or PDF files that contain linked video or audio. Best practices for each of the various types of files apply to the individual components of these documents.

Factors in determining which formats to use

We have identified a number of file formats that are considered suitable as the master and derivative versions of various types of digital resources. Of course, choosing which formats to use is not always straightforward. Issues that may influence the choice of which file formats are selected include:

- Analog vs. born-digital documents
- Total cost of ownership
- Goals of the collection
- Search and display functional requirements
- Availability of software tools, delivery systems
- Long-term management and preservation issues
- Support for embedded metadata

Analog vs. born-digital documents

When libraries digitise analog documents, they are able to choose which file formats to use for master versions. However, if a library inherits born-digital documents, converting the incoming files into the best formats for master versions may not be possible. In other words, if we inherit files, we have to work with what we get.

A common problem with born-digital files is that they do not meet the specifications (a certain pixel density for images, for example) that we would follow were we to create the files ourselves. Whereas is it possible to derive a low-resolution JPEG from a high-resolution TIFF and not lose significant detail, increasing the pixel density of an image only adds file size. The same applies to video and sound files. This technique, called 'upsampling', cannot add details missed during the creation of the digital file. Similarly, if a document that was created in an unstructured, presentation-orientated format such as PDF needs to be converted into a more structured document, the process for doing so will usually have to be a manual one. Finally, converting from proprietary formats to open formats poses its own set of problems: if the original file used data structures that are not replicable outside the proprietary format (which may be the case with some video or Geographical Information System data files), it may not be possible to do anything with the files other than provide them to users in their original formats. Long-term preservation of this type of file will be challenging to say the least.

Total cost of ownership

Formats suitable for master versions of files tend to have certain kinds of cost associated with them. First, some file formats cost more to create than others, simply because some formats require considerable staff time to create. XML will cost more to produce than PDF, unless the creation of the XML markup in the master version of a document can be completely automated; if it needs to be created manually, it will probably cost a considerable amount of money. Even the pixel density of image files can have an impact on creation costs: it may take over four minutes to scan a very high-resolution image whereas it may only take a fraction of that time to scan the same image at a low resolution. Over thousands of images, this difference in labour costs can be significant.

Secondly, costs for managing files over time include the costs of physical storage media and the cost of staff to back up the files regularly and to refresh the media the files are stored on. Over the long term, costs for storage media are likely to be relatively low, but if a library has large quantities of files to move from one generation of media to another (known as 'refreshing' the media), the cost of replacing hard drives, whether they are internal drives in a general-purpose server, part of dedicated file servers or standalone network attached storage arrays, needs to be factored into the appropriate budget cycles (probably every two or three years). Disk space is cheap, but managing it is not. Costs for optical media such as CDs and DVDs are low, but refreshing optical media is extremely time consuming and therefore expensive.

Finally, migration to new file formats, a common digital preservation technique, can be very expensive as well unless the migration is automated. Straight conversion from one image format to another will probably be fairly simple, but migrating complex document files or raw data files may require extensive planning, custom programming and careful quality control, and could therefore evolve into a large project in itself unless thorough preservation plans have been put into place.

Some libraries may choose to contract with what are known as 'trusted digital repositories', which are libraries and other institutions that have committed to ensuring that they meet a specific set of certification criteria defined by the Research Libraries Group and OCLC.[23] Even if libraries deposit their digital masters with a certified repository, it is likely that the repository will charge fees for their services, as they will need to recoup the costs of preserving large quantities of digital files and their associated metadata.

Goals of the collection

It is widely believed that libraries should always create the highest quality master versions of digital resources because doing so will (a) reduce the likelihood that new digital versions of the same resources will need to be created in the future to meet some currently unspecified use and (b) increase the likelihood that it will be possible to migrate the files to new formats as part of a preservation plan. This is in general a sound approach to creating digital resources but many libraries are realising that creating high-quality digital masters does not scale very well, and that a more pragmatic approach is to tie the specifications for the digital masters tightly to the goals of the particular collection or service they are developing.

The most common instance of this pragmatic approach is that resources that are not intended to have ongoing use or value do not require the creation of high-quality masters. Instead, the digital resources can be created in formats that are consistent with the intended use of the collection. In these cases there may be no need to create separate master and derivative versions, as the only version that is required is the one that is used for distribution to end users. For example, a service provided by a university library in which staff scan printed material (exercise keys, handwritten notes, etc.) created by course instructors for linking from their catalogue's course reserves listings probably do not need to be scanned into high-resolution TIFF files. In this particular case, the priorities of the collection are to provide access to students in the class as quickly as possible. The notes are only linked from the catalogue for the life of the course and are removed immediately after the course ends. It is perfectly justifiable to scan these notes directly into Adobe PDF and not into high-resolution TIFFs, as the TIFFs would serve no purpose.

This approach to determining which formats are most appropriate for certain types of collections does not advocate avoiding the creation of high-quality masters in general. For collections where the material is considered to have ongoing value, or where the source material is at risk (e.g. audio tape that is deteriorating), creation of master versions that are of the highest possible quality is justifiable. It does advocate comparing the potential total cost of ownership for digital resources with the planned use and managed lifespan of those digital resources, and making decisions about file formats based on the benefits of creating and maintaining high-quality masters.

Table 5.4 summarises the suitability of selected formats for achieving particular types of goals, broken down by document type; 'n/a' indicates that suitable formats do not exist to accomplish some goals. In the case of accessibility, the only feasible way to provide access to images, sound and video is to provide equivalent versions of the content that do meet acceptable accessibility criteria, as suggested in Principle 1 of the W3C's accessibility guidelines.[24]

Table 5.4	Summary of best practices for selecting formats based on collection goals			
Goals	Document types			
	Still images	Textual documents	Sound and video	Raw data sets
Access	JPEG	PDF	QuickTime, AVI, other delivery formats	Original formats
Accessibility	n/a	XML (Daisy)	n/a	n/a
Enhancement	TIFF	XML (TEI, DocBook)	n/a	n/a
Preservation	TIFF	TIFF plus XML (TEI, DocBook)	PCM, DV, MPEG-2	Original ormats, plain text, XML

Because a variety of derivative formats can be created from high-quality masters, it may be possible to achieve multiple goals (e.g. access and preservation). One benefit of creating high-quality masters is that they are typically more flexible in terms of the different types of formats that can be derived from them. However, this advantage does not apply if creation of multiple derivative formats is not important, as in the case of the scanned course reserve material.

Functional requirements

Related to goals of the collection are its functional requirements. Functional requirements are determined by the set of tasks that users of our collection are likely to want to perform. For example, if you anticipate that your users will want to perform full text searches of the resources you are creating, you will have to take this requirement into account when selecting file formats. The next chapter provides a detailed analysis of the different types of documents and collections, how the characteristics of each type influence how users typically interact with them, and how project managers can define functional requirements for digital collections.

Functional requirements of specific file formats should be considered as well. The US National Digital Information Infrastructure and Preservation Program[25] (NDIIPP) provides 'quality and functional factors' for various document types, including (for textual formats) integrity of structure; for still images, clarity and colour maintenance; for sound, fidelity and support for multiple channels; and for moving images, a combination of the factors for still images and sound.

Availability of software tools

The availability of software tools that can process a given format is a good indicator of a format's maturity and long-term viability. Library staff who are creating master versions of files, creating derivative versions, or performing activities related to file management or preservation need functional and reliable tools to perform their work. Unreliable or poor quality software tools can actually introduce errors into files that may go undetected for some time, even if careful quality control procedures are implemented during production. This potential problem is one reason for recording in administrative metadata the name and version of the software applications used to create and process files. In general, the more common and open the formats, the wider the selection of commercial and open source tools will be.

Some libraries choose formats for files that are delivered to end users based on native web browser support or the availability (and usability) of freely available browser plug-ins. If common web browsers do not natively support a file format, end users will have to install plug-ins, and this fact alone is enough to make some libraries decide to avoid Adobe PDF, Macromedia Flash, Java and other delivery formats. Again, the benefits of using a particular derivative format must be weighed against the requirement for a browser plug-in on an institutional or collection basis.

Preservation issues

As stated earlier, open formats should always be used for master versions of files in order to increase the likelihood that migration to newer formats in the future is possible. Compression of open formats, particularly lossy compression and proprietary compression achieved using algorithms, should also be avoided because it may inhibit format migration. Although few current file formats *require* the use of DRM (digital rights management) technologies, there is good reason to believe that formats may be introduced in the future that cannot be used without locking the content to a particular user on a particular computer for a given length of time or for a specific number of 'uses'. Some now defunct e-book formats used in conjunction with proprietary hardware devices in the late 1990s had several of these DRM characteristics. Any file format that requires the use of DRM should simply be avoided for master versions. Individuals and organisations that hold the rights to material in library digital collections may reasonably request the use of DRM in the formats that are delivered to end users, but master versions that contain DRM technologies are virtually guaranteed never to be migrated and therefore to die in their original formats. Chapter 11 will discuss preservation issues in greater detail.

Support for embedded metadata

As mentioned in the previous chapter, a number of file formats allow metadata to be embedded in the file itself. Including metadata within the file is becoming increasingly common, as are tools for extracting embedded metadata from a wide variety of file formats, such as the National Library of New Zealand Metadata Extraction Tool.[26] The ability of a file format to include textual metadata is useful for a number of reasons, but any metadata that is embedded in a file should also be stored in an external metadata management system.

Summary: making decisions about file formats

A number of criteria should inform your choice of file formats: how 'open' the format is, the type of content (still image, text and so on), the overall functionality of the resources in your collection, and your library's commitment to digital preservation. Ideally, the formats selected for master copies should be open, standardized, and free of compression and DRM technologies. Formats selected for distribution copies should balance quality and usability – they should be easy to distribute over the Internet and be easy to open, view or whatever else end users will want to do with them.

During the planning of a digital collection, the choice of formats for master copies is more important than the choice of distribution copies, as master copies contain all of the information captured when the source material was digitised (or all of the information available in the source material if it was born digital). In addition, master copies will probably form the basis for multiple derivative formats, so it is important to select formats that will be easy to manipulate and convert. Selection of robust master formats also decreases the likelihood that the files will be problematic for those responsible for preserving them in the future.

Further reading

Collaborative Digitization Program. (2005) *Digital Audio Best Practices*. Version 2. Available at *http://www.cdpheritage.org/digital/audio/ documents/CDPDABP_1-2.pdf*
This 40-page publication is an excellent source of information on the technical aspects of digital audio, including playback and digitisation hardware, software, quality control, and file storage and delivery. Also contains a useful glossary.

Jantz, R. (2003) 'Public opinion polls and digital preservation: an application of the Fedora digital object repository system,' *D-Lib Magazine* 9:11. Available at *http://www.dlib.org/dlib/november03/jantz/11jantz.html*
One of the few detailed case studies dealing with the preservation issues associated with raw data files. Describes the use of non-proprietary formats for the raw data and associated documentation, the use of METS as a general metadata format, and long-term management and migration strategies.

UK National Archives, 'PRONOM', *http://www.nationalarchives.gov.uk/pronom/*
PRONOM is a registry of technical information about file formats. Its database is searchable by file format, PRONOM unique identifier, vendor, compatible software and 'lifecycles', which are date ranges during which specific versions of the formats were current. Entries provide links to published specifications.

Puglia, S., Reed, J. and Rhodes, E. (2004) *Technical Guidelines for Digitizing Archival Materials for Electronic Access: Creation of Production Master Files – Raster Images*. Washington, DC: US National Archives and Records Administration. Available at *http://www.archives.gov/research/arc/digitising-archival-materials.html*
This publication is intended to provide standardised procedures for internal use at the National Archives, but it is useful to others because it provides detailed technical information on digital imaging, including colour management, image processing, quality control, and scanning specifications for specific types of images such as text, oversized and microfilm.

National Digital Information Infrastructure and Preservation Program, 'Sustainability of Digital Formats Planning for Library of Congress Collections', *http://www.digitalpreservation.gov/formats/*
Although this website is focused on the internal requirements of the Library of Congress, it provides detailed information on a wide variety of formats, criteria for selecting file formats, and a useful section entitled 'Preferences in summary' specific to text, images, audio and video that outlines best practices for each format. Complements PRONOM.

Tennant, R. (ed.) (2002) *XML in Libraries*, pp. 101–14. New York: Neal-Schuman.

The first and to date most comprehensive book devoted to using XML for library applications. Although the entire book is relevant to digital collection building in general, chapters directly applicable to our discussion of file formats include 'Publishing books online at eScholarship' (Tennant), which describes the use of XML by the California Digital Library to publish a set of books online, and 'Transforming word processing documents into XML: electronic scholarly publishing at the University of Michigan' (Brian Rosenblum).

Notes

1. NISO Framework Advisory Group. (2004) *A Framework of Guidance for Building Good Digital Collections*, 2nd edn. Bethesda, MD: NISO. Available at *http://www.niso.org/framework/Framework2.html*
2. Adobe Systems Incorporated. (2004) *PDF Reference*, 5th edn, pp.7–8. Available at *http://partners.adobe.com/public/developer/en/pdf/PDFReference16.pdf*
3. *http://flac.sourceforge.net/license.html*
4. *http://www.digitalpreservation.gov/formats/sustain/sustain.shtml #disclosure*
5. *http://j2karclib.info/*
6. *http://www.w3.org/TR/xhtml1/*
7. *http://www.tei-c.org/*
8. *http://www.docbook.org/*
9. *http://www.oasis-open.org/committees/tc_home.php?wg_abbrev=office*
10. *http://www.idpf.org/oebps/oebps1.2/*
11. *http://www.daisy.org/z3986/*
12. *http://www.aiim.org/documents/standards/ISO_19005-1_(E).doc*
13. *http://www.lizardtech.com/*
14. *http://djvulibre.djvuzone.org/lti-licensing.html*
15. 'Bit rate', Wikipedia, available at *http://en.wikipedia.org/wiki/Bitrate* (last viewed 12 December 2005).
16. *http://en.wikipedia.org/wiki/Mp3#Licensing_and_patent_issues*
17. Green, A., Dionne, J. and Dennis, M. (1999) *Preserving the Whole: A Two-Track Approach to Rescuing Social Science Data and Metadata*. Washington, DC: Digital Library Federation and the Council on Library and Information Resources. Available at *http://www.clir.org/pubs/reports/ pub83/pub83.pdf*
18. National Science Foundation. (2005) *Long-Lived Digital Data Collections: Enabling Research and Education in the 21st Century*. Available at *http://www.nsf.gov/pubs/2005/nsb0540/nsb0540.pdf*
19. Inter-university Consortium for Political and Social Research. (2005) *Guide to Social Science Data Preparation and Archiving: Best Practice Throughout the Data Life Cycle*. Ann Arbor, MI: ICPSR. Available at *http://www.icpsr. umich.edu/access/dataprep.pdf*

20. ESDS Access and Preservation, available at *http://www.esds.ac.uk/ aandp/create/depintro.asp*
21. *http://www.isotc211.org/*
22. *http://www.icpsr.umich.edu/DDI/*
23. RLG. (2002) *Attributes of Trusted Digital Repositories.* Mountain View, CA: RLG. Available at *http://www.rlg.org/en/page.php?Page_ID=583*
24. *http://www.w3.org/TR/WAI-WEBCONTENT/*
25. *http://www.digitalpreservation.gov/formats/content/content_ categories.shtml*
26. *http://www.natlib.govt.nz/en/whatsnew/4initiatives.html#extraction*

6

Search and display

The previous chapter examined the various types of digital file formats that are commonly used in digital collections found on the web. The first half of this chapter will focus on the conventional ways users interact with these files when they are assembled together into documents. It is important to understand how documents of the types we have identified – textual documents, still images, moving images and sound, and data sets – work both within collections and within the larger context of the web, because virtually every decision you will make during the planning of your collection will have an impact on how users will find items in the collection, how the items will be displayed and how users will navigate the various parts of the collection. Understanding your options for presenting your content on the web will allow you to make more informed decisions about the metadata you will use in your collection, the features you want in a content management system, and in deciding on the ways in which you put into operation the digitisation or conversion phases of your project. This chapter will define some basic decisions that have to be made early in the process of planning your digital collection.

Even though it is impossible to define a 'typical' user or set of interactions a user has with a website, it is reasonable to assume that users of organised collections of documents search and/or browse for documents, are presented with documents they find, navigate through those documents (if the documents consist of multiple parts) and navigate from document to document within the collection. Other activities may also be common, depending on the features that the collection's developers have included; users may be able to add documents or parts of documents to personal space in the system ('my favourites' etc.), save documents, annotate them, e-mail them and so on. Each general type of document poses its own challenges, and within each type, there are many variations that pose significant challenges to collection developers and users. When building digital collections of textual documents, for example, it is considerably simpler to present single-page letters than newspapers, because newspapers comprise multiple, separate articles that can span several pages. In this particular example, decisions made early in the planning process can have significant implications for how the collection is used.

It is important at this point to distinguish between a collection's functional requirements and the digital library content management system's user interface functional requirements. The collection's functional requirements describe broad structural aspects of the group of documents as a whole and of individual documents within the collection. Those of the content management system's user interface build on the collection's functional requirements and add specific aspects of functionality that are independent of the objects and metadata that make up the collection. For instance, the ability for users to view individual scanned pages of a book is a function of the collection, whereas the means provided for zooming in on a single page or for e-mailing the page or book is a function of the digital library content management system.

The fields of information architecture and software engineering provide relevant tools for the developers of digital document collections. In the second half of this chapter, I will borrow from these fields and build on the knowledge they have to offer by applying the techniques of use cases and storyboarding to the planning of digital collections. The fields of information retrieval, text retrieval and cognitive science have much to offer in the form of experimental models for improving the accuracy, scalability and sophistication of the systems used to provide access to digital collections. I will refer to several promising examples of search and retrieval applications from these fields as well.

Still images

Still images are probably the most common type of content that libraries and other types of cultural organisations make available on the web. Photographs (historical, architectural, etc.), photographs of paintings and sculptures, maps, posters and postage stamps all fall into this category of content. Many libraries develop online image collections because, in general, image collections are easier in many ways to implement than other types of collections.

Searching for images

Because most images do not contain any textual content that can be queried, users must rely on metadata such as creator, title and description for resource discovery.[1] Some search and retrieval interfaces to image collections do not rely on metadata but can perform queries based on the content of images. Examples of this type of interface (commonly known as CBIR or content-based image retrieval) include IBM's QBIC (Query By Image Content)[2] and imgSeek,[3] an open-source application that does not yet operate over the web. This type of searching has not been deployed widely and is still considered experimental, although a QBIC interface to a collection of paintings in Russia's Hermitage Museum is available.[4]

Display and navigation issues

Result sets generated by user queries or by browsing metadata elements frequently consist of one or two descriptive elements and thumbnail versions of the images (typically 200 pixels wide or high), and hyperlinks to either a full descriptive record or to a large version of the image itself. Brief records in results lists are often laid out in a table; this layout allows the user to see more thumbnails at once than other layouts, as illustrated in Figure 6.1.

The presentation of images on the web is usually fairly simple. Typically, the entire image can be shown on the user's screen at one time, and because there is no need for the user to navigate with the document, the navigational aspects of the web page can remain minimal, but often include mechanisms for moving on to the next record in the current result set, navigating back to a search or browse interface, and returning to the collection's homepage or appropriate top-level page of the collection's website.

Determining the size of the image to provide to the user is not straightforward, as the size of computer monitors varies widely. Typical monitor resolutions at the time of writing range from 800×600 pixels (common on 14-inch monitors) to 1280×1024 pixels (common on 17- and 19-inch monitors). Ideally, the images you provide should be as large as possible as the low image density of computer monitors (72–96 DPI) can obscure the details in an image, particularly if the image is a black and white or greyscale image. As illustrated in Figure 6.2, the impact that screen size has on the layout of the image display is dramatic.

Figure 6.1 List and grid views of the same result set, as provided by the Streetprint Engine content management system.[5] Used with permission of the CRC Humanities Computing Studio, University of Alberta.

(a)

(b)

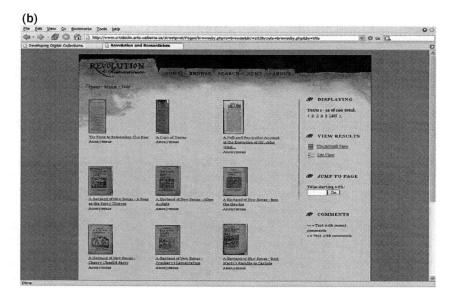

Figure 6.2 Screen space filled by the same image on monitors of two different sizes: (a) 1024 × 768 resolution monitor; (b) 1280 × 1024 resolution monitor.

(a)

(b)

The image of the kayak, water and mountains is 1000 pixels wide by 750 high. It is obvious that the proportion of screen space consumed on the smaller monitor is much higher than that consumed on the larger one. If the display contained any descriptive metadata, navigational elements or other elements on the web page, they would be totally obscured on the smaller monitor.

Some image collections present the full-sized images by linking from the descriptive record or thumbnail version to the full size file (for example, a .jpg) without wrapping it in HTML. Although doing this does allow the largest possible version of the file to be displayed, the context, even if it is a simple description of the content of the image, is temporarily lost. In addition, doing this requires the user to rely on the browser's 'back' button for navigation by removing the possibility of linking to the next record in the result set, a different size of version of the current image, etc. In general, if you decide to provide a link to the image file outside of any HTML wrapper, perform tests with potential users to see how they react to this type of presentation.

Most current web browsers will automatically resize images so that they fit on the screen properly, but this behaviour may be disabled by the user or not available at all in some browsers. Frequently, resizing the image may actually degrade its clarity or appearance. Therefore, you should not adopt the strategy of increasing the size of your images on the assumption that the web browser will always resize it to match the user's screen size.

One popular technique for accommodating a variety of monitor sizes is to provide several versions of the same image, all identical except for their pixel dimensions. In this way, users can view the version that best suits their monitors. Providing links to the different versions takes up little screen space. It is also possible to allow the web browser to detect the size of the monitor using JavaScript and to display the appropriate version of the image automatically. Creating multiple versions of the same image for this purpose (and for use as thumbnails in result set displays) is easy to accomplish using standard image manipulation software and takes up little hard drive space on the web server.

As indicated in the previous chapter, some image file formats such as JPEG2000[6] and DjVu[7] allow practical delivery of high-density image files. These types of file format are most effectively applied when users may want to view the entire image and zoom in to see specific areas of the image at higher magnification (Figure 6.3). Typical applications for this technology include rare books, maps, architectural plans and paintings. At the time of writing, both JPEG2000 and DjVu require browser plug-ins.

Figure 6.3 A double page image (above) from *The Latch Key of My Bookhouse*, and a magnified view (below), as viewed using the Internet Archives' DjVu applet. Used with permission of the Internet Archive.

(a)

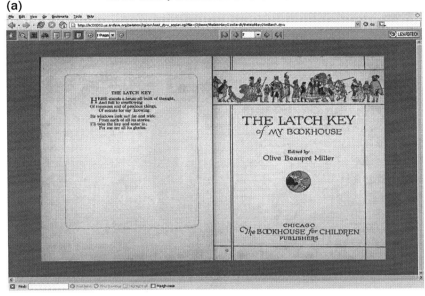

(b)

Up to this point we have been discussing static images – those that are created during a certain part of the production workflow and that are placed on a web server as files to be displayed whenever they are linked to from within an HTML page. The file that is presented to the user is identical to the file that is sitting on the web server waiting to be requested. However, images can be created dynamically, or *at the time of retrieval*. A simple example of this type of image is a map that shows the route from one street address to another. The map showing this route is not predefined, the route is added on top of an underlying map. Another query using a different origin and destination would generate a map that differed from the first one only in the line representing the route.

The most common use of this type of image is in collections of textual documents that display scanned images of the pages in response to a user's query. I will discuss textual collections and documents in detail below, but textual pages displayed as images is very common. Several commercial systems, including Olive Software's Olive collection management system,[8] will highlight in the page image the keywords that the user has entered. Google Print also uses this technique.[9] In these cases, the pixel coordinates that define the boundaries of the word in question are used to define the highlighted area. Other applications of this technique might include drawing a border around a person in a photograph whose name was used in a query, and identifying particular species of plants in photographs containing multiple specimens.

Some image-based documents comprise multiple images. Postcards, which many people would consider still images, are actually more like multi-page full-text documents than still images because their reverse sides are often of as much interest as their front sides. As we will see later in this chapter, some documents do not fit easily into convenient categories such as 'still image' or 'textual documents'.

Textual documents

After still images, textual documents are the next most common type of content that libraries make available online. Apart from containing text, this type of document is usually characterized by having multiple pages. Books, periodicals, and handwritten documents such as letters and postcards are commonly digitised or are born digital and made available in organised collections on the web. Some academic libraries are now developing collections of theses and dissertations produced at their institutions and making these widely available over the web.

Searching for textual documents

Unlike images, which require some sort of metadata to allow them to be retrieved by a user, textual documents can be retrieved using keyword searches on the text of the document or by searching metadata. Both approaches have their uses: full text searching is useful when the user knows specific words that might appear in the text, and metadata searching is useful when the user knows some attribute of a document that will aid in retrieval, such as the author, title or broad subject. Alternatively, searches can be performed on a combination of metadata and full text.

If you plan to allow your users to search full text, you must decide on the granularity of the full text search: the entire document, logical subdivisions such as chapters, individual pages, paragraphs, etc. The most common search granularity is the single page (i.e. when a user searches for multiple keywords in the 'full text', records will be returned if the words all occur on the same page). In this case the results are usually displayed as a list of pages matching the user's query. If more than one page within the same document matches the user's query, the results list may contain the document title only once or may contain an entry for each matching page.

Page-level granularity may not always provide effective retrieval. To illustrate the importance of selecting the appropriate full text search granularity, we can contrast what 'full text searching' means for single-page documents such as memoranda and what it means for complex documents such as long technical manuals. In the former case, each document contains only one page, and the full text of each document is its entire content. Full text searching on a collection of these documents will probably prove to be effective because all searches are performed within a limited scope. For technical manuals, which might contain multiple chapters, sections, subsections, tables, diagrams (with captions) and footnotes, defining the most effective 'full text' search granularity is problematic; here, searches for the same three keywords within the entire document (which could be hundreds of pages long), within a single chapter, within a single page or within a single illustration caption would probably yield very different results: more hits would be retrieved within the larger scope of 'full text' but they may not prove to be very relevant to the user. The challenge in planning a collection of this type of document is to define 'full text' at the level that would provide the best balance of search recall and precision.

Ideally, users would be able to select whether they want their full text searches to be on single pages, within chapters (when searching books) or within the entire document (without or in combination with searching descriptive metadata). Some search and retrieval systems allow this flexibility, particularly those that use XML as their native data structure. Of course, these options may not be of interest to most users but the small percentage that choose 'advanced' search options may be able to take advantage of this flexibility.

It is important to keep in mind that the technologies involved in making large quantities of full text searchable are fairly specialised, most notably (a) in their ability to perform queries efficiently on large numbers of documents, and (b) in their ability to calculate the 'relevance' of particular documents to a searcher's query. Particular technologies should not determine how collections are organised, but the size of a textual collection can have a direct impact on how much time is required for a user to perform a query. A number of products and platforms exist that will easily handle several million full text documents, but in some cases these tend to sacrifice granularity and flexibility for speed. For example, the well-known Greenstone Digital Library software can handle very large quantities of text and can perform queries very quickly, but has limited sorting capabilities.

Display and navigation issues

Results lists for textual documents can be similar to those for images; for example, if the page images make up a textual document, thumbnails are often used to represent the page returned by the query. Including the images of book covers in result lists is also popular. In some cases, standard bibliographic information is used in results displays, often consisting of author, title and data elements. As alluded to above, if users search at page-level granularity, the page (thumbnail or simple hypertext link) is sometimes displayed in the result list; another option is to display the page and also a link back to the first page of the document.

The display of and navigation through textual documents digitised for access on the web pose a number of challenges. The following are issues that planners of digitised collections of texts have to consider. Many of these issues apply to collections of born-digital texts as well.

First, many people do not enjoy reading long passages of text on screen. Many factors contribute to this, ranging from general feelings that a printed book offers a pleasing tactile experience to a dislike of sitting in front of a computer monitor. Some of these issues can be mitigated by providing versions of the text that facilitate easy reading, such as page images that fill the screen. Formats such as Adobe Acrobat allow flexible page resizing, so users can choose a page size that they find easiest to use. Also, texts marked up in structured formats such as XML can be dynamically resized when presented on the screen using Cascading Style Sheets and other technologies, offering readers various degrees of usability. Some collections that feature images of each scanned page also provide a simple textual version that facilitates easy reading, especially when the scanned page is not clear or is damaged.

Given that many people dislike reading texts on a computer screen, it is important to consider how users will print documents in your collection. Documents that are made up of many individual files, such as single-file page images, are very awkward to print. Documents that are contained in one file, such as an Adobe Acrobat file, tend to be much easier to print.

The second major challenge when dealing with textual collections is that the physical act of turning the pages of a book or other text must be translated to useful mechanisms within a piece of software. 'Page turners' of various sorts allow users to navigate inside long texts using a familiar metaphor. These can take the form of simple image-based turners that provide 'Next' and 'Previous' buttons on a web page (see Figure 6.4), to Adobe Acrobat files that contain thumbnail versions of each page in the file that link to the full size version of the page.

Documents that are highly structured, such as those marked up in XML formats including TEI format or DocBook, can be presented to end users in multiple ways, being converted to multiple formats either before being made available on a website or dynamically as they are requested by the user. Two examples of collections of XML-encoded documents that are provided in multiple output formats are the University of Virginia Library's Etext Center's Ebook collection[10] and the Alex Catalog of Electronic Texts.[11] Both of these collections offer versions of well-known works of literature in output formats including HTML for standard web browsers, e-book formats suitable for portable hand-held devices such as Palm and Microsoft Windows-based PDAs (Personal Digital Assistants), and Adobe Acrobat.

XML is the preferred format for complex documents that refer to other documents or to other parts of themselves, such as scholarly editions, variorum editions, and works within a larger context or group of significantly related documents. John Foxe's *Book of Martyrs Variorum Edition Online*[12] is an example of this type of document. This edition, hosted at the Humanities Research Institute of the University of Sheffield, is marked up in TEI, which is converted to HTML for presentation on the web. People's names and other references are identified by TEI tags, which are translated into hypertext links in the HTML.

Figure 6.4 A simple page turner from a collection of texts that provides one image for each page of text. Used with permission of Simon Fraser University Library.

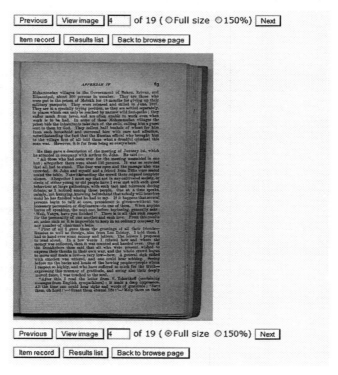

Standard newspapers provide an excellent example of the variety of ways textual documents can be presented online. The most obvious way to provide access to a newspaper would be to scan each page and make them available on the web. As planners of this hypothetical collection, the first decision we would have to make is how large the page images should be: as newspaper pages are very large compared with most computer monitors, we would have to make sure that the images were large enough so the text is legible but small enough so that users can navigate within each image easily. The second set of choices revolves around navigating between various parts of a single article: many newspapers split articles up over more than one page. Figure 6.5 illustrates the front page and second page of a newspaper, simplified but nonetheless realistic.

Figure 6.5 A simplified diagram of how standard newspaper layout can pose challenges for navigating between parts of a single article.

(a) Front page

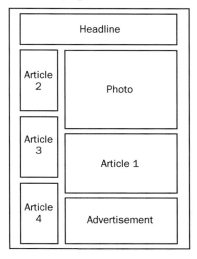

(b) Second page

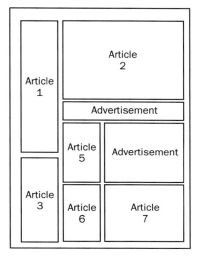

In order to allow our users to read all of Article 1, we would have either to allow them to turn to the next page (assuming they would expect that the article was continued on the second page) or to provide an explicit link from the bottom of Article 1 on the front page to the top of the continuation of Article 1 on the second page. Another option would be to piece both parts of Article 1 together for the user and provide the entire article at once, as in Figure 6.6.

The disadvantage of presenting the parts of the article using either of these options is that doing so for every article in the newspaper would be very labour intensive and therefore expensive. Software exists that will automate identifying parts of newspaper articles that span multiple pages, but it would have its own costs, which would not necessarily be lower than manually identifying, cutting out and reassembling individual articles. We could avoid these issues by providing the user with a transcription of the article without any images of the pages as they exist in the original newspaper, but then the context of the article as it appeared in the original would be lost.

Figure 6.6   A single newspaper article removed from its original context.

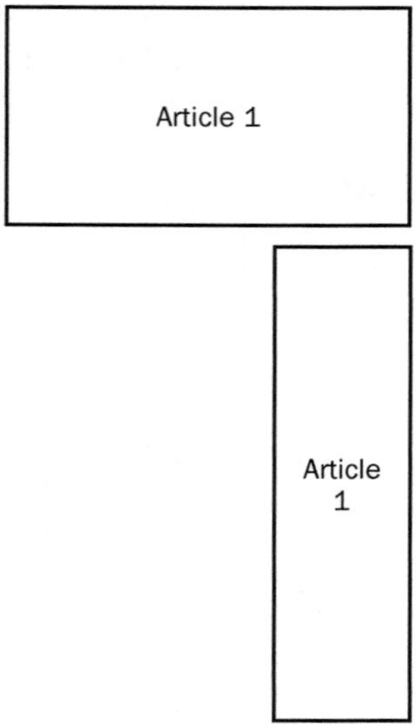

Article 1

Article 1

Moving images and sound

As networks become more robust and as improved file formats and software to read these formats become more common, video and sound recordings (together known as temporal media) are becoming increasingly common in digital collections created by libraries and other organisations. An excellent example of such a collection is the Internet Archive's Moving Image Archive,[13] which at the time of writing contained nearly 20,000 moving images and nearly 28,000 sound items.

Searching for moving images and sound

Like still images, video and sound files do not contain text that can be queried, so users must rely on metadata in order to find documents. And as also with still images, some progress is being made to develop automated methods of extracting 'full text' from temporal media that can then be searched or otherwise used for retrieval purposes. A leading example of this research is the work being done at the Centre de Recherche Informatique de Montréal.[14] Until this type of technology becomes widely deployed, the verbal content of temporal media will need to be manually transcribed and used in the same way as the content of textual documents. Technologies that automate generation of closed captioning for television are beginning to appear on the market, and mass-market voice recognition applications such as Dragon Naturally Speaking[15] are already common and may prove to be useful in converting the verbal content of temporal media into searchable text.

One type of metadata that is specific to temporal media is MPEG-7, which was designed specifically to address the unique retrieval challenges of multimedia content. As we saw in Chapter 4, MPEG-7 offers a standardised XML vocabulary for identifying structure, time points, and qualities such as colour and texture that allow precise retrieval and navigation within a moving picture or audio file. There are very few publicly available examples of MPEG-7 search and retrieval systems, however.

Display and navigation issues

A number of innovative display and navigation tools are included in the Internet Archive's interface to its moving images collection:

- On the details page for a moving image, a series of still images extracted from the moving image at one-minute intervals is displayed, giving the user an indication of the progression and content of the moving image.
- Beneath the rotating still images, a link with the text 'View thumbnails' leads the user to a grid view of all of the extracted images.
- Some videos in the collection can be viewed at an accelerated speed; for example, a moving image that is 15 minutes long can be viewed in 3 minutes, allowing the user to evaluate its usefulness or relevance.

The Internet Archive and other collections of moving images and sound provide multiple versions of the same file, each balancing quality and size, which are in general inversely related to each other. For example, typical moving images are provided in the following variations:

Streaming

- 64 kb MPEG4
- 256 kb MPEG4

Downloading

- 64 kb MPEG4 (109 MB)
- 256 kb MPEG4 (244 MB)
- MPEG1 (904 MB)
- MPEG2 (5.7 GB)

'Streaming' refers to a method of delivery whereby the files are sent from the web server to the user's computer in a constant stream, allowing the movie to start before the entire file is downloaded. The file is not saved on the user's computer but is played through special viewer software on the user's computer. 'Download' refers to delivery of the entire file at once; the user must wait until the entire file has been downloaded until the movie starts. The file is saved to the user's hard drive so it can be played later. The higher the quality or density (here expressed in kilobits or more properly kbit/s), the larger the files.

Sound files in the Internet Archive are provided in much the same way as video, allowing users to choose the highest quality version they can use given the speed of their Internet connection:

Download

- Lossless 621.6M
- Hi-Fi 151.9M
- Lo-Fi 49.1M

Stream

- Hi-Fi
- Lo-Fi

'Lossless' is the best quality file (also the largest); 'lo-fi' is, as the name suggests, the lowest quality but is also the smallest.

The reason it is important to provide a number of versions of moving image and sound files is that the files tend to be very large. As the examples from the Internet Archive show, the highest quality version of the video files is 5.7 gigabytes, the equivalent to a commercial movie DVD. Even the lowest quality version of the same file is over 100 megabytes, which would be unusable over a conventional modem.

Delivering moving image files over the Internet is not always reliable owing to the huge file sizes. Like still images, moving images are created at a specific pixel height and width, and resizing or enlarging them in the player software can cause the image to appear stretched and blurry. Therefore, providing several versions of each file allows users to select the best quality version that their Internet connection can transfer reliably.

Data sets

Data sets are the raw numerical data generated by research in the physical and social sciences. Non-numerical data such as qualitative survey responses can also belong to this type of digital content. Libraries of various types maintain collections of raw data, much of it already in digital formats but not easily accessible over the web, such as tapes, CD-ROMs and a variety proprietary formats. In the last few years, however, an increasing number of data sets are becoming available over the web. Factors that are increasing the need for libraries to create and maintain collections of data sets include increased interdisciplinary use of GIS data, a growing focus on 'e-science' and 'e-social science', and policy changes by national funding agencies in many countries that require grant recipients to make data generated with their funding support widely available.

Searching for data sets

Data sets, and collections of data sets, tend to be highly domain-specific, and therefore it is difficult to generalise about the search tools that accompany these collections. For example, the data sets available through NASA's Goddard Earth Sciences Distributed Active Archive Center, such as the *SIMBIOS-NASDA-OCTS On-line Data Products*, require knowledge of the particular variables that are described by the data, such as 'normalized water-leaving radiance', 'chlorophyll *a* concentration', and 'integral chlorophyll, calculated using the Level-2 values chlorophyll *a* divided by K_490'.[16] These and other variables are options that the user selects as part of the query.

Many collections of data do not have search interfaces as specialised as those described above. A much simpler user interface to raw data, in this case, XML files that describe molecules, is provided by the University of Cambridge's *WorldWideMolecularMatrix*.[17] This interface (which is the one provided by the DSpace repository software) provides a single search field and also allows users to browse the collection by title, author or date.

Although not a collection maintained by a library, Google Earth is a good example of information visualisation,[18] the use of visual search interfaces to facilitate the querying and use of numerical and other types of data. Users of Google Earth can enter street addresses and 'zoom right in' to a photo or map, 'tilt and rotate the view to see 3D terrain and buildings', and perform other types of queries on Google's vast datastore of geospatial data, satellite imagery and maps.[19]

Display and navigation issues

Tabular data in plain text format, tabular data in Microsoft Excel files, structured data in XML files and specialized formats associated with particular data-processing software applications are all common file formats contained in data collections. Some files that are part of data sets are extremely large (in the same range as larger moving image files), but issues associated with the size of the files are sometimes mitigated by systems that allow the retrieval of subsets or portions of the entire data set. Also, users of data sets are likely to be situated at universities and other institutions that will probably have fairly robust networks. In many cases, specific software applications (far more specialised than, say, Excel) are required to view or process the retrieved data.

In general, because the users of specialised data collections tend to have access to the knowledge, tools and infrastructure required to use the data, planning and design of these collections tends to focus less on the types of display and navigation issues associated with collections of images, textual documents, and moving images and sound, and more on creating specialized interfaces to extract the desired data.

Mixed document collections

Classifying all document collections as images, text, temporal media and data sets is somewhat artificial. Many collections contain several of these types of document, and some documents (known variously as 'complex' or 'compound' documents) comprise more than one type of content (e.g. textual documents that contain images). Some documents, such as sheet music, do not fit easily into the categories I have defined. The preceding analyses of each type's particular qualities and challenges is intended to make collection planners aware of some of the issues they will face when they start planning their collection, and to illustrate some of the complexities involved in creating organised collections of documents.

Collections that contain documents of more than one type ('mixed' collections) pose their own challenges. The first set of issues relates to the tools you will provide to the user for searching. Many search interfaces allow the user to limit his or her search to a particular type of document, which, as long as the metadata describing the documents contains the necessary information, may provide useful functionality. However, providing the same search granularity to users of collections containing heterogeneous documents as to users of homogeneous collections can be problematic. For example, a collection that contains both textual documents and photographs could provide users with options for searching on metadata elements such as 'writer/photographer', 'title' and 'subject'. If full text searching is provided for the textual documents, then the search tools should take into account the user's inability to search the full text of images. Because photographs do not typically contain full text, choosing clear and effective labels for search interface components can be challenging (as the example of 'writer/photographer' suggests). Although many users may not be confused by seeing a 'full text' field in the search form if they know the collection contains photographs, others may be. As usual, careful user testing early in the development phases of a collection's interface and search tools can help avoid usability problems later.

A second challenge is defining how search results will be displayed. We have seen how the various types of documents lend themselves to the use of different types of compressed or compact displays of results lists – image collections typically use thumbnails, textual collections use bibliographic information, collections of sound files use icons representing loudspeakers, and so on. The results list produced by a search that returns multiple types of documents will contain multiple types of compressed records. This is not necessarily negative, but does complicate decisions about how to display useful results lists. Another issue is how the results are grouped. In other words, are the results ordered by an attribute that applies to all the documents in the collection (such as date) or are all of the texts displayed together, then the images and then the sound files. This may not seem like a problem to many collection planners but some bodies of material may lend themselves to this type of grouped display, and some users may prefer to see the results displayed in this manner.

Planning your collection's interface

Planning the user interface to digital collections is a complex process. In addition to the issues surrounding the various types of digital content described in this chapter, factors that can have a direct influence on how your collection 'works' in a general sense include issues surrounding the production of the content, financial resources available for the development and maintenance of the collection, available technical infrastructure, the nature of the metadata applied to the items in the collection, and political factors such as donors' desires to see their material treated in ways that may not be consistent with best practices or user friendliness. To assist you in making informed and defensible decisions about providing access to your content, the remainder of this chapter will focus on techniques of use cases, storyboarding, and paper prototyping as they can be applied to online collections.

Use cases and functional requirements

It is useful to distinguish between the functional requirements of the software used to deliver your collection – the content management system – and the functional requirements of the collection itself. Reasons for separating the two types of requirements include:

- If you have not yet selected a content management system, determining the functional requirements of your collection will help you clarify certain aspects of the software during your selection process.

- You may migrate your collection from one content management system to another over the years; new versions of your current system may offer unplanned ways to access and use the collection; and in some cases, features disappear in newer versions of your current system.

- You may want to present your content to a number of different audiences (e.g. you have identified the two target audiences of a historical photo collection as historians and young children), and you may publish the content in multiple content management systems.

I will look closely at functional requirements of content management systems in the next chapter. The specific capabilities of these systems do have a real impact on how users interact with the documents in your collection, but ideally those capabilities should not drive how you plan and organise your collection; in other words, content and general search, display and use requirements should drive the overall architecture of your collection; the capabilities of a particular content management system should not. In the remainder of this chapter I will discuss how you can systematically define the aspects of your collection of documents that are independent of the software you use to deliver the collection on the web.

One technique for determining functional requirements for software applications is the *use case*. Use cases are scenarios that describe how a system should interact with the end user.[20] Even though our goal is to define how users should interact with our collections independent of any software, the same methodology that software designers use can be applied to collections of documents. This methodology typically involves using highly structured and standardised templates that identify the key aspects of each case; for example, some common template elements include a *summary* (a brief description which captures the essence of the scenario), *preconditions* (describing any conditions that must be true when a user enters the scenario), *triggers* (which describe the starting conditions when the scenario is entered), *basic course of events* (the essential actions in the scenario, in their required order and often numbered), *alternative paths* (exceptions, what happens when errors of various kinds occur), *postconditions* (describing the state of the interface at the end of the scenario) and *notes* (any additional information). Although there are a number of competing templates and ways of applying them, the goal of the use case methodology is to isolate and describe the ways that the application (or in our case, the collection) is intended to be used.

Table 6.1 is an example use case for an image collection describing the user's ability to find images by artist's name.

Use cases exemplify and document functional requirements. Each use case should describe a single aspect of your collection, and after you have completed writing all of your use cases, a listing of all of the individual summaries can act as your functional requirements list. To extend the example above, if you want your users to be able to find images through other access points such as subject descriptors or place names, you would write a use case for each of those access points, with the goal of documenting a complete list of desired access points.

The goal in writing use cases is to help us think systematically about certain aspects of our collection independent of the software used to deliver the collection. It is important to keep this distinction in mind when writing use cases, as it is very easy to fall into the habit of describing a user's interaction with a collection of documents and individual documents within the collection in terms of the user interface elements, application

Table 6.1 A sample use case

Summary	In this collection, users must be able to search for an artist's work by the artist's name
Preconditions	User must know how to spell the name of the artist. User must know how to enter the name of the artist (i.e. in direct or inverted order)
Triggers	User must be at a page on the collection website that contains the search field
Basic course of events	User enters the name of an artist, for example 'Vincent van Gogh'
Alternative paths	No records are found: user is presented with a list of names that are similar to the one entered
Postconditions	User has found all records by requested artist
Notes	The ability to search by artist's name requires a corresponding metadata element. In order for our search interface to support artist names entered in direct order, our metadata will need to use cross-references.

features and even application 'look and feel'. Use cases can be deployed in designing or evaluating a content management system (after all, they come from software engineering), but at the planning stage of a digital collection they describe required search capabilities, document attributes and navigational mechanisms, not a piece of software. At the end of this phase of planning, you will be able to state the following about each of your functional requirements: 'Users of this collection should be able to ...'.

Methods of generating use cases include interviewing potential users to determine how they would like to use the collection, and trying similar collections and enumerating the types of tasks that you can (or cannot) perform using their interfaces. It is important to be specific when generating use cases so that all of the parts of the template as illustrated above can contain sufficient detail to produce useful functional requirements. Another potential issue to be aware of is that your ideas of how your collection should work are probably not the same as a *typical* user's ideas. The classic example of this problem is advanced search functionality. Librarians frequently request the ability to use Boolean logic, granular limiting options and truncation, but most users of online collections never use anything more than the simple search functionality provided on the collection's homepage. Including both is perfectly acceptable, but if limited resources require deciding between the two types of search interface, the one most likely to be meaningful to typical users is probably the better choice.

An important functional requirement is adherence to standards that promote accessibility for users with disabilities. I will cover this in the next chapter.

Storyboarding and paper prototyping

After the functional requirements for a collection and its constituent documents have been defined, the requirements can be validated by using two techniques, storyboarding and paper prototyping. Combined, these techniques will minimise the likelihood that important aspects of your collection will be overlooked, and that the functional requirements for the collection are possible given the resources available for the development and maintenance of the collection.

Storyboarding is the process of representing graphically the typical tasks involved in using your collection. The technique originated in film making and has been adopted by instructional designers, software interface designers and others to allow them to test various combinations of screen layouts, conditional operations and navigational components (Figure 6.7).

Storyboarding can help planners of digital collections in the following ways:

- *By ensuring that functional requirements can be translated realistically into online documents and collections*: Storyboarding's purpose is to allow planners to walk through (more precisely, to *draw* through) tasks such as searching for documents, displaying them, and navigating within and between them. These tasks will have been identified in the functional requirements. If each functional requirement can be drawn as part of a storyboard diagram, planners will be able to demonstrate the tasks associated with each functional requirement.

- *By raising issues related to production of the documents*: Functional requirements such as whether or not each page will be displayed as its own image, or alternatively whether the entire document will be displayed as a single file, may determine workflows and procedures during production of the documents. Chapter 10 will deal with workflow in detail, but decisions made during the functional

Figure 6.7 A simple storyboard illustrating the steps required to get from the search page to the display of an image.

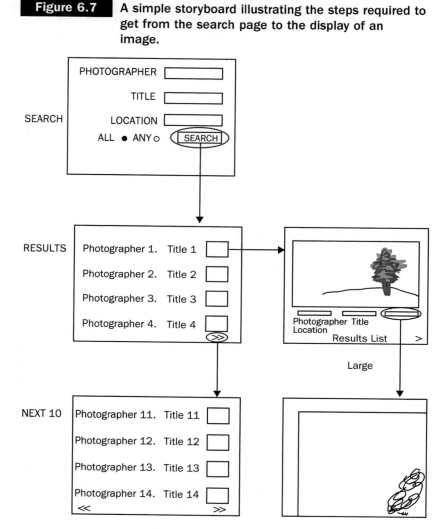

requirements stage of the planning process will have a direct bearing on how the documents and their constituent files will be created, and storyboarding can validate these functional requirements.

■ *By helping identify the descriptive and structural metadata required for the proposed architecture*: For complex objects (i.e. those that comprise more than one file), functional requirements relating to searching, display and navigation will determine what types of structural metadata will be required to enable these tasks.

Storyboarding can highlight the necessary descriptive metadata and the necessary structural metadata for fulfilling specific functional requirements, such as those associated with page turners, hyperlinking between sections of a document or linking between texts.

- *By highlighting functional requirements of content management software*: We have been separating the functional requirements of the collection and the functional requirements of software used to deliver that collection to end users. Storyboarding can illustrate how specific ways of searching, displaying and navigating might be embodied in general terms, independent of any particular content management application. The basic use cases and resulting functional requirements can help form the basis of the functional requirements of software packages that will either have to be developed locally, found among open-source applications or procured from vendors.

Paper prototyping is related to storyboarding, but involves users who interact with simple mock-ups of the collection. As the name suggests, these mock-ups are made of paper. Paper prototyping is a further refinement of storyboarding in that it takes testing away from the whiteboard and into the hands of users. Individual screens depicting user tasks that were represented as rectangles in a storyboard are transformed into corresponding sheets containing the hand-drawn (or roughly laid out using graphics software on a computer) equivalents, which are manipulated by typical users so that the steps in the tasks and the transitions between tasks can be tested. In software development, this interactivity even extends to having separate slips of paper representing various states that a menu can have, hypertext links on a web page, and buttons and other HTML elements. People acting as 'the computer' swap slips of paper representing changes in these interface components in response to user actions and choices, while someone else observes the user to see where he or she has difficulty interacting with the prototype. If any problems arise, they are documented and taken back to the interface designers.

Within the context of planning digital collections, it is not necessary (and not advisable) to achieve the same detailed level of interactivity with test users as software developers would achieve. For planners of digital collections, the purpose of paper prototyping is to allow representative users to validate the choices depicted in the storyboards. Collection planners may find it enlightening to observe how users interact with search forms, browse lists, navigation buttons and drawings depicting documents; again, it is important to remember that it is the collection and its constituent documents that are being tested, not a particular software application. Also, it is extremely important to remember that any problems users have with the prototype are the result of a poorly designed interface (or prototype) and are *not* the fault of the user. Staff who are running the test session must train themselves to remind the user of this tenant of paper prototyping whenever the occasion arises.

Multiple user interfaces

Some collections may warrant multiple user interfaces. For example, a collection of historical diaries may have one interface that is suitable for specialists (hobbyists, genealogists, historians) and another that is suitable for children. The first interface may feature advanced search tools and may present the diaries such that users can read the entire book using a page turner built into the website; the second interface may present selected pages from a group of diaries that all describe the same event, linked from an artist's pictorial rendition of the event. Multiple interfaces that provide access to the same content (in this case the same scanned pages from a group of books) allow you to provide the most effective access to the collection possible, as specialised interfaces can meet the specific needs of a particular group of users without the risk of being cumbersome, difficult and ineffective for general or non-specialist users.

Providing multiple interfaces to the same content is only possible if you produce that content with either all the planned interfaces in mind or without reference to a particular interface. The second approach is obviously the desirable one, as you are unlikely to be able to predict what specialised interfaces you might want to develop in the future. As Clifford Lynch puts it:

> [L]earning materials, interpretation and presentation seems to me to typically – or at least often – have shorter lifespans than the primary source materials that they draw upon. If you look at the processes of scholarship they include a continual reinterpretation of established source material (as well as the continued appraisal of new source materials). Source material persists and generation after generation of scholars and students engage it, yet we typically rewrite textbooks every generation or so at least.[21]

Each interface you develop will have its own development, cost and maintenance issues, but multiple interfaces to the same content can often be justified if the benefits to specialised audiences are defined, tracked and documented. In addition, specialised interfaces allow the use of features that enable tasks other than simply viewing images, reading texts or downloading raw numerical data. For example, CONTENTdm allows users to compare two images selected by the user side by side;[22] MDID features a drag-and-drop 'light table', which uses the metaphor of the traditional tool used to view and arrange photographic slides.[23] An increasingly popular feature is the ability for users to annotate items in a digital collection and to discuss the item with other users, within the context of the collection's website. The variety of features that allow users to perform engaging tasks can be overwhelming to planners of digital collections because some features (but not all) require unproven, non-standard or proprietary technologies. Technologies such as Macromedia's Flash[24] are extending the capabilities of what standard web browsers can allow users to do without specialised software. Multiple, specialised interfaces allow collection planners to test new technologies without necessarily committing to integrating them into the collection's sole interface.

A good example of a collection that uses multiple user interfaces is the International Children's Digital Library,[25] which provides three different ways to read each book: 'standard' (one page image at a time, with links for navigating to the next and previous pages), 'comic' (a zooming interface in which all pages are laid out in panels like a comic book) and 'spiral' (a zooming interface like 'comic' but the pages are laid out in a spiral pattern that rotates so that the current page is brought to the front of the spiral). Books that are still under copyright are also provided in Adobe Acrobat format.

Summary: making decisions about search and display

Grouping the content that we are likely to organise into collections on the web into still image, text, video and sound, and raw data allows us to identify and address issues in searching for these types of content and in displaying them to the user. Although this classification is admittedly simplistic, it can prove useful in planning our collections as long as we acknowledge that many collections contain content of various types. Also, users tend to want to do more than simply search for and display documents; they may want to manipulate them in various ways, save them for use later, comment on them, e-mail them to friends or print them for reading offline. Planning how we anticipate users to interact with our collections in general can be challenging because it is difficult to separate the 'collection' or 'documents' from the 'software' and in fact it is not possible to do so completely. We can assume that the digital content we have created will have a longer life than any particular content management or digital library system we use to deliver that content, however, and we may even want to provide more than one 'view' of our content in order to meet the needs of specific audiences. Being conscious of the particular qualities and attributes of the basic types of digital content typically organised by libraries into online collections can assist us in our efforts to organise our collections so they can be used effectively.

Every library will develop its own protocols and methods for planning a digital collection, influenced by any number of internal and external factors. I will look at some of those factors closely in the chapter on project management. This chapter introduced several techniques from the fields of software and usability engineering that can be applied to the planning of digital collections. These techniques can help us identify possible issues that might impact our work significantly in other stages of developing our collection, and demonstrate that the tools we intend to provide to users are effective. Most importantly, these techniques can help us validate assumptions we make when organising content into coherent digital collections.

Further reading

Horton, W. (1994) *Designing and Writing Online Documentation.* New York: John Wiley & Sons.
Even though Horton's book pre-dates the web as it currently exists, the book focuses on aspects of online documentation that are directly relevant to designing collections of digital documents, such as planning strategies, access methods, differences in reading texts in print and online, and effective use of multimedia. Horton also cites a large body of scholarly research and examples from commonly known software systems that is still relevant although somewhat outdated.

Nielsen, J. (2000) *Designing Web Usability: The Practice of Simplicity.* Indianapolis: New Riders.
Jacob Nielsen is a leading usability expert and the author of the popular useit.com columns on web usability. His book *Designing Web Usability*

documents websites that exhibit good and bad user-centred design, and although it does not address the particular challenges involved in planning collections of documents, Neilsen's constant focus on the user should be a model for anyone who is involved with putting content online.

Rosenfeld, L. and Morville, P. (1998) *Information Architecture for the Word Wide Web*. Sebastopol: O'Reilly.
This book was the first to articulate in detail the principles of 'information architecture', the study and practice of user-centred organisation of information. The chapters on 'Organizing information' and 'Designing navigation systems' are directly relevant to the development of digital collections and the websites that bring them to users. The authors are librarians by training and this background is evident.

Snyder, C. (2003) *Paper Prototyping: The Fast and Easy Way to Design and Refine User Interfaces*. San Francisco: Morgan Kaufmann.
This comprehensive handbook is the standard resource for people who want to employ paper prototyping in software development, but most of the techniques Snyder describes can be used outside of software application development and can be applied to the planning and development of digital collections. Snyder covers everything from the political implications of paper prototyping to the types of paper and glue you should use in your testing.

Witten, I. and Moffat, A. (1999) *Managing Gigabytes: Compressing and Indexing Documents and Images*. San Francisco: Morgan Kaufmann.
A well-respected textbook on building digital libraries, *Managing Gigabytes* focuses on the techniques involved in high-performance text retrieval (although as the title suggests, image retrieval is also covered). The popular Greenstone digital library software (*http://www. greenstone.org*) is the result of Witten's application of information retrieval research to a sophisticated and feature-rich digital library content management system.

Notes

1. A comprehensive overview of theories of and applications in image retrieval is given by: Jorgensen, C. (2003) *Image Retrieval: Theory and Research*. Lanham, MD: Scarecrow.

2. *http://wwwqbic.almaden.ibm.com/*
3. *http://imgseek.python-hosting.com/*
4. *http://www.hermitagemuseum.org/fcgi-bin/db2www/qbicSearch.mac/qbic?selLang=English*
5. Revolution and Romanticism, *http://www.crcstudio.arts.ualberta.ca/streetprint/*
6. *http://j2karclib.info/* [but this is covered in the preceding chapter]
7. *http://www.djvuzone.org/wid/index.html* [but this is covered in the preceding chapter]
8. *http://www.olivesoftware.com/*
9. *http://print.google.com/*
10. *http://etext.lib.virginia.edu/ebooks/*
11. *http://infomotions.com/alex2/*
12. *http://www.hrionline.ac.uk/foxe/*
13. *http://www.archive.org/details/movies*
14. *http://www.crim.ca/en/*
15. *http://www.scansoft.com/naturallyspeaking/*
16. *http://daac.gsfc.nasa.gov/data/datapool/OCTS/index.html*
17. *http://www.dspace.cam.ac.uk/handle/1810/724*
18. The best introduction to information visualisation is: Bederson, B.B. and Shneiderman, B. (2003) *The Craft of Information Visualization: Readings and Refelections*. San Francisco: Morgan Kaufmann.
19. *http://earth.google.com/*
20. Wikipedia contributors, 'Use case,' *Wikipedia: The Free Encyclopedia, http://en.wikipedia.org/wiki/Use_Case*
21. Lynch, C. (2002) 'Digital collections, digital libraries and the digitization of cultural heritage information,' *First Monday* 7:5, *http://www.firstmonday.dk/issues/issue7_5/lynch/*
22. *http://www.contentdm.com/*
23. *http://mdid.org/*
24. *http://en.wikipedia.org/wiki/Macromedia_Flash*
25. *http://www.icdlbooks.org/*

7

Content management systems

A content management system (or CMS) is software that allows efficient organisation and presentation of content on the web. From the perspective of digital library collections, a CMS should at a minimum provide (1) tools for assisting staff in creating content and metadata and (2) tools for end users to find and display resources. This chapter defines some common terminology associated with CMSs, defines some characteristics that CMSs need for digital library applications, describes a number of CMSs suitable for digital library collections, and provides a list of evaluative criteria for CMSs.

Types of CMSs

The phrase 'content management system' is used to describe a number of different types of software applications. They all help their users manage content, but differ in the types of content they are designed for and the tools they provide.

Several common types of CMSs, from the general to the specific, include:

- *Enterprise CMSs*: Enterprise Content Management deals with documents and content related to organisational processes. AIIM (the Enterprise Content Management Association) provides more information on this type of CMS.[1]

- *CMSs for the publishing industry*: Products such CrownPeak CMS[2] and IXIASOFT's TEXTML Server[3] provide functionality tailored specifically to the workflow needs of magazine, newspaper and book publishing industries and often integrate tightly with other standard technologies used by publishers.

- *General website CMSs*: A bewildering number of commercial and open-source products have been designed to assist in maintaining general-purpose websites. Common features include use of a relational database or XML files to store content that is then wrapped in templates to define the HTML sent to the end user, management of news feeds and other rapidly changing content, and account-based personalisation features. Services such as CMS Matrix[4] offer comparisons of a huge array of general website CMSs. Popular general website CMSs include Drupal, Mambo and Plone.

- *Specialized website CMSs*: This category includes products that limit their functionality to managing specific types of websites, such as blogs (WordPress is a popular blog CMS), discussion forums (such as phpBB) or personal photo collections (such as Gallery). CMSs for digital library collections, which I will discuss in the next section, fall into the category of specialised website CMSs.

- *Course Management Systems*: These are educational technologies that assist in the management of online courses, and can include tools such as lesson modules, quizzes, glossary and chat. Course Management Systems (confusingly also known as CMSs) are described here to disambiguate them from the more general category of 'Content Management Systems'. Common examples of Course Management Systems include Moodle and WebCT. A comprehensive list of open-source Course Management Systems is available on the EdTechPost wiki.[5]

CMS for digital library collections

For lack of a better term, I will call content management systems suitable for collections of digital resources 'digital library content management systems', or DLCMSs. The defining features of DLCMSs are:

- They should be able to define a 'collection' of individual resources; in other words, they should allow libraries to present a group of resources that has its own distinct identity within the DLCMS.

- They should be able to present each discrete resource to the user.

- They should include metadata that describes each discrete resource, and provide searching and/or browsing mechanisms that allow users to discover resources using that metadata.

- They should allow staff to add and edit content.

Additional functionality includes the ability to manage administrative, structural and preservation metadata, even though these types of metadata are typically not presented to end users.

Types of DLCMSs

Within DLCMSs, there are a number of subtypes:

- DLCMSs that are custom built for a particular collection or group of collections;
- digital library toolkits, which provide programming libraries, utilities and other components that enable digital library functionality but which require an application (typically staff workflow and end-user presentation web applications) to be built on top of them;
- general DLCMSs, which are distinguished by handling multiple types of documents and by including features of interest to a variety of end users;
- specialized DLCMSs, which are optimised for one type of collection or document type, often accompanied by specialised workflow tools;
- general website CMSs modified or configured for use as a DLCMS.

Examples of DLCMSs

The following selected list of DLCMSs represents all of the types defined in the previous section, but the accompanying descriptions are simply intended to provide a brief overview of each product. They provide insufficient information to allow to you judge whether they are applicable to a given collection or set of collections. More information on each product is available at the URLs supplied in the endnotes. The systems are presented alphabetically by vendor or product within each section. I will compare the advantages of custom-built, open-source and proprietary DLCMSs later in this chapter.

Custom-built DLCMSs

Some libraries choose to develop their own CMSs from the ground up, without using the toolkits described below or without basing the CMS on an existing open-source product. However, custom-built CMSs often use commonly available components such as relational databases, software libraries for handling XML and utilities such as ImageMagick[6] for handling image processing. Software developers use a variety of programming languages for these applications but tend to favour those that are suitable for web applications, such as Java, PHP, Perl or Python. In many cases, particularly if the library needs a DLCMS that can manage resources encoded in XML, web application frameworks such as Cocoon[7] and Axkit[8] are sometimes used as the basis for the CMS. Some institutions release their locally developed CMSs as open-source software (as was the case with MDID, described below) or ommercialise it (as was the case with DLXS, also described below).

The most common rationale for developing a DLCMS in-house is that a suitable product cannot be found. However, as with creating your own metadata schema or XML DTD, developing your own DLCMS carries significant risks, the most significant of which is lack of user community, or more specifically the *size* of the user community (probably just your own institution). Users of both vendor and open-source products benefit greatly from being able to discuss implementation strategies, technical problems and other issues with other users of the same DLCMS. A second risk is sustainability: if only a single library is using a product, ongoing development of that product is less likely to occur, unless it is released later under an open-source licence (but simply releasing a product under an open-source licence does not guarantee ongoing development). Lack of interoperability is not as much of an issue with locally developed software as it is with locally developed metadata and XML schemas, particularly if the software is built using open and common standards.

Digital library toolkits

DLXS[12] is a set of tools for managing collections of books, images, finding aids and metadata encoded in XML or SGML. It is based on the XPAT search engine originally developed by OpenText Corporation and relies heavily on XSLT for transforming encoded content into HTML for presentation on the web. DLXS is developed and maintained by the University of Michigan's Digital Library Production Service. Pricing and support options for the full version of the software are available on the DLSX website, and a Lite version is freely available under an open-source licence.

Fedora[9] is described on its website as a 'digital repository system'. Even though basic tools for adding and maintaining documents and metadata come bundled with Fedora, a number of programming interfaces are available that can be used to create specialised applications such as digital assets management systems, institutional repositories, digital archives, scholarly publishing systems and digital libraries. A number of applications based on Fedora and made available under open-source licences include the Fez[10] digital library system and the VTLS VALET[11] electronic theses and dissertation management system. Fedora is developed and maintained at Cornell University and the University of Virginia.

General DLCMSs

CONTENTdm[13] supports multipage documents, Adobe Acrobat files, images, video and audio files in any format. It also has a JPEG2000 option that is useful for presenting large images such as blueprints and maps. In addition to a web-based administrative interface, CONTENTdm provides a staff tool called the Acquisition Station that allows staff to create and describe objects and import batches of prepared objects. CONTENTdm supports Dublin Core, OAI-PMH, Z39.50, METS and a number of other standards. It includes an interface to the popular PHP programming language, which allows libraries to create customised search and display pages for their collections. One distinguishing feature of CONTENTdm is its 'multi-server' option, which allows collaborating libraries to host collections in a distributed manner but present them to users as if they were hosted on one installation of CONTENTdm. Pricing information is available on the CONTENTdm website.

Greenstone[14] is an open-source digital library platform that supports full text documents of various types, images, video and audio. Object and metadata creation, bulk importing and other staff functions are performed using a Java application called the Greenstone Librarians' Interface. Greenstone supports a variety of standards including Dublin Core, OAI-PMH and METS. One of its distinguishing features is that it supports a wide variety of languages and character sets, including Chinese, Maori and Hindi. Greenstone also provides tools for distributing collections on CD-ROM. Greenstone is developed and maintained at the University of Waikato in New Zealand.

Streetprint Engine[15] is a simple, easy to use open-source DLCMS written in PHP. Streetprint was originally developed to provide a platform for putting literary and historical texts online to support teaching, but it is also suitable for general digital collections. It includes functionality for allowing users to leave comments about individual resources, for building a glossary for the collection and for adding a course syllabus to the collection. Streetprint supports page-image-based textual collections (and searching full text), images, and other files such as Adobe Acrobat, audio and video files. Streetprint Engine is developed and maintained by the Canada Research Chair Humanities Computing Studio at the University of Alberta.

Specialized DLCMSs

DSpace[16] is an open-source institutional repository management system that provides tools for both library staff and end users to ingest items and create metadata. Even though DSpace is used primarily for institutional repositories, it is also being deployed in learning object repository and electronic theses applications, which also use similar workflows. DSpace supports Dublin Core, OAI-PMH, METS and a number of other standards. Unlike most DLCMSs, DSpace provides a number of features to support digital preservation activities, such as a checksum generator (and auditing tools) and compliance with the Open Archival Information System Reference Model. DSpace is developed and maintained by MIT Libraries and the Hewlett-Packard Company.

ePrints[17] provides similar staff and end-user workflow tools that DSpace does, but is tailored more to disciplinary archives than institutional repositories (although it is used for the latter as well as for the former). It supports Dublin Core, OAI-PMH and several other important standards. ePrints organises content differently from DSpace: whereas DSpace allows administrators to define 'communities' and 'collections' within those communities, ePrints provides facilities for creating multiple 'archives' using one instance of the software, in much the same manner that CONTENTdm, Greenstone and other systems organise content into discrete collections. ePrints is available under an open-source licence and is developed and maintained at the University of Southampton.

Luna Insight[18] is a suite of tools for creating digital images, audio and video, and for presenting them on the web. It includes an administrative client for creating collections and for bulk importing objects and metadata, a cataloguing tool, a set of database administration tools, and two different end-user clients, one that does not require a browser plug-in and one that does (although the second one offers greater functionality). Pricing information is available on the Luna Imaging website.

MDID[19] is an open-source collection manager for digital images and, like Streetprint Engine, was developed to support collections used for teaching. MDID provides workflow tools for instructors and curators (people who can define certain properties for a collection), and allows instructors to upload their own images and to generate 'slideshows', which can be annotated, placed online for student study, or archived for testing or future use. MDID is developed and maintained at James Madison University.

<teiPublisher>[20] is an open-source platform for publishing collections encoded in Text Encoding Initiative XML that provides administrative tools for uploading and deleting documents, creating search and browse indexes, creating HTML links within and between documents, and configuring the appearance of the public search interface. <teiPublisher> is built on the native XML database eXist[21] and the text engine search library Lucene.[22] <teiPublisher> was originally developed at the University of Maryland and is supported by a team of developers and collaborators from various institutions in North America and Europe.

General website CMSs used for library applications

The applications described above are developed specifically for managing collections of digital documents and associated descriptive metadata. Some general web CMSs can be used to manage digital collections as well, and although they do not have the same level of specialised functionality seen in DLCMSs, they may be useful in cases where libraries are willing to give up specialised functionality in order to gain the flexibility of general website CMSs, or for prototyping digital collections that will eventually be managed in a DLCMS.

CWIS is 'software to assemble, organize, and share collections of data about resources, like Yahoo! or Google Directory but conforming to international and academic standards for metadata.'[24] Although CWIS does not have functionality for processing documents or the files that make up documents, its metadata capabilities are remarkably sophisticated and flexible. They include the ability to allow administrators to create their own record structures, to add qualifiers to elements, to use controlled vocabularies and to define taxonomies that allow hierarchical browsing of resources. Its search capabilities are as powerful as its metadata management capabilities and provide automatic generation of advanced search forms that include keyword, date and controlled vocabulary searching. To use CWIS as a simple DLCMS, each document would have to be placed on the web independent of CWIS (i.e. documents would have to be uploaded to a website outside of CWIS), but because each document would then have a URL, the descriptions in CWIS would simply provide the URL to each resource. Like Drupal, CWIS has user management functionality, community features such as commenting and forums, and other features that complement its ability to manage and provide access to collections of digital documents and that potentially make it a suitable CMS for some types of collections and situations, such as the ability for users to receive e-mail notifications when new resources that match their saved queries are added to a collection.

Drupal[23] is an open-source CMS that is frequently used for community sites (i.e. sites that allow users to create accounts for participating in discussions) and blogs. Drupal's principal benefits include comprehensive navigation mechanisms (menus, breadcrumbs, etc.), a full user management system including permissions based on groups and roles, and a sophisticated system of modules that allow addition of new functionality without impacting on the core application. Drupal can be transformed into a simple DLCMS by enabling a small set of these modules to provide fielded metadata records, controlled vocabularies and simple staff workflow management.

Integrated library system vendor products

Not mentioned in any of the types above are DLCMSs from integrated library system (ILS) vendors. Many vendors offer products for the creation and management of digital content, including but not limited to Endeavor[25] (ENCompass), Ex Libris[26] (DigiTool), Innovative Interfaces[27] (MetaSource) and Sirsi[28] (Hyperion Digital Media Archive). Advantages of using products supported by ILS vendors include integration with a library's ILS and the fact that you are dealing with a known vendor. As we saw above, some vendors, such as VTLS, are building digital content modules based on open-source technologies.

Evaluating DLCMSs

The remainder of this chapter provides criteria with which libraries can evaluate DLCMSs. The exact evaluation process will vary from library to library, and will probably depend on a number of factors other than strict functional requirements. For instance, some libraries will choose to avoid open-source DLCMSs because they may not have the staff resources required to support open-source applications, while other libraries will choose to acquire a DLCMS module from their ILS vendor because they have a good relationship with the vendor or because integration with the ILS is very important to that particular library. In addition, as commercial DLCMSs frequently cost substantial amounts of money, public and academic libraries in particular may be bound by their parent institutions to issue a formal Request for Information (RFI) and Request for Proposal (RFP), which may require local, institutional criteria not identified here. Another factor that may override strict functional evaluation is whether a DLCMS is hosted on servers maintained by the library or on servers maintained by the parent institution's centralised information technology services.

One common evaluation strategy that can be used regardless of the general factors described above is to create a checklist that is then applied to candidate DLCMSs. A more structured and at the same time more flexible variation of the simple checklist is to add weighted values to individual criteria. For example, a score between 1 and 5 (or some other number) is applied to the features of all candidate products and the total score is used to narrow the list of candidates or to choose a single DLCMS. Once the list of systems is narrowed to a few candidates, other evaluative techniques can be used, such as demonstrations of the product by the vendor (or a company supporting an open-source product), visits or phone calls to other sites that use the system, or having access to a copy of the system on a trial basis. This last option can be useful but requires that the library is able to perform hands-on tests with the system in a short period of time, as vendors typically do not grant access to trial versions of their systems for more than a month. Open-source systems do not suffer this problem, but trial installations must be hosted on servers managed by the library or parent institution.

The following criteria are applicable to commercial, open-source or locally developed DLCMSs:

- Proprietary/open source/custom built
- Pricing

- - Acquisition
  - Annual licence fees
  - Third-party licence fees
  - Hosting fees
- Support options
- Hardware/infrastructure requirements
  - Hardware and operating systems requirements
  - Compatibility with library IT environment
  - Compatibility with parent institution's IT environment
  - Underlying components (web server, database management system)
  - Client requirements for staff and users
  - System administration requirements
- Collection-level functionality
  - Ability to support multiple collections
  - Ease of creating new collections
  - Support for variety of document types
  - Suitability for collection functional requirements
- End-user interface
  - Search options
  - Browse options
  - Display options
  - Proprietary features
  - Ease of configurability/customisation
  - APIs for custom interfaces
  - Personalisation, community features
  - Native authentication/authorisation (such as IP addresses)
  - Application programming interfaces (APIs) for external authentication/authorisation
- Creation, maintenance of content
  - Tools for single and bulk tools
  - Tools for staff user account management
  - Configurable workflows

- – Tools for managing complex documents
- – Conversion tools
- ■ Creation, maintenance of descriptive metadata
  - – Tools for single and bulk tools
  - – Tools for staff user account management
  - – Configurable workflows
  - – Support for authority control
- ■ Standards compliance
  - – Support for a variety of metadata types and formats
  - – Import/export capabilities
  - – Interoperability using standard protocols
  - – Accessibility
- ■ Scalability
  - – Number of documents
  - – Number of users
- ■ Digital assets management
  - – Administrative functions
  - – Preservation functions
- ■ Migration functionality
  - – Standards compliance
  - – Use of common components/infrastructure
  - – Licence restrictions

When using this list, it is important to be as specific as possible. For example, simply asking whether a DLCMS provides 'support for a variety of metadata formats' is not very meaningful; asking if the DLCMS supports the specific descriptive metadata formats that your library is likely to use in the near future (e.g. MARC, Dublin Core and MODS) is a much more thorough approach. Similarly, a checkmark next to the 'accessibility' criterion does not indicate what level of accessibility the system complies with, W3C Conformance Level 'A', Conformance Level 'Double-A' or Conformance Level 'Triple-A'.[29] Libraries using this (or any other) checklist will have to ensure that their own specific needs are articulated and incorporated into the evaluation process. Each top-level group of criteria in this outline will be elaborated upon below.

Proprietary vs. open-source vs. custom built

A number of factors can influence a library's decision to 'buy, build or borrow', as this set of options has become commonly known. Table 7.1 summarises some of these factors:

Issues not identified here include the need for RFIs/RFPs, licences for both proprietary and open-source systems, and the importance of systems' user communities.

Issuing RFIs and RFPs is not uncommon if the estimated cost of a DLCMS is above a certain limit, which varies among institutions but is set by purchasing policies (particularly in publicly funded institutions). Open-source DLCMSs, which generally do not have any direct acquisition or licensing costs, may also be included in RFIs and RFPs to compete with commercial products. The process of developing, distributing, and evaluating RFIs and RFPs requires a substantial amount of work, and some libraries choose to avoid the entire process if doing so does not contravene local procurement policies.

Licence agreements apply to both commercial and open-source products, and even custom-built DLCMSs. Particular aspects of licences that are worth paying particular attention to include the presence of non-disclosure agreements (NDAs) that limit a library's ability to discuss certain aspects of the product with other libraries; whether or not the library can continue to use the software if it decides to stop paying for support from the vendor; and the number of simultaneous users who can access collections managed by the DLCMS at one time (known as 'simultaneous users' or 'SUs'). Libraries that are very cautious will

Table 7.1	Summary of the advantages and disadvantages of the three types of DLCMSs	
	Adavantages	**Disadvantages**
Proprietary	Vendor supplies software, training support. Software can offer desired functionality	Acquisition and licensing cost can be issues. Relations with vendor can deteriorate
Open source	Low initial cost. Reduced dependence on vendors. Flexibility	Often require more staff resources than option. Outside support for many products can be difficult to find
Custom built	Local requirements can define functionality. Can be specific to collection. Flexibility	High staff requirements for development and maintenance. May not be most cost-effective option

require that they are allowed access to the DLCMS source code should the vendor go out of business, and will require that language to that effect be included in the licence agreement.

The nature of licences that apply to open-source software varies widely, from a 'public-domain' licence that effectively eliminates any rights the original author of the application had, to what some people consider restrictive open-source licenses such as the GNU Public License (GPL), which requires that any software derived from applications released under the GPL be distributed under the same licence.[30] Most restrictions of this nature only apply if you plan to redistribute software based on the open-source application; if you simply want to use GPL software to manage a digital collection, you can modify it in any way you want. As with licences for commercial software, it is important that libraries are aware of the implications of the licences attached to open-source applications early in the DLCMS evaluation process. Locally developed, custom DLCMSs often use open-source software libraries and components, and their licences can have an influence on how a local DLCMS can be distributed, if the developers choose to do so later.

A final aspect where proprietary and open-source products need to be compared is their user communities. A good indication of the overall health of a DLCMS is how large and how active its user community is. The most common form that this user community takes is an e-mail discussion list or web-based forum. Vendors who do not permit potential customers temporary access to user discussion forums during the evaluation period (or at least to the forum archives) should be told that libraries cannot make sound decisions without being allowed access to the forums, at least to the forum archives. Similarly, if the archives for an open-source application's user forum show little activity, you have every reason to suspect that developer and community support for the product is stagnant.

Pricing

Pricing for commercial DLCMSs can have the following components: acquisition costs, annual licensing fees, third-party licensing fees and hosting fees. Acquisition costs are one-time fees, analogous to a purchase price. In addition, many vendors charge annual fees called either licence or support fees, typically ranging between 10% and 15% of the acquisition cost. In some cases, vendors will charge either a one-time or an annual fee to cover the costs of incorporating technologies from other companies (sometimes called a 'third-party licence fee') into their product such as specialised image manipulation toolkits or optical character recognition software. These costs are usually included in their acquisition and annual fees but if the third-party technology is optional, these costs may be separated out from the DLCMSs vendor's fees.

Some vendors offer the option of hosting a library's collections, in which case there may be no acquisition cost. This option may be preferred by libraries that do not maintain their own servers or that are not planning to develop their digital collection building beyond one or two collections.

Even though open-source DLCMSs usually do not have any acquisition costs, they should be considered 'free as in puppy' [ZAP1] – their upkeep has real costs, either in local staff costs or in fees paid to external support services. These costs will vary from product to product, and usually include time spent on documentation, local modifications, and regular maintenance such as security patches and bug fixes. All of these costs can be associated with commercial products as well (depending on the product's licence and support agreements), but they are a certainty with freely acquired open-source products and should be incorporated into the total cost of ownership of open-source products.

Support options

DLCMS vendors generally offer technical and operational support for their products, either as part of the initial acquisition fee or as part of a separate support agreement. All software licences should contain clear definitions of the type and amount of support the vendor offers. Support for much open-source software is limited to developers or users on the product's forums (and whatever in-house technical support a library can provide), but some companies create open-source software, give it away freely and earn income by providing fee-based support packages for libraries. In addition, some companies, such as DL Consulting,[31] provide commercial support for specific DLCMS products (in this case, Greenstone); others, such as LibLime,[32] offer commercial support for a variety of open-source library applications.

Hardware and infrastructure requirements

If a library plans to host a commercial or open-source DLCMS on its own servers or those of its parent institution, it is important to consult with IT staff while evaluating potential products. Locally developed

DLCMSs assume a certain level of IT staffing that should ensure local infrastructure requirements are considered early in the development process. Some issues to clarify include:

- *Hardware and operating system requirements*: Does the DLCMS require particular server hardware (or more likely operating system), such as Microsoft Windows, a particular Linux distribution or Sun Solaris?

- *Compatibility with library IT environment*: Are the server hardware and operating system requirements supported by the library's IT staff, or in cases where the DLCMS will be hosted by a unit or organisation other than the library, by their IT staff? Local expertise and experience, and the amount of resources that IT staff can devote to supporting new operating platforms, are important factors to consider and clarify.

- *Underlying components*: Some DLCMSs are built on commonly available web servers (such as Apache or Microsoft IIS) and relational databases (such as MySQL, PostgreSQL, Oracle, Microsoft SQL Server). Local support for these underlying components must be clarified.

- *Client requirements for staff and users*: Do the staff and end-user interfaces require special browser plug-ins or specific web browsers to operate properly? If so, are all of the required plug-ins and browsers available for the operating systems commonly used by staff and end users (such as Microsoft Windows, Mac OS and Linux)?

- *System administration requirements*: Finally, what routine system administration tasks does the DLCMS require? Scheduled backups, routine security patches and bug fixes are common to all DLCMSs, and some require that utilities such as indexers, file integrity checkers and database maintenance scripts be run at regular intervals. Backups and utilities can often be configured to run automatically, but security patches and bug fixes typically need to be performed by systems administration staff.

Collection- and document-level functionality

Some DLCMSs can host multiple collections, whereas others can host only a single collection. Systems that can host multiple collections allow system administrators to define collection-level HTML presentation, descriptive metadata structures, and staff and end-user access permissions for each collection. DLCMSs without this functionality require that a library run a separate instance of the DLCMS for each collection. If a system supports multiple collections, it should provide efficient and easy-to-use tools for creating a new collection, customising HTML elements in the collection's display pages, configuring the metadata elements for the collection, and so on.

Another important aspect of the DLCMS is the types of documents it supports. As we saw earlier in this chapter, general DLCMSs should support all major document types (still images, textual documents, audio, video and data sets), while specialised ones (such as those intended to organise collections of images only) will only support specific document types. Regardless of whether the DLCMS is general or specialised, candidate systems should be evaluated on their ability to meet stated collection-level functional requirements, as explained in Chapter 6. Specific areas of functionality that should be evaluated carefully include the DLCMS' ability to display multiple versions of the same still image (e.g. small, medium, large), its full text search granularity and its ability to display complex documents (documents that contain multiple types of files).

End-user interface

In Chapter 6 I distinguished between the functional requirements of a collection and those of a content management system's user interface. To reiterate that distinction here (it is an important one), the collection's functional requirements describe broad structural aspects of the group of documents as a whole and of individual documents within the collection. The functional requirements of the content management system's user interface build on the collection's functional requirements and add specific aspects of functionality that are independent of the objects and metadata that make up the collection.

Typical end-user interface functionality that should be evaluated carefully to ensure that it meets a particular library's needs includes:

- *Search functions*: Simple and advanced searching; limiting by resource type, dates and other fields; truncation.
- *Browse functions*: Browse lists of specific metadata elements such as title, creator and subject; support for browsing hierarchical categories.

- *Display functions*: Full records-displaying in separate browser windows or in same browser window as results/browse list; user options for viewing brief full record or all record details.

- *Ease of configurability/customisation*: DLCMS administrators should be able to implement user interface configuration options easily, and should be able to modify the user interface's appearance so that it matches the library's general website, if desirable.

- *APIs for custom interfaces*: APIs are documented toolkits for allowing an outside application to interact with the DLCMS. Some DLCMSs provide APIs that allow libraries to create custom or specialised user interfaces in popular programming languages such as PHP and Java.

- *Personalisation, community features*: Shopping carts, folders and other tools for allowing users to collect and organise resources are popular, as are tools for adding end-user comments to individual resources. These features may require end users to have or to create accounts, or may allow anonymous use.

- *Authentication and authorisation mechanisms*: Authentication is the verification that a user is who he or she claims to be, generally using a matching username and password; authorisation is the granting of permission to perform specific tasks or access specific content based on predefined user privileges. DLCMSs should provide multiple mechanisms for restricting access to content, including IP-address-based authentication, tools for end users to create accounts (if applicable), and APIs for common external authentication/authorisation services such as LDAP, IMAP and Active Directory.

Creation and maintenance of content

DLCMSs should provide tools for the creation and maintenance of content. In most cases, content is created independent of the DLCMS using procedures such as those described in Chapter 9 and then 'ingested' into (imported into, added to or submitted to) the DLCMS.

DLCMSs should provide tools for ingesting a single document and for batch loading multiple documents. In addition, systems that support multiple types of documents should provide tools that are tailored specifically for each type of document. For example, still images will require a thumbnail version for use in results and browse lists, and complex documents consisting of multiple files and accompanying structural metadata will need to be assembled into usable documents.

If the DLCMS does not itself provide ways of dealing with the various types of content, additional processes will need to be devised to prepare documents for loading. In addition to tools for creating resources, DLCMSs should provide tools for maintaining resources after they have been loaded. Resources that are made available to the public should not usually need to be updated, but no matter how thorough the quality control process during content production, occasional problems slip through, and it is not unheard of to receive complaints or comments from users that images are not of good enough quality or of misspellings in full text.

Ideally, system administrators should be able to create staff user accounts and associate specific types of privileges with each account or with groups of accounts. This type of capability is useful not only to ensure that staff with the appropriate training can ingest content, but also for creating 'roles' that are authorised to perform specific actions and to create corresponding workflows incorporating those roles. For example, it may be desirable to create a group of users who can only ingest content into the DLCMS, another group who can create descriptive metadata and another group who can approve the completed resource for appearance to the public.

Some DLCMS provide tools that are tightly integrated with content creation processes, such as the ability to scan images directly into the DLCMS' staff interface (as opposed to requiring that the images be scanned into another application such as Adobe Photoshop). DLCMSs that include this type of functionality simplify content creation by reducing the number of workflow steps required to ingest a resource into the collection, but unless the DLCMS allows for alternative methods of adding content prepared outside the DLCMS, libraries' options for content creation are severely limited as they cannot take advantage of other, possibly more efficient tools and procedures.

Creation and maintenance of metadata

Tools for creating and maintaining metadata can be evaluated using criteria similar to those applied to content, but additional functionality includes (1) the extent to which metadata tools provide data validation and (2) the tools' support for controlled vocabularies. Data validation restricts staff from entering values in fields that do not meet certain criteria, such as dates like '03/12/2006' that must be in YYYY-MM-DD format. Support for controlled vocabularies varies widely, from no support at all to full-featured tools for maintaining controlled lists, and tools for importing standardised vocabularies from outside sources such as the *Thesaurus of Graphic Materials*.[33] Additional features to look for include support for multiple controlled vocabularies within the same collection, and support for multiple vocabularies within the same descriptive record.

Standards compliance

In Chapter 4 I covered a number of important metadata standards. The importance of which specific standards a DLCMS supports will be determined by the overall importance you give particular metadata formats within your collections and the importance you give interoperability. However, 'support' and 'compliance' are vague terms, so to evaluate the extent to which a DLCMS can allow effective use of a given standard, it is helpful to specify exactly what types of functions a DLCMS can perform with information structured according to that standard. For example, a set of questions that could be included in an RFI for a DLCMS that supports MODS metadata could take this form:

- Does the product allow staff to create and edit MODS records according to Version 3.1 of the MODS Schema as published at *http://www.loc.gov/standards/mods/v3/mods-3-1.xsd*?
- Does the product allow staff to import and export records structured according to the same version of the MODS Schema?

Cynthia Hodgson's *RFP Writer's Guide to Standards for Library Systems*[34] provides compliance criteria for MARC 21, Z39.50 and other library standards commonly used by integrated library systems, and also for non-MARC metadata in general (Hodgson does not provide compliance criteria for individual descriptive standards such as Dublin Core or MODS), for Open Archives Initiative for Metadata Harvesting, and for the Web Accessibility Initiative's Guidelines.[35] Although Hodgson's *Guide* does not explicitly mention DLCMSs, it does provide useful examples of the language that is conventionally used to describe standards and that libraries and vendors both understand.

Scalability

Scalability is the ability of a software application to remain efficient as the amount of data it has to process increases and as load on the system increases. Applied to DLCMSs, scalability should be evaluated as the number of documents (and their associated metadata) added to the system increases and as the number of simultaneous users of the system increases. A DLCMS that is not scalable will respond more slowly as either the number of documents or the number of users increases; conversely, a scalable system will not show signs of decreased performance as numbers of documents or users increase. These two variables can also have an aggregate effect: response time can remain acceptable in systems that contain large numbers of documents as long as the number of users remains low, but degrades as the number of users increases. Symptoms of poor scalability include poor performance when first connecting to or visiting the DLCMS, slowness during searches and slowness during record updates by staff. One area that is particularly susceptible to scalability problems is the indexing of full text (a staff function) and end-user searching of full text. Vendors should be able to provide reasonable responses to questions regarding their systems' scalability, and any responses from vendors should be confirmed by asking other sites that use their product.

Scalability not only applies to the use of a system's public and staff interfaces. DLCMSs that support bulk importing of documents and metadata can also exhibit poor performance when either the number of documents already in the system is large or the number being imported is large. This type of scalability may not be a significant issue, as bulk importing can be done at times other than when the DLCMS is being used heavily by end users. However, libraries that intend to perform batch importing on a regular basis should clarify with the vendor what type of performance to expect.

Digital assets management

'Digital assets management' (or DAM) describes the broad set of policies associated with managing, preserving and re-using digital resources. A digital assets management system (DAMS) is 'a set of coordinated technologies that allow the quick and efficient storage, retrieval, and reuse of digital files that are essential to an organisation.'[36] As applied to digital collections created by libraries, a DAMS would provide a comprehensive set of functions including creation and management of administrative metadata from the content production process throughout the life of the digital resource, such as inventory control of the files that make up the resource (both masters and derivative versions), original permission to digitise or use the resource, licences granted by the library for re-use of the digital resource, use of the resources within the library's parent institution not covered by standard policies (such as printed course packs at a university), and creation and management of preservation metadata.

Unlike in some industries such as publishing and even to a certain extent in other heritage sectors such as museums, libraries for the most part suffer from a lack of comprehensive DAM policies, not just a lack of tools to perform the required functions. Commercial products such as Artesia DAM[37] and IBM Content Manager[38] are available but have not been widely deployed in libraries. General awareness of DAM in libraries is growing, as witnessed by the 2005 symposium 'Managing Digital Assets: Strategic Issues for Research Libraries', sponsored by the Association of Research Libraries, Coalition for Networked Information, Council on Library and Information Resources, and Digital Library Federation.[39] DAMS for library use are starting to emerge, such as the tools being developed by the National Library of Australia's Digital Services Project[40] and Columbia University's Metadata Master File,[41] but in general specialised DAM applications and mature DAM functionality in DLCMSs remain uncommon.

In practice, very few DLCMSs deal with anything other than descriptive metadata, apart from the minimum amount of structural metadata needed to present resources to the end user and basic administrative metadata such as the username of the staff member who ingested the resource into the DLCMS and the time it was ingested. Similar details for descriptive metadata records are also commonly recorded by DLCMSs. Many libraries manage administrative and preservation metadata in applications outside their DLCMS such as spreadsheets or relational databases, and link information in these tools with metadata and resources in the DLCMS through unique identifiers.

Migration functionality

Any DLCMS will have a shorter lifespan than the content that it contains, for any number of reasons: the vendor of your current system goes out of business or stops supporting its product, community support for the open source CMS you are using dries up, or you require more functionality than your current system can provide. DLCMSs should be evaluated on their migration functionality, which is a DLCMS' overall ability to enable resources and associated metadata to be moved to another system (in which case the DLCMS is said to be the 'source' system) and its ability to import content and metadata from other systems (in which case it is the 'target' system).

Two important indicators of migration functionality are the level of support a DLCMS has for various standards for structuring data, and the extent to which a DLCMS relies on commonly available components such as relational databases. Structured metadata exported in MARC, qualified Dublin Core and MODS can usually be imported into other systems that support those formats. METS is a fairly comprehensive metadata standard that can encapsulate any descriptive metadata and that also provides structural metadata elements that are theoretically transferable between systems. In practice, METS sometimes fails to accommodate architectural differences between DLCMSs, as the developers of Greenstone and DSpace discovered when they explored using METS to integrate those two systems.[42] However, METS is still an important standard, and its potential as a migration format is maturing as it is deployed. Current work in this area includes development of METS profiles to document implementation-specific usage. A number of METS profiles exist,[43] including a Greenstone profile; MIT is developing a METS profile specifically for ingesting material into DSpace.[44]

Another important aspect of migration functionality is the extent to which DLCMSs use technologies such as commonly available relational databases, proxy servers and authentication mechanisms. Use of a standard relational database is important because if the metadata and content cannot be simply exported from the source system and into the target system, the likelihood that it will be possible to create custom migration utilities is increased substantially if the data being migrated are structured in standardised means such as those used in relational databases. Support for common authentication mechanisms such as LDAP, IMAP, the patron databases of common integrated library systems and authenticating proxy servers is also important because of the complexities in managing high numbers of users.

Migration functionality applies to target DLCMS as well. If a library is moving from an old DLCMS to a new one, the most pressing requirement is that existing collections can be imported into candidate systems. Vendors of new (target) systems should be asked what migration services and support they provide. Another reason to pay attention to a given system's functionality as a migration target is that libraries sometimes license collections from content providers, such as art image collections and locally hosted electronic journal collections, and importing these born-digital collections into a DLCMS can be an extremely complex task if the target system does not support common standards.

Licence agreements for DLCMSs should contain language clarifying the library's ability to extract its data in commonly used formats. NDAs that limit a library's ability to share information about a DLCMS with third parties should be negotiated to include a clause specifically for migrating collections to new systems.

Summary: making decisions about content management systems

Libraries have a wide range of options when they select a DLCMS. A number of vendor and open-source products are available that allow libraries to make their digital collections available to end users. Whether a library should acquire a vendor product or deploy an open-source product depends on a number of factors, but in either case, the total cost of ownership of a DLCMS can be quite high. As with any large-scale application that libraries use, thorough definition of the required functionality combined with sound evaluation processes will ensure that the system chosen will meet the needs of end users, staff involved in the creation of content and metadata, and staff who must maintain the DLCMS's technical infrastructure.

Further reading

Digital Asset Management Systems for the Cultural and Scientific Heritage Sector (2002). Available at *http://www.digicult.info/ downloads/html/1039519224/1039519224.html*
Part of DigiCULT's Thematic Issues series,[45] this volume collects nine articles, including two case studies and a report from a forum on digital assets management held in September 2002 in Essen, Germany. Also includes a brief but useful bibliography on DAM. Readers interested in DAM will also find useful the presentations given at the October 2005 forum 'Managing Digital Assets Strategic Issues for Research Libraries', held in Washington, DC, and sponsored by the Association of Research Libraries and others (*http://www.arl.org/ forum05/*).

Open Society Institute. (2004) *A Guide to Institutional Repository Software v 3.0*. Available at *http://www.soros.org/openaccess/software/*
Although this document only covers content management systems for institutional repositories (similar to DSpace and ePrints described in this chapter), it offers a very useful model for evaluating other types of DLCMSs. In particular, the Guide contains a 'Features and

Functionality' table that compares nine platforms using a large number of very specific criteria.

Hodgson, C. (2002) *The RFP Writer's Guide to Standards for Library Systems*. Bethesda, MD: NISO. Available at *http://www.niso.org/ standards/resources/RFP_Writers_Guide.pdf*
This Guide is 'intended for those who are writing Request for Proposals (RFPs) for library systems or evaluating RFP responses and software products', and although it is more relevant to RFPs for integrated library systems, it provides sample RFP language and assessment criteria that are also useful for evaluating DLCMSs, as are the Summary table of standards and Glossary.

Perens, B. (1999) 'The open source definition', in *Open Sources: Voices from the Open Source Revolution.*. Edited by C. DiBona, S. Ockman and M. Stone, pp. 171–88. Sebastepol: O'Reilly. Available at *http://www.oreilly.com/catalog/opensources/book/perens.html*
This chapter from O'Reilly's well-known book on open source provides clear distinctions between the most popular open-source licences, including a section on 'Choosing a license'. Perens' chapter will prove useful to libraries that are planning on redistributing modified versions of open-source software or who are developing their own DLCMS that may be distributed in the future (commercially or as open source).

Rhyno, A. (2004) *Using Open Source Systems for Digital Libraries*. Westport: Libraries Unlimited.
This is a comprehensive handbook on open standards and open-source technologies that are useful in all types of digital libraries, not only content management systems. Rhyno covers the basics of World Wide Web protocols, XML, metadata, relational databases, object databases, scripting and programming languages (with a focus on regular expressions), and DLCSMSs. It also contains a useful glossary.

Notes

1. *http://www.aiim.org/*
2. *http://www.crownpeak.com/*
3. *http://www.ixiasoft.com/*
4. *http://www.cmsmatrix.org/*
5. *http://www.edtechpost.ca/pmwiki/pmwiki.php/EdTechPost/Open SourceCourseManagementSystems*

6. *http://www.imagemagick.org/*
7. *http://cocoon.apache.org/*
8. *http://axkit.org/*
9. *http://fedora.info*
10. *http://espace.library.uq.edu.au/documentation/*
11. *http://www.vtls.com/*
12. *http://www.dlxs.org/*
13. *http://contentdm.com/*
14. *http://greenstone.org/*
15. *http://streetprint.org*
16. *http://dspace.org*
17. *http://www.eprints.org/*
18. *http://www.lunaimaging.com/*
19. *http://mdid.org/*
20. *http://teipublisher.sourceforge.net/*
21. *http://exist.sourceforge.net/*
22. *http://lucene.apache.org/*
23. *http://dupal.org/*
24. *http://scout.wisc.edu/Projects/CWIS/*
25. *http://www.endinfosys.com/*
26. *http://www.exlibris-usa.com/*
27. *http://www.iii.com/*
28. *http://sirsi.com/*
29. *http://www.w3.org/TR/WAI-WEBCONTENT/*
30. *http://www.gnu.org/licenses/gpl-faq.html#GPLRequireSourcePostedPublic*
31. *http://www.dlconsulting.co.nz/*
32. *http://liblime.com/*
33. *http://www.loc.gov/rr/print/tgm1/*
34. Hodgson, C. (2002) *The RFP Writer's Guide to Standards for Library Systems*. Bethesda, MD: NISO. Available at *http://www.niso.org/standards/resources/RFP_Writers_Guide.pdf*
35. *http://www.w3.org/WAI/eval/Overview.html*
36. Geser, G. (2002) 'Introduction and overview,' *DigiCULT* Thematic Issue 2, 5. Available at *http://www.digicult.info/downloads/html/1039519224/1039519224.html*
37. *http://www.artesia.com/*
38. *http://www.ibm.com/software/data/cm/cmgr/*
39. *http://www.arl.org/forum05/*
40. *http://www.nla.gov.au/dsp/*
41. *http://www.columbia.edu/cu/libraries/inside/projects/metadata/mmf/*
42. Witten, I.H. *et al.* (2005) 'StoneD: A bridge between Greenstone and DSpace', *D-Lib Magazine* 11:9. Available at *http://www.dlib.org/dlib/september05/witten/09witten.html*
43. *http://www.loc.gov/standards/mets/profiles/*
44. *http://cwspace.mit.edu/docs/xsd/METS/SIP/profilev0p9p1/metssipv0p9p1.pdf*
45. *http://www.digicult.info/pages/themiss.php*

8

Project management

As we saw in Chapter 2, the development of a digital collection can be broken down into a number of distinct phases:

1. Define goals and scope of the collection (covered in Chapter 2).
2. Evaluate and select source material (Chapter 2).
3. Clear permission to use the source material (Chapter 3).
4. Define project objectives and preliminary milestones (this chapter).
5. Determine technical specifications (Chapters 4–7).
6. Develop workflows (Chapter 10).
7. Develop budget (this chapter).
8. Execute the project (this chapter, Chapter 9).
9. Evaluate the project (this chapter).
10. Evaluate the collection (this chapter).

So far, I have covered in detail a number of these phases, such as defining the goals and scope of the collection, evaluating source material, dealing with copyright issues, deciding what types of metadata to use, determining how users of the collection should find and display items in the collection, determining what file formats to use, and selecting a CMS. This chapter introduces a number of topics not reflected in the high-level outline of phases provided above that deal specifically with project management, including planning the implementation of a project, writing funding proposals, staffing, vendor relations and project evaluation. The following two chapters, 'Project operations' and 'Developing workflows', focus on the operational aspects of project management.

The term 'project' can be misleading, as it implies a period of activity with a defined start and end. In many cases, particularly with collections that are intended to grow over time, there is no specific end to the work – it continues indefinitely. In other cases, the work stops when either the goals defined for the collection have been met or the money allocated to the work has been spent. In this chapter (and in others throughout the book), 'project' is used primarily to describe the work required to create and maintain a collection of digital content. 'Project' also refers to the entire set of activities surrounding development of a digital collection, including promotion, user education and ongoing evaluation, but in general this chapter focuses on the narrower meaning of the word. 'Project management' includes overall planning of this work, overseeing of project operations, project staff and project funding. Whether or not the actual work stops at a specific point in time or whether it continues as the collection grows is not important because both types of projects need to be managed.

Typically one person (a project manager) or a small group of people (a management committee) is responsible for the planning and execution of a defined project. Depending on the size of the library or the number of staff involved in the development of locally created digital collections, this person may or may not be the same one who is responsible for other aspects of the collection, such as advocating for its development, gaining financial commitment from their library, or defining the collection's goals and scope. The production of content and the related work required to make the content available to users frequently occur quickly, with firm deadlines and limited resources, and it is important that libraries creating collections take the role of project manager seriously, as managing any project is usually a time-consuming and intense activity.

Sequence and timing

Not surprisingly, the above list of phases hides a good deal of complexity. To begin with, the fifth phase, 'Determine technical specifications', is really a catch-all that involves defining the metadata that the collection will use, determining the search and display functionality, determining the file formats that will be used, and selecting a CMS. As we have seen, all of these tasks are themselves fairly complex, and ideally should be completed before actual production of content begins, given that each has implications for tools, workflows and procedures. For example, during this phase, desired search and display functionality may influence file formats, which may in turn determine the tools that are used during the creation of the files.

Likewise, search and display requirements and the functionality of the CMS will determine what types of structural metadata need to be created.

Second, even though it is convenient to view the phases as a sequential list, in practice it is not always possible to complete one and move on to the next sequentially. Two examples:

- The original goals for a collection may need to be revised later because of technical or budget issues that arise.

- Securing the rights to include a large amount of material could take more time than initially anticipated, resulting in delayed digitisation and the need to alter workflows in order to finish the work on time.

In addition, some of the activity that is defined early in our list of phases may continue past the beginning of later phases. The best example of this is the clearance of permission to include material in the collection. Depending on national copyright laws, material should not be digitised before permission to do so has been secured, which means that some material may be 'held back' from the project execution phase. However, this material can remain in the clearance queue while the project moves forward and other material is digitised and made available. One of the most challenging roles of a project manager is balancing the complex relationships between the various phases in a project.

One phase that should happen at a specific point in the planning of a digital collection is the development of the budget. This activity should happen after the workflows and project objectives have been finalised, not before. Later in this chapter I will cover 'evidence-based budgeting', which requires that workflows and procedures be sufficiently developed to perform representative samples of the work in order to determine how much time they take. It is important that the creation of a budget follows the development and testing of workflows; otherwise, cost and estimates and production milestones will be highly speculative. The more information available before the budget is created, the more accurate the budget will be.

To summarise, even though we can identify a fairly linear progression between distinct phases in the development of a digital collection, in many cases it will be necessary to adopt a more flexible approach. The exception is developing the budget: accurately projecting the cost of executing a project requires that as many decisions are finalised early in the planning process as possible.

Planning the implementation

Another area of complexity not reflected in the list of phases provided above is planning the implementation of the project itself. This activity, broken down into specific tasks, clusters around phases 5, 6 and 7:

a. Define project objectives and preliminary milestones

b. Determine technical specifications

c. Develop workflows

d. Determine preliminary procedures based on workflows; begin project documentation

e. Determine what resources you need (hardware, software, staff)

f. Decide if you will outsource

g. Develop budget

h. Evaluate and acquire necessary resources

i. Finalise milestones

j. Finish project documentation

k. Hire and train staff, if necessary

l. Start production

This series of tasks begins with identifying objectives and milestones and ends with the start of production work. The remainder of this section will cover each of these aspects of planning the implementation.

Defining project objectives and preliminary milestones

A collection's goals are the starting point for defining the objectives of the project. Objectives should describe the desired outcomes of the project, specifically the deliverables expected at the end of the project (if a specific end point has been defined). Milestones describe desired outcomes at specific points in time throughout the project and are used to assist in monitoring the progress of the work being completed.

As an example, I will use the following statement of a collection's goals developed in Chapter 2:

> The Southeastern Regional News Collection contains selected issues of the *County Herald* and *Crighton Daily* newspapers

published between 1900 and 1920. The collection, which will be freely available to everyone over the World Wide Web, will be of interest to local historians, to genealogists, and to the students seeking primary source material from the early part of the 20th century. Access to the major articles and in each issue will be aided by the addition of subject keywords. Each newspaper issue will be presented as a single Adobe Acrobat file for easy printing.

Once we have a clear statement of the project's goals, we can determine how much work needs to be done by compiling an inventory that lists all of the major groups of content that will be included in the collection based on physical format, and within each group, the number of documents that need to be digitised. It is useful to define these groups by physical format (text, image, audio, video), as the ultimate purpose of this inventory is to help us plan the amount of work that will need to be competed and how long it will probably take. Each format group will require its own workflow (or at least major section of a workflow). Finally, in addition to the number of documents within each format group, it is necessary to calculate how many components or parts of each document will need to be processed. For text, the countable unit is pages; for graphic materials, it is usually the entire document (e.g. a single photograph); for audio and video, it is each separate document, but as these two formats must be digitised in real time they are generally quantified by their duration. Again, the goal of this inventory is to determine the amount of work that will need to be completed during the project, so the inventory needs to be fairly granular. It is better to define more format groups than fewer because you can combine similar groups later; by contrast, defining your format groups too narrowly can introduce unnecessary complexities into your cost estimates.

To proceed with our example, during the content evaluation and selection phase of collection planning, the following calculations were used to estimate the total number of pages published in the period 1900–1920. As stated above, the two newspapers are of the same physical format, but we are putting each newspaper in its own group simply to assist in determining the total number of pages (Table 8.1):

The number of issues to include in the collection was determined during the evaluation phase. The staff evaluating the material concluded that in general one issue per month of the *Herald* and one issue every 2 weeks of the *Daily* would provide a representative sample of the articles, advertisements and other content in the newspapers. Based on this assessment, approximately 9840 pages need to be digitised.

Table 8.1 Sample calculations for estimating extent of source material

Newspaper	Average no. of pages per issue	No. of issues per week	No. of issues in collection	Approx. no. of pages in collection
County Herald	15 pages/issue	1	240 (one per month)	3600
Crighton Daily	12 pages/issue	5	520 (one every 2 weeks)	6240

The project is to be performed over a period of 10 months (that is the period during which the funding is available). Therefore, 984 pages need to be scanned every month (or 246 every week), on average, during this time. This figure will be used to determine preliminary production milestones.

Based on the information we have at this point, the preliminary monthly milestones for the project can be represented as in Table 8.2:

Table 8.2 Sample production milestones

End of month	No. of pages to be digitised
1	984
2	1968
3	2952
4	3936
5	4920
6	5904
7	6888
8	7872
9	8856
10	9840

These milestones are preliminary at this point because we have not performed the detailed calculations necessary to determine how many staff we will need (and we do not have enough information to do that at this point). We will almost certainly need to revise these milestones as information about funding and resources becomes available, but it is good to have a general idea of how much content we will be expected to produce at this point so that we can at least start planning for staff, hardware and other resources.

In some cases, the project is not intended to complete all of the work required to fulfil the collection's goals, such as when the collection has open-ended goals or when the collection is intended to be completed in specific phases over an extended period of time. In these cases, defining milestones and using them to track project status is still essential, if only to track how much is being spent in staff salaries.

The role of workflow

As suggested by its position in the implementation list, workflows need to be developed as early as possible. From a project management perspective, a clearly defined workflow provides information necessary to:

- Determine the tasks required to achieve a specified set of outcomes and the order in which these tasks must be completed.

- Determine costs. As already mentioned, the only sound method of determining the resources required to perform a given set of tasks (and the costs of performing those tasks) is to perform a representative set of those tasks and document actual costs carefully. Workflow modelling and evaluation is therefore necessary *prior* to estimation of costs associated with the production of digital content.

- Clarify duties and responsibilities. Systematic workflow definitions can help clarify who is responsible for what and can serve as the basis for negotiations between partner libraries, vendors, consultants and other participants in the creation of a digital collection.

Chapter 10, which deals exclusively with workflow development, will expand on these three functions, but at this point it should be apparent that workflow development is a crucial component of project management.

Project documentation

In the next chapter I will cover documentation as it relates to project operations: documentation of detailed procedures, rationales for decisions, administrative metadata and general best practices for creating operational documentation. A number of other kinds of documentation that are not particular to digital collection development must be managed efficiently. These types of documentation are required for any type of project (e.g. they apply to retrospective cataloguing of print materials as well as digitising content) but are worth mentioning here nonetheless. These include:

- *Finances*: Financial aspects of a project need to be documented very carefully. Financial audits are a real possibility, particularly if funds have been received from public agencies, and any funder has the right to ask for documentation on how project managers are spending its money. Many institutions rely on centralised financial services (at the library or parent organisation level) to assist in this documentation. Periodic reporting to funders is much easier if sensible documentation procedures are established early in the project.

- *Staffing documentation*: Job descriptions, documentation regarding position creation, applicants' forms and resumes, and other types of documentation should be handled in accordance with your institution's normal practices.

- *Results of monitoring the project*: I will discuss the importance of documenting the results of monitoring later in this chapter.

- *Meeting minutes*: Notes and minutes from project staff meetings should document the status of the project, issues that require attention and action items.

Documentation should be viewed as a regular activity and not one that is performed on an as-needed basis, and it should be built into each of the phases identified earlier as part of large-scale collection planning, from defining the goals and scope of the collection to project and ongoing collection evaluation. Every phase needs to be documented in some way, but in particular, evaluating and selecting source material, clearing permission to use the source material and determining the technical specifications for the collection all require considerable documentation. Given that creating and maintaining useful documentation is time-consuming, it can take considerable staff resources, and therefore should be included in the overall staffing and budget for a given collection or project.

Staffing

The tasks that operational staff perform will be defined in project workflows. Similar tasks should be grouped into roles, which are general types of staff positions that can be used in planning and in developing job descriptions. Stephen Chapman provides the following list of staff roles typically involved in digitisation projects:

- Project manager
- Selector
- Conservator, curator, or other analyst of the source materials
- Preparations technician (may also be curator, who, in turn, may also be the selector)
- Cataloger to create or enhance bibliographic records and to withdraw materials for conversion
- Scanning technician or photographer
- Quality control technician (may also be the scanning technician)
- Metadata analyst (may also be the cataloger)
- Data entry technician
- Programmer or other database expert who integrates metadata and images into a coherent resource (also known as the digital object)
- Systems administrator or other manager of electronic records and systems
- Network administrator to implement security and other access requirements (may also be the systems administrator)
- Developer or designer of the user interface[1]

These roles may not apply to every project, depending on the nature of the source material and the workflows that you have defined. For example, the staff required to work on a collection of born-digital material will differ from the staff required to work on a digitisation project. Also, some of these roles, such as cataloguers and network administrators, may be assumed by existing staff who perform these functions as part of their regular jobs. Having existing library staff perform work in short-term projects is a good way to save on staff costs, and many funders consider existing staff time to be 'in kind' contributions (discussed further below). However, if existing library staff are to work on the digitisation projects, they must be allowed to devote the required time and not have the extra work simply added to their existing responsibilities. In some cases this means that the digitisation project takes priority over other activity or that someone else can take on work displaced by the digitisation project without exceeding their own normal workloads.

A number of factors should be considered when creating job descriptions for project staff. First, new positions may be based on existing ones if they exist, particularly for roles such as cataloguers, systems administrators and software developers as the skills required for these positions are in general not specific to the work that is required in digital library development projects. On the other hand, many positions in Chapman's list are quite specialised and project managers may have difficulty finding models for suitable job descriptions. Second, much digitisation work is repetitive and detail-orientated, particularly that of scanning or digitisation technicians. Therefore, it is important to build variety into their job descriptions. Two strategies for ensuring variety are (1) have each staff member fill multiple roles or (2) have each role perform a variety of tasks. The disadvantages of setting up positions in this way is that it may be more difficult to fill such positions because of the variety of skills required, and when a person leaves a project, multiple roles are left vacant.

Planning for staff training in digitisation projects can be challenging. In short-term projects that have a defined duration, staff filling positions created specifically for the project will need to be trained early in the project period. For training to occur, hardware and software must be operational, and procedural documentation must be ready. Staff taken from other parts of the library will also need to be trained on project operations but this can sometimes be done before the training of new staff happens, provided documentation and tools required for their work are ready.

As stated earlier, an individual project manager should be identified as being responsible for the project. This person is directly involved in the planning of the project, assembling and allocating the required resources, monitoring the progress of the work, managing the budget, and for evaluating the project and often for evaluating the collection after the work is complete. Project staff should report directly or indirectly to the project manager; if there is a separate supervisor of project operations, most project staff will report to this person, who in turn reports to the project manager. In small operations, the project manager and supervisor can be the same person, but in larger operations, the demands of both of these roles can quickly surpass a single person's capacity. In fact, larger projects will probably need more than one supervisor, especially if the production work is done in shifts that exceed a normal work day or if it is done at more than one physical location.

In some cases a committee, instead of a single individual, performs the role of project manager. Committees are common in large-scale or long-term projects, and in multi-institution projects. However, smaller, shorter projects are often best managed by a single individual who can draw on the expertise of others when needed.

In Chapter 9, 'Project operations', I will cover the roles of project supervisor, digitisation technician and quality control technician in detail.

Hardware and software resources

If your library does not already have the hardware and software resources necessary to create the desired content, you will have to acquire them. Unfortunately, acquiring scanners and other digitisation hardware is not as straightforward as it might sound, so project plans must include suitable lead times if production is to start on a given date.

A number of factors will help you determine the requirements for the hardware and software you will need to create your collection's content. First, information gathered during the source material evaluation phase, such as format (still images, sound, etc.), physical dimensions and physical condition, should be considered when selecting digitisation hardware. Second, fully developed workflows can assist in the selection of hardware and software by helping define the most efficient set of steps in which to create content and metadata. The desired set of steps can then be used to define criteria for evaluating hardware and software. For example, if you know that you will in general be using TIFF as the format for the master versions of image files you are creating, you can include the ability to create TIFF files in your scanner evaluation criteria. Limitations in hardware and software can often be compensated for in workflows, but usually this compensation involves additional tasks, which add to overall project costs. The next chapter, 'Project operations', will provide additional, detailed information on evaluating suitable hardware and software.

It may be tempting to evaluate and acquire hardware and software based on the requirements of a single collection or the workflows of a single project, particularly if these resources will be purchased from funds allocated specifically for that collection or project. However, if a library intends to develop additional digital collections or participate in collaborative collection development initiatives, acquiring hardware and software that can produce files meeting a variety of criteria is a much sounder strategy. Acquiring a scanner whose maximum output resolution is the exact resolution required in the current project is less preferable to acquiring a scanner that can output images at much higher resolutions. Typically, the better the hardware, the more expensive it is, but all other things being equal, if you can afford hardware that exceeds the requirements of your current project, you should consider acquiring it as future projects may have more demanding technical specifications than the current project. Realistically, however, you need to work within your budget, and if you can only afford digitisation hardware and software that meets but does not exceed the requirement of your current project, then that is what you should buy.

To a large extent, exactly when you evaluate and acquire any new hardware and software does not matter, except that you will need to know the minimum technical specifications that content in your collection will adhere to, and you need to know if you have the funds to buy the required resources. Obviously you will need to have all tools in place in time to document procedures prior to training new staff. This applies to hardware, software used in the production of the content and metadata, and the CMS you will be using. Project deadlines and staffing levels can have an impact on how much hardware and software you will need. For this reason, many project managers wait until they know the final deadlines and staff budgets before acquiring new hardware.

Outsourcing

Producing digital content, even on a small scale, requires a substantial investment in hardware, software, space and staff resources. Many libraries are not in the position to make these investments or are otherwise happy to avoid making them. Instead, they send original material to a vendor, who creates the digital content and then delivers it to the library, ready for loading into the library's CMS. Alternatively, the vendor may be responsible only for digitising the material and the library will perform other required tasks, such as creating derivative versions for presentation on the web. The latter case applies to libraries that wish to avoid investing in digitisation hardware but still want to be involved in the production of their content. Some libraries also outsource the creation of descriptive metadata, whereas others choose to create their own even if they outsource digitisation or conversion. In some cases, the library does not host its own collections, but contracts with a vendor to host them on its servers.

When deciding whether to invest in the infrastructure necessary to develop and maintain a digital collection, a library may choose from a number of options:

- performing all work internally,
- hiring a commercial vendor to perform all or parts of the work required to produce the content,

- hiring a consultant to plan and oversee the project, with the work done either internally or by a vendor,

- collaborating with other libraries, and

- a combination of the above options.

Janet Gertz's chapter cited in the 'Further reading' section at the end of this chapter provides extensive information on the relative benefits of doing the work internally or contracting with a vendor, on selecting a vendor and on developing the various documents that are necessary when outsourcing such as Requests for Information and Requests for Proposals. The information Gertz provides is thorough and detailed and will prove to be extremely useful to libraries considering contracting with commercial vendors for the production of their digital content and metadata.

Contracting with other libraries that act as 'vendors' is becoming increasingly common. This type of relationship differs from multi-institutional projects (discussed below): the 'client' library is simply contracting with the 'vendor' library to do specific types of work instead of contracting with a commercial vendor. Many libraries that have invested in digitisation hardware, software and staff have the extra capacity to do external work, particularly during periods of low activity from their own projects. In these cases, the client and vendor libraries must come to an agreement that is satisfactory to both parties, and the vendor library must be able to perform the work at rates comparable with those charged by vendors. This type of relationship may be preferred when the client libraries feel most comfortable dealing with other libraries, particularly if they cannot find a commercial vendor that meets their needs. Also, it is not uncommon for larger university and public libraries to act as digitisation and metadata production centres for smaller libraries within their geographical region that may have interesting collections but not the resources to digitise them. On the other hand, some libraries may prefer to deal with commercial vendors because they feel that it is easier to establish business-like relationships with commercial entities or that it is best to collaborate with other libraries on a more equitable basis than the client–vendor relationship often implies.

Hiring a consultant to assist in planning and to oversee project operations is yet another option. A good consultant will have experience in digital library content development, will balance the goals of the collection with the resources available for the project, and will demonstrate flexibility in how problems are solved. Avoid consultants who are tied to a particular set of technologies (unless the library would adopt those same technologies independent of the consultant's recommendations). Keep in mind that a consultant cannot assist a library with a digital collection project (or any other type of project) unless library staff assist the consultant: clearly communicating the expected outcomes of the consultant's work and freely providing the information the consultant needs are essential. The best possible outcome of hiring a consultant for this type of project (other than a successful digital collection, of course) is successful knowledge transfer; in other words, library staff should be able to plan and manage similar projects on their own in the future, if doing so is part of the library's long-term digital collection development programme.

In addition to outsourcing the production of digital content and metadata, some libraries choose to make their collections available using CMSs hosted externally. Options for making the collection available to end users include:

- host the collection on servers maintained by the library's parent institution,
- host the collection on a commercial vendor's servers, or
- host the collection on another library's servers.

Like selecting an external source for content production, selecting a vendor or other library to host a collection allows libraries with content to create digital collections without investing in the required infrastructure. Many libraries do not run their own servers or do not have the technical staff required to maintain a CMS. On the other hand, many libraries would rather host a CMS than acquire scanners and specialised software, and employ the staff necessary for creating digital content.

Preparing a budget

Preparing a budget for a digitisation or conversion project can be somewhat complex because of the following factors:

- *Variability in workflows for different projects*: Digitising or converting still images, text, video and audio source material all require different sets of tasks, and even within each type of source material there can exist a wide range of workflows (we have seen, for example, that there are several substantially different approaches to digitising texts). Collection functional requirements can vary widely as well, as can options for creating metadata. This matrix of implementation variables can result in real challenges for project managers who need to estimate how much it will cost to create a given collection. Costs are determined by the nature of the project workflow, and if mangers cannot predict workflows, they cannot predict costs with much accuracy.

- *Inconsistency in source material*: Even though careful project managers will base cost estimates on representative samples of the source material they are working with, many collections of source material contain hidden surprises that complicate production significantly and therefore have a real impact on a project's overall budget. This impact can be considerable given the cumulative effect of high numbers of unexpected exceptions.

- *Limitations of technology*: Whether due to temporary problems or due to systemic limitations, problems with technology can dramatically affect the likelihood that a project will be completed on time and within its budget.

As already stated, by far the safest way to estimate the costs involved in producing specific digital content is to develop appropriate workflows and procedures, perform trials, document the cost of the trials, and then using those costs extrapolate the cost of processing the entire collection of source material. Any other method of determining costs is an educated guess. Even in the unlikely event that your institution will accommodate budgets that are off by 50–200% (to pick arbitrary figures), it is safe to say that few external funders will. They will typically want to know exactly how much it will cost to accomplish the goals you describe in the grant applications.

This type of evidence-based budgeting is not easy. It is difficult if not impossible to do on short notice, it can require resources (such as hardware) that are not available prior to receiving the funding you are applying for, and it can be inaccurate if staff performing the trial runs are not proficient at using the available workflows and tools, which they may not be without a few weeks' experience. It can also create a misleading sense of confidence in cost estimates, particularly if the workflows and procedures are not fully developed or if the source material being tested is not typical of the entire collection. Finally, even though evidence-based budgeting provides fairly accurate data for estimating the costs of staff who are performing the tasks, it does not necessarily provide accurate data on how much time supervisors and project managers spend on tasks not directly related to production, such as documentation, supervision and writing reports. Despite these drawbacks, using empirical evidence to estimate costs lends authority to budgeting, and even if these informed estimates prove to be inaccurate, the information derived from trials will allow you to identify the areas that are inflating actual production costs.

In some cases it is not necessary to perform trials on representative samples of source material in order to derive an accurate budget if the project you are planning is very similar to ones you have performed in the past. In these cases, the known costs from the previous projects can act as a reliable indicator of the likely costs in the new project. However, this method is reliable only to the extent that the source material, metadata requirements and workflows of the two projects are the same. Even slight differences between source material and technical specifications can cause estimated costs to be inaccurate, particularly if the number of items in your collection is large.

Cost components

The largest costs for a digitisation project are operations staff (staff performing permissions clearance, metadata production and content creation; supervisors; project managers, etc.), hardware, software, copyright clearance fees and a CMS, whether a vendor product or open source. If your library already has suitable hardware or software, or a suitable CMS, those items will not represent additional real costs (although they may be applicable as in-kind contributions on grant applications, as described below). The most common type of cost for any project is staff. It is difficult to generalise about the relative proportions of the various types of cost in a project because of the wide variability in hardware, software and CMS prices, and because staff costs are unknown for any project until workflows have been tested. Using documented costs from a series of large-scale digitisation projects, Steven Puglia found that roughly one-third of the cost of the production of those collections accounted for digitisation, one-third for metadata creation, and the final third for administration, quality control and other activities.[2] Although these findings were derived from actual recorded costs, they should be used as a general guide only and not as an accurate planning formula, for reasons stated earlier.

After production is complete, ongoing costs include collection maintenance, promotion and evaluation. Preservation of the digital content will also have real costs, and as we saw in Chapter 5, these are at best difficult to predict.

An example budget

The following example illustrates how project managers can develop a budget based on performing trials of the tasks identified in a project's workflow. The example is simple but realistic, and includes every aspect of the digitisation and metadata creation activities necessary to put a small collection of audio tapes online. It includes estimates for two positions other than the staff involved in content and metadata production, a web developer who is configuring a CMS for the collection, and a project manager who is responsible for supervision, documentation, training and quality control. It does not include the work necessary to clear permission to mount the material on the web. The collection consists of 110 tape recordings of authors reading short fiction or excerpts from longer works.

In preparation for developing this budget, we have developed a workflow and digitised a number of samples. From these trials, we have determined that the following are reasonable average amounts of time for processing each reading (Table 8.3):

Table 8.3 **Workflow tasks and average times for processing sample audio recordings**

Task	Estimated time required
Retrieving and preparing each tape	15 minutes
Converting audio tape to WAV and naming the file according to documented procedures	20 minutes
Converting each WAV file to mp3 format for the web and copying it to the designated archive directory	10 minutes
Creating descriptive metadata for each sound file	20 minutes
Adding administrative metadata to the CMS, copying the master WAV file to the archive drive, and adding the mp3 file into the CMS	10 minutes

A note about converting from audio tape to WAV: the conversion must be done in real time (i.e. a tape that is 15 minutes long takes 15 minutes to convert). Even though the technician does not have to sit at the workstation during the conversion but can do other tasks – in theory he or she could be preparing the next tape while the previous one is playing and being digitised – we have decided to account for the times as if the technician did not perform other tasks while waiting for the tape to finish playing.

Another note, this time about how to perform the budgeting trials: for most projects where textual content is being produced, the number of pages is a useful unit to base timelines on as each page needs to be scanned separately. For image-based collections, the number of images that are required would be an appropriate unit; for collections of audio or video that must be digitised, the number of minutes or hours may be more appropriate as these formats must be digitised in real time.

The Conversion Technician, who retrieves each tape, digitises it and converts the files from WAV to mp3, earns $15.00 an hour plus 8% benefits, and the Metadata Specialist, who applies all metadata and adds the files to the archive directory, earns $20.00 an hour plus 9% benefits. To calculate the cost of digitising the entire collection and creating the accompanying metadata, we multiply the average times identified above by the number of tapes (Table 8.4):

Table 8.4   **Estimated time required to digitise entire collection and create metadata**

Task	Estimated time required to complete the project	Total time required to complete the project
Retrieving and preparing each tape (Conversion Technician)	15 minutes/tape	0.25 hours/tape × 110 tapes = 27.5 hours
Converting from audio tape to WAV and naming the file according to documented procedures (Conversion Technician)	20 minutes/tape	0.33 hours/tape × 110 tapes = 36.3 hours
Converting each WAV file to mp3 format for the web and copying it to the designated archive directory (Conversion Technician)	10 minutes/tape	0.17 hours/tape × 110 tapes = 18.7 hours
Creating descriptive metadata for each sound file (Metadata Specialist)	20 minutes/tape	0.33 hours/tape × 110 tapes = 36.3 hours
Adding administrative metadata to the CMS, copying the master WAV file to the archive drive, and adding the mp3 file into the CMS (Metadata Specialist)	10 minutes/tape	0.17 hours/tape × 110 tapes = 18.7 hours

The costs for the Web Developer and the Supervisor are calculated separately (Table 8.5). The former is a freelance consultant who charges a flat rate and has supplied a quote indicating that the work will not take more than 10 hours to complete. The Project Manager/Supervisor's salary is more difficult to estimate accurately, but based on similar work done

Table 8.5 Tasks and salaries for the Web Developer and Supervisor

Type	Estimated time required	Estimated cost
Web Developer, who has to modify some of the CMS web templates for publication of these files. This activity does not include any other activity. (Position 3)	10 hours	$40/hour, no benefits
Administration, including project development, documentation, staff training and supervision, and quality control (Position 4)	50% of all staff time including the Web Developer	$32/hour, plus 12% benefits

at the library, we estimate that the Supervisor will need to spend half of the total time required by the Conversion Technician and Metadata Specialist to digitise the material and create metadata. This estimate is relatively high but it includes the time required to write the procedures manual and to perform quality control on the digitised sound files (by listening to the beginning, middle, and end of each reading, for example).

Now that we have estimated costs for all of the staff, we can add them together in the following spreadsheet (Table 8.6; numbers of hours are rounded up to the nearest hour):

Table 8.6 Total staff costs for processing the audio recordings

Title	Conversion Technician
Number of hours	28 + 37 + 19 = 84 hours
Hourly rate and total salary	$15.00/hour × 84 hours = $1260.00
Benefits (8% of total hourly wage)	$100.80
Total cost for Position 1	$1360.80
Title	Metadata Specialist
Number of hours	37 + 19 = 56 hours
Hourly rate and total salary	$20.00 × 56 hours = $1120.00
Benefits (9% of total hourly wage)	$100.80
Total cost for Position 2	$1220.80

Table 8.6 Total staff costs for processing the audio recordings *(Cont'd)*

Title	Web Developer
Number of hours	10
Hourly rate and total salary	$40.00
Benefits (0% of total hourly wage)	$0.00
Total cost for Position 3	$400.00
Title	Supervisor
Number of hours	70
Hourly rate and total salary	$32.00 × 70 hours = $2240.00
Benefits (12% of total hourly wage)	$268.80
Total cost for Position 4	$2508.80
Total staff costs	$5490.40

This example illustrates a linear workflow, which means that all of the tasks are performed sequentially. To budget for parallel workflows, in which independent tasks are performed at the same time and the output from each is combined later, we need to add additional rows in our spreadsheet for each of the parallel tasks and then add up all of the costs. In other words, the time required to digitise the source material using parallel workflows is cumulative – we need to pay the salaries of all the staff who contribute to the creation of a digital document, even if they are working at the same time but on separate tasks. For example, if we had someone transcribing the audio tapes as they were being digitised in order to create a searchable 'full text' for each tape, the salaries for both of these staff would need to be included in our budget.

Additional planning considerations

Once the amount of staff time required for a project is known, we can estimate the number of staff we need to hire, the amount of hardware and software we need to procure, and the amount of physical space required to do the work.

After fully developed workflows, the next issue to resolve is how much time is required to complete the project. The number of work days available to you will let you determine how many staff to hire, which in turn will determine how much hardware you need and how much physical space you need. These numbers can be determined by various factors, such as the amount of time a funder gives you to spend their money, the end dates of fiscal years, the availability of staff (e.g. scheduling work shifts around major holidays is often problematic), or other factors. Ultimately, you will need to determine when you plan to launch your collection. This date may or may not be flexible, and you may need to launch the collection before all the content and metadata are ready, but in practice you will probably have to juggle all of the timing factors listed here in order to get a fairly accurate idea of how long your project will take.

Given the total amount of time required to complete the tasks defined in our workflow, and the number of days available within the project timeline, we can estimate the number of hours of work per day that need to be completed. Given the total number of hours of work, we can determine the number of staff required, and from that number, the amount of hardware and physical space they will need to complete the work. This formula is only a guide – adjustments may need to be made in response to contingencies such as unpredictable availability of staff (e.g. most students do not want to work at exam time) and delays due to hardware and other problems. However, the total number of hours of work required to complete a project is a useful basis on which to estimate associated resources.

First, for the conversion technician and metadata specialist, we need to calculate the number of work hours per day required to complete our project:

Number of hours per day required to complete all work = Total number of hours required to complete all work/number of available days

For the sake of this example (Table 8.7), we are told by the library administration that we need to spend all of the money allocated to this project within 4 weeks (or 20 working days):

Table 8.7   Hours of work per day required to complete all work

Position title	Hours required to complete all work	Days available	Hours per day required to complete all work
Conversion Technician	84	20	4.2
Metadata Specialist	56	20	2.8

Using this figure of 4 weeks and the number of hours in a standard working day (in this case 7 hours per day for full-time equivalent staff, or FTE), we can determine the number of positions we need for the conversion technician and the metadata specialist in order to complete work within the given timelines (Table 8.8):

Table 8.8 Positions required to complete all work in days available (FTE)

Position title	Hours in standard working day (1 FTE)	Hours per day required to complete all work	Positions required to complete all work in days available (FTE)
Conversion Technician	7	4.2	0.6
Metadata Specialist	7	2.8	0.4
Supervisor	7	3.5	0.5

Number of positions required to complete all work = Number of hours per day required to complete all work/number of hours in a standard working day (for 1 FTE)

The right-most column shows that the number of positions required is less than one FTE for each position title. This figure is useful in determining how many people to hire, and whether their positions will be full time or part time. In our example, because all of the positions are less than one FTE, we may be able to complete the project in fewer than 20 days if we make the positions full time; if the number of positions were more than one FTE, we would need to hire more than one person, or increase the number of days in which we would be able to complete the project (which the library administration says is not an option).

At this point we should finalise our project milestones. In the earlier example in which we devised some preliminary milestones for the digitisation of the local newspapers, we did not have much information – only how much content was intended to go into the collection and an estimate of how long we had to complete the project. In this example, however, we know an additional and important piece of information: how many staff we will need to complete the project. Once we know that, we can finalise our project milestones. If we monitor the project's progress carefully, we will be able to detect any significant deviations from these refined milestones and take corrective measures if necessary.

Also, now that we have determined the number of staff we will need to hire, we can determine the amount of work space and hardware required. In our example, we will need a separate workstation for the Conversion Technician and Metadata Specialist, and a separate workstation for the Supervisor (the Web Developer will work at home). The Conversion Technician will need to have the tape player arranged near his or her computer workstation in order to capture the audio. If circumstances were such that we needed to hire more than one FTE staff member for each position (if, for example, we had 80 hours of audio to capture and catalogue in the same number of days), we would need to hire more than one person for each position, which would require more work space, more computer workstations (each with the necessary software), and in the case of the Conversion Technician, more than one tape player and audio capture card.

Executing the project

At this point we are ready to finish project documentation, hire and train staff, and begin the actual production of our content and metadata. Any required hardware, software and work space must now be in place as well. The next two chapters deal with project operations and workflow development, and expand substantially on the topics introduced here.

Proposal writing

Project managers are usually required to prepare formal proposals for funding. Funders can be internal (to the institution), private (individuals, foundations, corporations or other organisations) or public (government bodies at any level, from municipal to international). In this section I will introduce some general information about proposal writing. The jurisdiction that a library is part of can have a significant impact on its eligibility for a particular source of funds, so I will not identify specific sources of funding.

The process of applying for funding will be defined differently by each funder. In some cases, the funder will provide a standard form that needs to be completed, sometimes with attachments or appendices containing narrative responses to particular questions. The form and all supporting documentation must then be submitted by a given date. In other cases, particularly where the amount of available funds is high and the time over which they can be spent is long (e.g. from a full year to several years), the application process may involve multiple submissions delivered at different deadlines. In these cases, funders will issue invitations to applicants to submit to the next phase of the process, with each submission containing more detailed information. Finally, some funding organisations rely on a less formal application procedure that does not involve standardised forms, but instead defines criteria (ranging from general to quite specific) that applicants address in their proposals.

Proposal components

Despite this variety of requirements, most funding proposals contain at least some of the following components. Both this list of components and the list of terms described in the next section are general and not necessarily comprehensive. However, they do include some of the more common aspects of funding proposals that you may encounter.

- *Letter of intent*: In application procedures where multiple components must be submitted at different times, the first component often takes the form of a 'letter of intent' indicating that the institution intends to pursue the grants in question and that may give very general information about the proposed collection or project. The funder responds to this letter with an invitation to proceed with the remainder of the application or a statement of why the applicant is not being invited to proceed.

- *Executive summary*: A brief summary of an application, typically containing information such as the name of the applying institution, names of major partner institutions, title and nature of the collection, fund(s) being applied for, amount being applied for, and a brief indication of the relevance of the collection or activity to the funder's stated objectives.

- *Description of your organisation*: Brief and selective description of the library applying for the funds. Frequently this information is detailed in a form that may ask basic information such as principal contact person, year founded, charitable organisation status, number of employees, and so on, while in other cases the funder may require detailed information about the library's previous projects, partners and funders.

- *Project objectives*: A clear statement of what the funds will be spent on, using language that the funders will understand.

- *Description of how funder's objectives will be met*: Not all funders support 'digitisation', but many support job creation for students, building databases of local content or some other activity that you can incorporate into your project. Funders want to know that their money is being spent on things that matter to them, and you should be prepared to explain why *your* project meets *their* objectives.

- *Project work plan*: Some funders require a work plan, which is typically an outline or table indicating major milestones in the project.

- *Project budget*: Budget formats vary widely, from simple forms to sophisticated Excel spreadsheets that include formulas to calculate items such as administration charges, salary calculations, and maximum allowable amounts in various categories such as hardware or copyright licensing fees.

- *Appendices*: Some applications may require other documentation, often grouped together as appendices, attachments or schedules. These documents can vary widely depending on the requirements of the application, but can include letters of support from partners (both for the current project and for previous projects), letters or special forms from officials in the library's parent institution, screen captures or printed pages from prototype websites if applicable, and sample job descriptions or job advertisements.

Assembling the information required for most applications can be time consuming and difficult. For large grants it is not uncommon to treat the application process itself as a 'project' that requires hiring consultants or providing temporary replacements for existing staff. Although the amount of effort required to complete most application procedures should not require additional staff, you should assume that any formal, structured application process will take considerable coordination, particularly if you must involve people outside your library for letters of support, financial information or other reasons. Most funders will not accept applications past their stated deadlines.

Proposal terminology

The following terms are used frequently in funding applications. In some cases, application documentation will actually contain definitions of the terms used throughout the application and even some examples of how the terms are intended to be used. Obviously, paying close attention to the instructions for completing applications is extremely important. Missing components or misinterpreted questions can disqualify an application, and if the funder receives many more applications than they intend to fund, they will be looking for opportunities to make their adjudication easier.

- *Partners*: Many funding agencies favour applications submitted on behalf of multiple institutions – in fact for larger grants this may be a requirement. Typically, one institution must be identified as the 'lead' or 'principal' partner, if for no other reason than to simplify the funder's accounting procedures (the lead partner would be responsible for distributing funds to partners). The term 'partner' will probably be defined within the application documentation, but participants of all types, from individuals to entire organisations such as commercial companies, universities or government departments, may be considered partners.

- *In-kind contribution*: 'In-kind' describes resources that the institution, as opposed to the funder, is expected to supply. As this term is generally used within the context of a project budget, it will usually be defined very specifically; for example, some funders consider staff salaries to be in-kind, whereas others do not. In-kind contributions are also often subject to formulas that qualify the value of the contributions in some way, such as reducing the value of a $5000 scanner to $500 that can be applied to the institution's contribution. In addition to staff resources, other typical in-kind contributions include hardware and physical space for digitisation and related activities.

- *Cash*: In contrast to in-kind contributions, cash is typically money that an institution must contribute to a project that they would not spend if they were not participating in the project (in other words, it must be additional to their normal operational costs). The most common costs that cash contributions apply to are staffing and hardware. In general, the same resources cannot be considered cash and in-kind contributions, although some funders allow claiming staff time as a 'cash in-kind' contribution.

- *Outcomes*: Funders will frequently ask for a statement of 'outcomes', which are generally equivalent to your project's goals. To be effective, outcomes should be worded such that they are understandable to readers of your application (i.e. free of library jargon) and consistent with the funder's objectives. Many funders will use language that is tied very closely to their mandate or organisational objectives. For example, government agencies at various levels may allocate funds to supporting projects that employ youth; some large private foundations have been requiring any software created with their funds to be released under a specific open-source licence. When describing outcomes, it can be advantageous to adopt some of the language used in the proposal documents, particularly when discussing how your project's objectives align with those of the funder.

- *Deliverables*: Deliverables tend to be more concrete and countable than outcomes. Items that might be expected in response to a question about what deliverables a project will produce include a description of the website/CMS, the number of documents, any standards or reports, or other documentation or software developed during the creation of the content (CMS platforms, software utilities, etc.).

- *Evaluation*: Many grant applications will ask how you plan to evaluate the success of your project, and may even ask you to write a final report and sign a release so they can use the report for their own purposes. I will cover project evaluation later in this chapter.

- *Sustainability*: Finally, some funders are interested in how long their investment will pay off. If they fund early stages of a project, they may ask what its long-term sustainability is and what the library's long-term goals for the project are. Your response to this type of question will depend on your institution's and your partner's commitment to the project. If a collection is open (content will continue to be added), a statement of sustainability should address how the ongoing activity will be funded; if a collection is intended to be closed (for example, the scope of the collection is narrow and the content appropriate to that scope is likely to make it into the collection within the defined life of the project), a statement of sustainability may only need to address issues of preservation and ongoing evaluation.

Reporting

If your grant application is successful, you will be expected to report to the funders periodically. Many funders will require clear and comprehensive reports of how their money is being spent. This is as true of funds allocated internally from the library as it is of funds awarded from an external organisation. Every funder will define its own reporting requirements, but typically they will include periodic statements of how much money has been spent, statements of periodic quotas or milestones for deliverables, and progress on other work that is being funded.

Monitoring

Monitoring is essential for any type of project, not just projects producing digital collections. Periodic checks on the progress being made and the identification and correction of any problems as they occur will dramatically increase the chances that a project will meet its defined goals and will do so without exceeding the allocated resources.

The most important aspects of monitoring digital content creation projects are ensuring that objectives and milestones are being met, ensuring that the available budget is not being overspent, holding regular staff meetings and documenting the outcomes of issues resulting from those meetings. First, it is more efficient to keep production on schedule throughout a project than to try to make up for low production at the end of the project. Available space, hardware and staff resources will probably be insufficient to increase the output required toward the end of the project to meet overall objectives. Second, production milestones should be linked to ongoing costs, so that at any time during the project you can predict if the funds allocated to the work will be sufficient. Third, communicating with production staff regularly through regular meetings ensures that problems they encounter are dealt with as early as possible. Finally, because one of the goals of monitoring a project is to address potentially serious issues as early as possible, documenting problems as they arise and are resolved will allow even faster resolution of similar problems should they arise again.

Evaluating the production phase of the project

In a general sense, the content production phase of a digital collection project should be considered successful if it reaches the project's stated goals. However, evaluating projects according to specific criteria is desirable for a number of reasons: evaluating a project after its completion can demonstrate to funders that their money was spent the way they intended it to be spent, can validate a project and can identify areas for improvement. The most useful strategy for evaluating a project is to build evaluation into the project's goals. In other words, one of the project's goals should be to undergo a systematic evaluation. Explicitly stating this goal will help keep the project focused and will encourage project managers to maintain accurate and thorough documentation.

The exact criteria by which projects will be evaluated should be determined by the desired outcomes of the evaluation, which should be defined by the project manager(s), the library administration and the project funders. Criteria will fall into the following categories:

- *Production milestones*: Typical criteria include the project's ability to meet defined production milestones and objectives, and what constitute acceptable deviations from defined objectives.

- *Budget*: Obviously, the project's ability to accomplish its goals within the defined budget is important. Using substantially less money than the amount defined in the budget is less likely to happen than overspending, but funders may not look favourably on what they would perceive as an overestimation of the funds required to complete the project. Careful monitoring will help avoid this situation.

- *Quality benchmarks*: Evaluating the ability to meet defined levels of quality over the duration of the production activity is relatively easy (provided standards of acceptable quality have been clearly defined and documented) and should provide no surprises if quality control has been performed throughout the project.

- *Operational aspects*: Evaluation of the suitability of the hardware, software and workflows is useful as a planning tool for subsequent projects. Staff job descriptions, scheduling and other aspects of staffing should also be reviewed at the end of each project.

To summarise, careful monitoring during the project is a form of formative evaluation, but summative evaluation of the work involved in creating digital content is an important aspect of overall project evaluation.

Evaluating the overall project

Content production is only one aspect of the 'project' associated with a digital collection. Initial and ongoing promotion, the benefits to users, financial sustainability and ongoing maintenance issues should also be evaluated. The NISO *Framework of Guidance for Building Good Digital Collections* defines four principles by which projects should be evaluated:

1. A good collection-building project has a substantial design and planning component.

2. A good project has an evaluation plan.

3. A good project produces a project report and broadly disseminates information about the project process and outcomes.

4. A good project considers the entire lifecycle of the digital collection and associated services developed through the project.[3]

The second principle may sound tautological, but it actually emphasises the need for systematic evaluation. As the *Framework* states, 'An evaluation plan demonstrates the commitment of a project to its stated goals and objectives.' To support development of effective evaluation plans, the *Framework* cites the Institute of Museum and Library Services' list of resources on Outcome-Based Evaluation (OBE).[4] As the IMLS describes it, OBE determines the impact of digital collections on users' knowledge, attitudes, skills and behaviours. This impact is evaluated by using techniques such as online questionnaires that test users' knowledge. The IMLS website offers this example:

> In order to know if online availability had a benefit, an institution needs to measure skills, attitudes, or other relevant phenomena among users and establish what portion of users were affected.
>
> To capture information about these kinds of results, a library or museum could ask online visitors to complete a brief questionnaire. If a goal is to increase visitor knowledge about a particular institution's resources, a survey might ask questions like, 'Can you name 5 sources for health information? Rate your knowledge from 1 (can't name any) to 5 (can name 5).' If visitors rate their knowledge at an average of 3 at the beginning of their experience, and 4 or 5 (or 2) at the end, the sponsoring institution could conclude that the web site made a difference in responders' confidence about this knowledge. It should be clear that such a strategy also lets you test your effectiveness in communicating the intended message![5]

Regardless of whether the narrowly defined activity involved in content production is being evaluated or whether the entire set of activities surrounding the development of a digital library collection is being evaluated, a thorough and effective evaluation plan should be part of the overall project goals.

Evaluating the collection

The third type of evaluation that project managers should perform is evaluation of the collection. This evaluation is actually part of ongoing collection management, and will happen after the 'project' has ended, whether defined narrowly by its production phase or more broadly by a larger set of activities.

The NISO *Framework of Guidance for Building Good Digital Collections* provides seven principles of 'good' collections (good meaning generally appropriate for the user groups the collection is aimed at) that are independent from aspects of projects described above. These principles can be used both as planning tools and as evaluation criteria:

1. A good digital collection is created according to an explicit collection development policy that has been agreed upon and documented before digitisation begins.

2. Collections should be described so that a user can discover characteristics of the collection, including scope, format, restrictions on access, ownership, and any information significant for determining the collection's authenticity, integrity and interpretation.

3. A collection should be sustainable over time. In particular, digital collections built with special internal or external funding should have a plan for their continued usability beyond the funded period.

4. A good collection is broadly available and avoids unnecessary impediments to use. Collections should be accessible to persons with disabilities, and usable effectively in conjunction with adaptive technologies.

5. A good collection respects intellectual property rights. Collection managers should maintain a consistent record of rights-holders and permissions granted for all applicable materials.

6. A good collection has mechanisms to supply usage data and other data that allows standardised measures of usefulness to be recorded.

7. A good collection fits into the larger context of significant related national and international digital library initiatives.

Project managers should develop mechanisms during production that will capture the information needed for testing these attributes, such as entrance or exit surveys on the collection website, usage loggers, in-person interviews, focus groups or general feedback forms that users can complete. Part XII of the NINCH *Guide to Good Practice in the Digital Representation and Management of Cultural Heritage Materials*[6] provides detailed discussion of the types of mechanisms that can be used to collect information from a collection's users. OBE, described above, can also be applied to the collection on an ongoing basis if desired.

Multi-institution projects

Increasingly, libraries are collaborating on digital collection-building activities. This collaboration is different from the client–vendor relationships between libraries described earlier. Partner libraries come together to create digital collections for the same reasons they come together co-operatively to subscribe to commercial databases and electronic journal collections or to share virtual reference services: to form strategic alliances, to pool resources and to please funding agencies, which to a large extent favour multi-institution projects over ones undertaken by a single institution.

The advantages of collaborating that are specific to digital collection building are that the costs of specialised hardware and software can be distributed, expertise can be shared, large projects can be delivered in shorter timeframes, and libraries that are not able to invest in hardware and software can participate by performing other types of necessary tasks, such as clearing copyright permissions and creating descriptive metadata. Collaborative efforts also have the disadvantage of increased administrative overhead, which can manifest itself in a number of ways, including record-keeping requirements that are not compatible with all partners' local institutional practices, scheduling meetings and holding them via teleconference or video conference, etc., and making sure that all partners meet project milestones and deadlines.

From a practical perspective, multi-institution projects introduce a number of complications that need to be taken into account. First, development of workflows that are distributed among multiple partners can be challenging simply because having multiple sites provides more ways of getting the work done: in some multi-institution projects, most or all of the work is carried out in parallel at multiple sites, whereas in others, each partner performs different sets of tasks that are then integrated centrally. In order to maximise efficiencies, the implications of distributed workflow should be explored carefully during the planning phases of multi-institution projects.

Second, all participating institutions must conform to the project's technical specifications. Care must be taken that file formats, file densities, colour depths, sampling rates, metadata formats, the application of metadata creation guidelines and file naming conventions are consistent across all partners. Use of the same hardware and software at all contributing institutions promotes consistency, but in reality being able to use identical resources at each site is not common, particularly if each site possessed its own hardware and software prior to the start of the project. However, regular checks of output from partners will ensure that inconsistencies are minimised.

Third, the number of participating institutions can have a considerable impact on the project's ability to meet production milestones. The more partners fall behind, the harder it is to recover; by contrast, the more partners are involved in producing digital content, the more likely it will be that shortfalls can be taken on by other partners if they have the extra capacity. All of these issues can be mitigated with sufficient planning and continuous communication among partners.

Summary: managing digital collection projects

Developing a digital collection encompasses a relatively complex set of tasks. However, if the collection's goals have been defined clearly, those tasks can be grouped together and performed in an effective order. The group of tasks surrounding the production of the digital content can be considered the core of the overall set of activities required to make a collection available to users, but it cannot happen without considerable planning and preparation. In particular, the development of workflows early in the overall project timeline is essential for the success of the project. Budget, the role of digitisation vendors, the roles of partners in multi-institution projects, local hardware, software and staffing requirements all depend on effective, tested workflows (so much so that I will spend an entire chapter on this topic).

The production of the digital content is not the only aspect that must be planned carefully. Effective documentation, proposal writing, evaluation of both the production phase of the project and the project as a whole, and ongoing evaluation of the collection over time are also tasks that project managers must perform or oversee.

Further reading

Gertz, J. (2000) 'Vendor relations', in *Handbook for Digital Projects: A Management Tool for Preservation and Access*. Edited by M. K. Sitts. Andover, MA: Northeast Document Conservation Center, pp. 141–53. Available at *http://www.nedcc.org/digital/viii.htm*
Gertz explains the benefits of both digitising in house and outsourcing, and covers all important aspects of working with digitisation vendors not covered in this chapter, including selecting a vendor, writing a Request for Information and Request for Proposal, evaluating responses from vendors, drawing up contracts and dealing with quality control issues.

Library Hi Tech. Special issue on collaborative digitization projects. Vol. 23:2 (June 2005).
This special issue contains eight articles describing collaborative digitisation projects from the USA, including articles on sustainability, partnerships between libraries and museums, multi-institution training and support, CMSs, and benefits to end users.

New York Public Library. Picture collection online project documents. Available at *http://digital.nypl.org/mmpco/documents.cfm*
This site contains links to documents NYPL submitted to the IMLS for their Picture Collection Online funding application, including the proposal abstract and narrative, general workplan, deselection criteria (for identifying images that would *not* be included in the collection), quality control procedures, metadata guidelines and OBE proposal and workplan.

NISO Framework Advisory Group (2004) *A Framework of Guidance for Building Good Digital Collections*, 2nd edn. Bethesda, MD: NISO. Available at *http://www.niso.org/framework/Framework2.html*
Cited several times in this chapter and elsewhere in this book, the NISO *Framework* provides a number of principles of digital collections, objects, metadata and projects that will be useful to project planners and

managers, and also provides links to selected resources that support and expand on those principles. Each section contains a brief case study.

Notes

1. Chapman, S. (2000) 'Considerations for project management', in *Handbook for Digital Projects: A Mangement Tool for Preservation and Access*. Edited by M. K. Sitts. Andover, MA: Northeast Document Conservation Center, p. 27. Available at *http://www.nedcc.org/digital/iii.htm*
2. Puglia, S. (1999) 'The costs of digital imaging projects', *RLG DigiNews*, 3:5. Available at *http://www.rlg.org/preserv/diginews/diginews3-5.html#feature*
3. NISO Framework Advisory Group (2004) *A Framework of Guidance for Building Good Digital Collections*, 2nd edn. Bethesda, MD: NISO. Available at *http://www.niso.org/framework/Framework2.html*
4. *http://www.imls.gov/applicants/obe.shtml*
5. *http://www.imls.gov/applicants/basics.shtml*
6. The Humanities Advanced Technology and Information Institute and the National Initiative for a Networked Cultural Heritage. (2002) *The NINCH Guide to Good Practice in the Digital Representation and Management of Cultural Heritage Material*. Available at *http://www.nyu.edu/its/humanities/ninchguide/*

9

Project operations

Project operations is the set of activities related directly to the production of digital content, such as scanning analog material, converting files from one format to another, preparing master files for long-term management, creating metadata and making content available on the web. The activities required to achieve the goals defined in the planning phase of the collection are performed within the context of a workflow, which is a structured list of deliverables and tasks presented in logical sequence. This chapter introduces the processes typically performed during the production phase of a digital library collection, and the software and hardware used in those processes. Specifically, the following topics are covered: staffing, project documentation, strategies for metadata creation, quality control, hardware, software and processes used in project operations, and file management. The next chapter deals with workflow development. In many ways the two are tied closely to one another and could easily form a single chapter. Consider the components of project operations to be the tools and techniques that you will use to assemble rooms and buildings. If you prefer to learn about drawing blueprints before becoming familiar with materials and tools, you may prefer reading Chapter 10 before reading this one.

As we saw in the last chapter, some libraries choose to outsource the production of their content. This choice is justifiable. Libraries that choose to create their own content must be prepared to assemble the necessary resources. Although some of the hardware and software used during content production may not be familiar to most libraries, requirements for physical space and staff are in many ways similar to those that would be involved in other common library activities such as retrospective cataloguing, projects involving attaching barcodes or radio-frequency ID tags, or other technical services operations. Libraries that have undertaken these types of projects are well suited to digital content production as they involve similar operational aspects. At anything but a small scale, both types of operations take on qualities typical of any type of factory: raw material enters, processes are applied and a new product exits. Reducing digital content production or the activities performed at any type of factory to a black box trivialises a great deal of skill, effort and expense, but essentially that simple model applies.

A closer look at staffing

Staff roles

We have already discussed staffing requirements for the creation and maintenance of digital collections. Other than the project manager and cataloguers, the three roles that are most focused on the production of content are the supervisor, the digitisation technician and the quality control technician. Supervisors in digital collection production environments perform the same types of functions that supervisors in general perform, but owing to the highly technical and detailed nature of the work, strong problem-solving skills and familiarity with the computing environment, software applications, and project hardware are very important. In conjunction with project managers, the supervisor will need to develop a mechanism for handling source material that is so dissimilar from the rest that it cannot be dealt with according to standard operating procedures. (This situation seems to occur even if every source document is inspected during the evaluation stage of the project.) Two specific supervisor functions, scheduling and work queuing, will be discussed below. These two tasks are tied closely to the high-level workflow used in the production of digital content, the available hardware resources, and the amount of work that can be performed by scanning and quality control technicians. Work queuing and scheduling are challenging because all of these factors have to be balanced in order to keep production levels consistent and, if there are tight deadlines for completing the production of the content, on schedule.

Digitisation technicians perform the actual digitisation or conversion, process the resulting files, and create administrative and structural metadata. In projects that involve particularly fragile or unusual source material, a conservation specialist may be involved in preparing the documents for digitisation, but for most projects the digitisation technicians will prepare and possibly even retrieve the material being scanned. Qualifications for digitisation technicians include a high degree of capability with the operating environment (including skills such as file copying and renaming using the operating system), the ability to follow prepared documentation, and the ability to identify problems and resolve or report them according to established procedures. The reality of digital content production is that it is repetitive, detailed and often boring work. People working as digitisation technicians should be prepared to perform the same procedures over standard work shifts while also paying sustained attention to detail.

If project operations deal exclusively with born-digital resources and do not involve digitisation, the same qualifications apply to technicians who process the born-digital files. In this chapter, the term 'digitisation technician' is used in a number of places regardless of whether the task being described is digitisation, processing the files resulting from digitisation or processing files that make up born-digital resources.

Justification for quality control and strategies for carrying it out are covered in detail later in this chapter, but with regard to staffing, it is extremely important to allocate staff to ensure that all content and accompanying metadata consistently meet project specifications. In many small to medium-sized operations, the supervisor performs this role, whereas in larger operations a separate position may be allocated to quality control. Like the work performed by digitisation technicians, quality control staff need to be able to do repetitive, detailed work over extended periods. Descriptive metadata may be generated by library staff outside of the digital production workflow and therefore may be inspected by cataloguers, but administrative, structural and preservation metadata needs to undergo quality control as well, and because these types of metadata are closely tied to the files that make up digital resources, the task of verifying that they are accurate needs to be integrated into the production workflow appropriately.

Work queuing

Work queuing is the task of making sure that staff have enough material to work on. All tasks other than ones at the beginning and end of a workflow both require input and produce output. Ideally, material (in our case, the files and metadata that make up resources at each stage in the workflow) should move through the workflow at an even pace, with a small but controlled queue of items at all points in the workflow. It is desirable to maintain a controlled queue so that no staff member is ever without material to work on. If the queue gets too short, staff may have

Table 9.1   A sample item status board

Ready to scan	Ready to process	Problem	Ready to QC
dfoe0145	dfoe0131	dfoe0123	dfoe0099
dfoe0129	dfoe0138	dfoe0120	dfoe0104
dfoe0122	dfoe0141		dfoe0101
dfoe0135	dfoe0143		
dfoe0142	dfoe0125		
dfoe0124			

nothing to do; if it gets too long, it may be difficult to restore the even and regular flow of items through the workflow.

Maintaining a balanced queue can be challenging when some tasks are inherently more time consuming than others. For example, scanning books frequently takes longer than preparing the master and derivative versions of the page images. Therefore, ensuring that the queue is the same length for the scanner operator and the staff processing the files requires careful monitoring. The most obvious strategy for balancing the two queues is to ensure that the total number of hours that the scanner is active is greater than the total number of hours that the processing work will take. Another strategy is to acquire a second scanner and pay for additional staff to use it.

One simple method for monitoring work queuing is to use a whiteboard to record the status of individual resources as they move through the workflow. An illustration of this technique is shown in Table 9.1. The entries in each column are locally assigned, unique identifiers assigned to works by Daniel Defoe by cataloguers when they created a descriptive metadata record for the books (the identifier naming scheme is borrowed from Chapter 4). The project supervisor adds the identifiers to the 'Ready to scan' column once he or she receives notification that the book has been inspected by the special collections librarian and catalogued. After the digitisation technician scans a book, he or she erases the identifier from the 'Ready to scan' column and writes it in the 'Ready to process' column. The technician who is responsible for the next set of steps (checking to see if all pages have been scanned, creating structural metadata, deriving JPEG versions of the TIFF files created by the scanner, etc.) then knows which items are ready to be worked on. Once the book has been processed, its identifier is moved to the 'Ready to QC' column, alerting the quality control technician that the files are ready for inspection. If a problem of sufficient severity is discovered with either a printed book or the files generated by the scanner, its identifier is entered into the 'Problem' queue and the exact nature of the problem is noted in the problem log (a word processor file in a specific shared network location); upon seeing an entry in the Problem column, the supervisor investigates and takes appropriate action. Any staff member can add an entry to the Problem queue.

This general technique for monitoring the status of an item as it moves through the workflow is fairly effective, and is flexible enough to accommodate even moderately complicated workflows. Some libraries automate the process by using a simple database application, particularly if all staff are not working in the same physical space.

Scheduling

Scheduling is tied to project timelines, space and hardware availability, number of staff, and their availability for work. Supervisors must schedule staff with these restrictions in mind. Within an overall project timeline, the average number of hours of work per day (i.e. the total number of hours of work required to accomplish the project's goals divided by the total number of work days within the project's timeline) must be scheduled within normal work periods (eight hours per day, for example). If monitoring daily or weekly production reveals that deadlines may not be met, the only two options available to supervisors for achieving the average quota of work each day are to schedule more staff to work at the same time or to increase the number of work hours per day.

Increasing the number of staff who work at the same time is an effective way to increase overall output. Doing so requires careful planning, as work queuing becomes more complicated as the numbers of staff working at the same time increases. In addition, workflows that operated smoothly with a small number of staff working at the same time may not scale very effectively. Regardless of whether the workflow is linear (i.e. steps in the workflow are performed sequentially) or parallel (related tasks can be performed simultaneously and their output is integrated after the tasks have been completed), accommodating extra staff will probably require establishing additional streams of the same work. In either case, care must be taken in order to make sure that bottlenecks in the workflow are identified and resolved quickly.

One of the most common challenges when increasing the number of staff working at once is providing sufficient space and hardware resources for the additional staff. This is particularly true when specialised hardware is being used: acquiring and deploying additional computer workstations is fairly straightforward compared with adding additional scanners and other digitisation hardware, if only due to the relatively high cost of specialised hardware. A related issue is the additional data storage space that is often required during increased production. The more staff are producing content, the more files enter the work queues, and if additional staff are not added at all stages of the workflow, disk storage space that seemed ample at lower levels of production can fill up unexpectedly. Constantly monitoring available disk space is worthwhile at all times but especially at times when staff levels are higher than usual.

Increasing number of hours that staff work per day can be accomplished by increasing the number of shifts. The length of standard work shifts will vary depending on the nature of the work (put simply, how boring and repetitive it is), local regulations (either as defined by government regulations or by agreements with trade unions), or the nature of the staff (who may be defined as full time or part time). Adding an additional four-hour shift to a standard eight-hour working day can increase productivity by 50%; adding an additional eight-hour shift can double productivity. Depending on the project timelines, adding additional shifts might be the best way to meet hard deadlines imposed by funders, for example. Of course, adding additional shifts requires staff (digitisation technicians, supervisors and quality control technicians) who are willing to work outside standard hours.

One other aspect of scheduling for digital content production is to plan for times when staff cannot perform their regular or principal duties. Common problems that arise include a lack of material to work on (possibly the result of queuing problems) or problems with computer hardware, software or networks. Having a plan for this situation is always desirable but not always possible given the nature of the work – if the network is down for an hour, sometimes staff simply cannot do anything useful. Some workflows incorporate preparation of original source materials, and if this work does not require the specialised skills of a conservator, it may be a suitable activity when ordinary work is not possible. Less specialised activity is simply retrieving source material from where ever it normally resides. Having a contingency plan is always a good idea. Specific suitable tasks will vary from project to project.

Documentation in project operations

As we saw in the previous chapter, clear, accurate and thorough documentation of all aspects of a digital collection, from the planning process through to ongoing evaluation, is essential. During the production of digital content, operational documentation identifies the procedures that staff need to follow, codifies standards of acceptable quality and records the rationale behind decisions made during production. Operational documentation may also include general workflow outlines and diagrams that provide context for the specific details required at the most practical levels of production activities.

Most documentation for project operations is printed. Online documentation may be more suitable in some situations, such as when work is taking place in a number of physical locations. Documentation that is best formatted for printing but needs to be distributed electronically can easily be converted to Adobe PDF. Wikis, websites that can be modified easily by a large number of people, are popular forms of project documentation. If a wiki is used, a project manager or supervisor should be responsible for editorial control as the fact that the documentation can be modified by a number of people means that inaccuracies or inconsistencies can become common. E-mail lists, blogs and other ways of distributing information about changes in documentation are also extremely useful.

Administrative metadata is a form of documentation in that one of its functions is to record details about the production process such as the date of creation of a digital resource, dates of significant steps in the production process, the names of people involved in the production process, and the locations of master and derivative copies of the resulting files. It is therefore a type of structured record keeping. The obvious difference between project documentation and administrative metadata is that documentation is structured as narrative text, whereas administrative metadata is usually structured like other forms of metadata, using pairs of elements and values. More fundamentally, project documentation applies to all the resources created using the documented procedures, whereas administrative metadata applies to a single resource and its constituent files. Documentation is specific to a project, but administrative metadata is specific to a resource. Each can refer to the other, but they serve two different purposes and should be created and managed as separate and distinct kinds of information.

Some best practices for project documentation include:

- *Re-use when appropriate*: Some types of detailed procedural documentation can be used in more than one project, particularly if a library uses the same hardware and software over multiple projects. Being able to re-use documentation from previous projects can save considerable amounts of time while planning a new project. References to version-specific software features, and to project-specific workflows, file naming schemes and directories can cause confusion and errors if not updated, however.

- *Assume the audience is someone in your position two years from now*: Although the most important audience for procedural documentation is the staff performing the work, a useful criterion for evaluating the completeness and clarity of the documentation is whether it could be used two years in the future by another manager working on the same project. Two years is an arbitrary amount of time, but in that period most of the technology described in the documentation will not seem overly antiquated, and two years is sufficient to erase any unwritten details from most people's minds. The objective of this 'future proofing' is of course to ensure that documentation is clear, sufficiently detailed and comprehensive.

- Use examples, illustrations, screen captures, and decision tables where they suit the content: For example,

Table 9.2   A sample decision table

If...	Use...
A long explanation can be replaced by a succinct example	Examples
The material you are describing is graphical in nature (such as quality of a scanned image)	Illustrations
You are describing a detailed dialog box or configuration settings in a software application	Screen captures
Staff need to choose one of several courses of action based on specific conditions	Decision tables (like this one)

- *Test documentation thoroughly*: Having someone (preferably a member of the intended audience) test detailed procedural documentation is useful as it can reveal missing background information, missing steps in processes, inconsistencies between wording in documentation and labels in software, and other problems that will confuse or mislead staff. One method for testing procedural documentation is to watch someone work through it, noting where they make mistakes (or rather, where the documentation is not clear), much like usability testing in software engineering.

- *Learn from problem reports*: Patterns in problem reports can indicate flaws in documentation. If the same problem occurs more than once, the relevant documentation should be reviewed to see whether it can be improved in areas that might prevent the same problem from happening again.

- *Document unusual cases*: Similar to patterns in problem reports, patterns in the occurrence of unusual cases (such as a printed book with fold-out maps, or an audio recording with muffled segments) indicate that documentation may need review. If the same case occurs frequently, it should be documented. However, deciding where to document unusual cases may not be easy. Including every unusual case that comes up may bloat operational documentation, but unusual cases should at a minimum be recorded for the use of supervisors and quality control technicians. Documentation of unusual cases intended for supervisors should include a description of the case, any decisions made about the case and the rationale supporting the decision.

- *Feedback from technicians*: It goes without saying that feedback from the people using the documentation is extremely valuable. Operational staff should be encouraged to suggest improvements both to processes and to the documentation itself.

- *Keep documentation current*: It should also go without saying that it is extremely important to keep documentation current. Despite careful planning, changes in workflow and in specific procedures are normal occurrences during project operations, and all documentation should be updated promptly to reflect any such changes.

Creating metadata

Descriptive metadata for resources being digitised or processed from born-digital files can be created separately from the processes involved in creating the digital resources themselves. In fact, many libraries choose to create descriptive metadata separate from other aspects of resource production, or alternatively to create brief descriptive metadata early in the workflow and add more detail at a later date. The second strategy is useful if metadata such as the Dublin Core type and format elements will be part of the description, as this information is often not known until after the resource takes its final form in master and derivative files. Finally, descriptive metadata used in some collections is based on records describing the original source material, and is created in a batch using conversion utilities or custom scripts. In some cases the process of creating descriptions will be tied much more closely to the production of the digital resources, for example, as the first step in processing an item. The best method for creation of descriptive metadata will need to be determined for each local workflow.

Descriptive metadata can also be extracted automatically from many born-digital document formats such as Microsoft Office formats and Adobe PDF, both of which add 'document properties' as a normal part of file creation, usually derived from the network or computer username of the person creating the document, the user's institutional affiliation, and so on. This is the type of metadata creation and extraction that is the focus of the 2004 AMeGA report mentioned in Chapter 8.[1] Extracting embedded descriptive metadata can be efficient, although in many cases cataloguers or other metadata specialists perform quality control to the metadata after it has been extracted. The Greenstone digital library content management system employs a large repertoire of 'plug-ins' to extract embedded descriptive metadata from digital resources and insert it into uniform record structures for searching and display. As of Greenstone version 2.61, metadata extraction plug-ins for 29 file formats were available, with an additional 35 listed as 'potential' (i.e. technically possible but not yet complete).

Most types of administrative, structural and preservation metadata are best created at the same time as the files they describe. Some of this metadata can be created manually, while metadata that describes technical aspects of the files themselves must be generated using software. Information that can be derived using software includes timestamps for file creation or modification, attributes of files such as size, pixel dimensions and pixel density (for images), and file type (TIFF, JPEG, PDF, etc.).

Some content management systems are capable of generating administrative and structural metadata automatically. Streetprint Engine, for example, will detect the pixel dimensions of images that are uploaded for attaching to descriptive metadata records and will use these dimensions to generate HTML links to small, medium and large versions of the images. DSpace will generate checksums (unique numbers based on the integrity of the uploaded files) for files as they are ingested, which can be regenerated later and compared to see if the file has been altered since the first checksum was created. Most content management systems will generate timestamps that indicate when the item was created or loaded into the system.

When these types of metadata generation capabilities are lacking or not applicable, it is possible to use other technologies to generate metadata. All popular programming and scripting languages have the capability to generate timestamps, information based on file attributes, and some operating systems environment variables such as the username of the person logged into the computer. Gathering this information using locally developed scripts and then adding it to content and metadata management systems is common practice. In addition, a number of specialised tools for generating metadata are available that run on all major operating systems. The most comprehensive utility for extracting metadata from files is JHOVE (the JSTOR/Harvard Object Validation Environment),[2] introduced in Chapter 4. JHOVE is a utility and set of accompanying modules for generating administrative metadata for AIFF, GIF, HTML, JPEG, JPEG2000, PDF, TIFF, WAVE, XML and plain text. JHOVE will generate the file pathname, last modification date, byte size, format, format version, MIME type, and a number of different types of checksums for all of the formats above, format-specific information such as NISO Z39.87 technical metadata for still images,[3] and compliance with various specifications for XML and PDF. JHOVE can output this information in plain text or XML, so relevant elements of the output can be imported into other applications and combined with other metadata.

Creating some types of structural metadata automatically can be challenging because, like descriptive metadata, structural metadata is often the result of complex analysis and interpretation. In fact, the need for structural metadata suggests that the relationships between the files that make up a complex resource cannot be easily or reliably reconstructed by software. In METS, which offers the most robust specification for structural metadata, creating structural maps for identifying the files that make up the resource, the sections of the files that have structural significance, the order of the files in the reconstructed resource and the labels that identify the structural parts of the content ('Table of Contents', 'Chapter 1', 'Chapter 2' and so on) cannot be automated to any useful degree. Because METS is represented in XML, it is frequently assembled by software of some sort (from a database, for example), and METS <fileSec> elements can be populated programmatically based on patterns in file names, but creating useful METS structural maps is for most resources a manual process that requires extensive knowledge of the resource being described.

Quality control

Quality control (abbreviated QC and sometimes known as quality assurance or QA) is the process by which the results of digitisation and processing are monitored to ensure they meet expected levels of accuracy, consistency and various format-specific criteria. Quality control is essential for a number of reasons: digitising source material and processing the resulting files is repetitive and often boring work, so errors can easily occur; attention to detail is extremely important; multiple people may be doing the same work, so uniformity must be achieved across all output; and errors can occur owing to unclear or incomplete documentation.

In addition, the creation of derivative files often introduces compression of image (and image-based textual documents), audio and video files. If this compression is lossy, as is JPEG compression for images and as are most popular audio and video compression codecs, the quality of derivative versions must be checked to ensure that reduction in file size has not had an unacceptable effect on the content. The conversion of XML into HTML for use within web browsers also introduces potential quality problems, such as broken hypertext links and image references.

Expected levels of quality should be defined according to the goals of the collection. The discussion in Chapter 5 relating the goals of the collection to file formats is relevant here. In cases where source material is at risk, or the source material and digital collections based on it have ongoing value, expected levels of quality will usually be high; in cases where the digital collection is intended to be short lived (using my earlier example of scanned course material), expected levels of quality may be considerably lower. Consistency is always desirable, regardless of the level of expected quality. Format-specific criteria typically include clarity and colour quality for still images and video, fidelity for sound, and preservation of document structure for text. One set of format-specific criteria that libraries may find useful is provided by the Library of Congress, through its National Digital Information Infrastructure and Preservation Program (NDIIPP).[4] Again, specific criteria will depend on the goals of the collection, and should be developed in consultation with experts who may be advising on the content and goals of the collection. These criteria should be documented clearly so they are understood by staff doing the work and by quality control technicians, supervisors, project managers and advisors.

Quality control applies to the creation of metadata as well as to the creation of content. The checking of descriptive metadata can be separated somewhat from the content creation workflow, but checking of structural metadata is best done in conjunction with quality control checks of the content files, as the structural metadata determines the relationships among the files. Checking the accuracy of the agent and event components of administrative metadata can be challenging because they describe staff activity. Technical administrative metadata, describing file attributes such as type, size and so on, can be checked as part of the quality control processes defined for checking the content files and accompanying structural metadata. Preservation metadata that documents data storage refreshing, file format migration and other event-based attributes of digital resources should be checked as part of those activities.

Quality control should be incorporated into project workflows, and quality control events should be documented by administrative metadata. For the purposes of workflow development it is useful to define two types of quality control, formative and summative. Formative quality control is performed throughout the various stages in a workflow, and can be performed by digitisation technicians as part of normal procedures. For example, if a technician is supposed to create structural metadata for a group of page images, he or she can make sure that there are no missing pages before beginning the task. If there are missing pages, the problem is reported according to documented procedures and can be corrected before creation of structural metadata. Summative quality control is performed after all the tasks in a workflow have been completed, and should be performed by quality control technicians or supervisors as it is the final set of checks before the resources are made public. Formative quality control is not a substitute for summative quality control but it does ensure that problems are discovered early and therefore lowers the rejection rate at the end of the workflow, after effort and money have been spent on problematic files and metadata. In workflows that incorporate activities performed by vendors, the best place to perform formative quality control is at the point at which the files (and metadata, if applicable) are delivered by the vendor, so that problems can be caught before the files enter the rest of the workflow. This inspection should probably be performed by a quality control technician or supervisor as problems with these files need to be reported to vendors according to provisions written into the contract to perform the work.

Before moving on to a brief survey of some specific quality control techniques, I should clarify that the costs of performing quality control must be balanced against its benefits. This balance is embodied in the expected levels of quality referred to above. The higher the expected quality and the more rigorous and thorough the quality control processes, the more expensive they are; the less rigorous they are, the more errors will go undetected. Quality control processes should therefore be designed and implemented in order to achieve a balance that is acceptable to the collection's planners. For instance, project managers may decide that the potential consequences of not knowing for certain who converted a group of TIFF files into JPEGs do not justify the effort required to verify that aspect of the project's administrative metadata. Similarly, inspecting every derived JPEG for compression artefacts would not be worth the required effort, if project managers decide that inspecting every 50th image will provide a cost-effective level of quality control.

Quality control techniques involve monitoring the results of processes (in our case, files and metadata) and reporting unacceptable deviations from expected levels of quality. Reported cases are then dealt with in whatever way is most efficient for the given workflow, either by being completely redone (which may be necessary if analog source material was not digitised properly) or simply corrected (which may solve a problem with metadata, for instance). Below are some general quality control techniques that can be applied in digital library project operations:

- Incorporate formative quality control into workflows whenever possible. This activity is most effective if performed at the very beginning of the task that modifies the incoming files or metadata in some significant way, such as converting files from one format to another, or exporting metadata from the software application it was created in. Formative quality control is a supplement to summative quality control, not a substitute for it. Formative quality control is intended to catch problems as early as possible in the workflow.

- Some checks can be automated. Ensuring there is a one-to-one correspondence between master and derived versions of files, comparing checksums before and after mass file copying and format validation are all best handled by customised scripts or specialised utilities such as JHOVE (for format validation).

- When appropriate, check every item. If expected quality levels are very high, or if the collection is very small, performing quality control checks on every image or other file and on all metadata may be appropriate. The costs of being this thorough will be substantial, however.

- When appropriate, perform quality checks by inspecting a sample of items. Typical samples are every 10th, every 50th or every 100th item, depending on the total number of items and the amount of time allocated for quality control. If problems are found with a sampled item, it is common practice to check every previously produced item and every subsequently produced item (e.g. all 10 previous and all 10 subsequent items) to determine if the problems are systemic or isolated.

- Sampling can be recursive: checking every 10th item but only checking every 10th page within the item may be sufficient. This technique is also useful for checking sound and video; checking for quality at intervals of 5 or 10 minutes within long items, as opposed to checking the entire resource, can save a lot of time while providing effective results.

- Checking the digitising hardware is recommended where high quality and consistency is expected. For example, scanners need to be calibrated for colour accuracy, lenses need to be cleaned and tape players need to be demagnetised. Performing hardware maintenance according to manufacturers' schedules can prevent quality problems from occurring in the first place.

Part of quality control procedures is effective reporting. Many libraries use problem logs, which provide a structured means for recording information required to resolve the problem. Log entries typically include the unique identifier of the problematic resource (and often the specific files or sections within the resource), the stage in the workflow that the problem was discovered, the name of the person who discovered the problem, the date and time it was discovered, a description of the problem, and steps taken to correct the problem. Local implementation of problem logs varies widely and is determined by local resources and workflows, but they often take the form of simple word processor files, spreadsheets or locally developed database applications. Using problem logs allows the separation of normal production tasks and specific tasks intended to address quality problems, as reported issues do not have to be dealt with as they are discovered. In this case, the problem log acts as a work queue for the staff members responsible for addressing quality problems. Problem logs are a form of administrative metadata and are an important aspect of quality control procedures. They also function as documentation in that they contain a history of the problems that have occurred throughout a project.

Readers interested in other views of quality control should see Stuart Lee's section on 'Benchmarking and quality assurance'[5] and Oya Y. Rieger's 'Establishing a quality control program.'[6]

General hardware and software used in project operations

The hardware and software used during project operations is a mixture of commonly available and specialised products. I will cover general requirements first and then move on to specialised requirements, focusing on the special aspects of capturing and processing printed content and then audio and video content.

Computers

The choice of computing platform should be influenced by local preference. In other words, no one platform is better overall at digital library content production than any other. The Macintosh has traditionally been preferred for tasks involving graphics, but other platforms are equally capable of creating high-quality images. A considerable amount of specialised hardware and software used in project operations requires the use of Microsoft Windows, although the availability of peripheral devices that connect to computers using USB and FireWire, and the use of uniform internal expansion card interfaces (particularly the PCI interface) on both Mac and Windows platforms means that a large number of hardware devices can be used on either platform. Linux is maturing as a desktop operating system and a large amount of open-source software that is worth considering for use in project operations runs only on that platform (but there is also a large amount that runs on Windows and Mac as well).

Given the rate at which computing power evolves, detailed recommendations about processor speed, memory and hard drive capacity are pointless. It is safe to say that most tasks involved in digitising or converting content benefit from powerful computers, but given the continuously increasing capabilities of commonly available PCs and Macs, it is not necessary to use professional-grade graphics, video or audio editing workstations except in fairly specialised or demanding digital library content production environments. Buying at the higher end of mainstream computers should suffice. In general, hardware budgets are better spent on specialised scanners and audio and video capture devices than on specialised workstations. An exception is when the vendor of a specialised scanner or capture device recommends a specific computer for use with its hardware; in these cases, the vendor's specifications are worth following if only to lessen the likelihood of compatibility and reliability problems with the specialised hardware.

Hard disk storage

One aspect of hardware planning that catches some project managers off guard is the disk space required during project operations. The size of high-resolution image, sound and video files, and the need to hold potentially large quantities of these files in queues during production, justifies investing in as much disk storage as possible given the scope of the project and available funds. Options for hard disks include the following (Table 9.3), listed in order of capacity and cost:

Table 9.3　Typical capacities for the most common types of hard disk storage

Type	Typical capacities	Advantages	Disadvantages
Internal	300 GB to 1000 GB (or 1 TB/terabyte)	Fast, inexpensive	Limited expandability, reliability
External USB or FireWire	300 GB to 1 TB each unit	Flexible	Less reliable, slower than internal
Network Attached Storage (NAS)	1 TB and up	Reliable, expandable	Relatively expensive for smaller operations, lower speeds
Storage Area Network (SAN)	100 TB and up	Reliable, fast, very expandable	Expensive, high administration costs

The capacities listed in Table 9.3 for internal and external drives are intended to illustrate the relative sizes for each type of disk storage, and will no doubt appear out of date quickly, as the capacities of the individual hard drive units that can be installed internally in a computer or added to external hard drive enclosures are constantly increasing. External drives are popular because they easily attach to USB or FireWire ports on computers, and are reasonably fast compared with internal drives. One way of using external drives is to move them from computer to computer as files move through the workflow; for example, files that are scanned at one computer are copied onto an external drive, which is then unplugged from the scanning computer and plugged into the computer used for processing the files. This method can be more efficient than copying files over local area network. Network attached storage (NAS) devices are like external drives but instead of plugging into a USB or FireWire port on a single computer, they attach to the network and are therefore sharable among multiple computers. Storage area network (SAN) configurations are used in very high capacity environments such as corporate data centres and are not typically managed by individual libraries. RAID (redundant array of independent disks) is a common option in all types of hard drives and can increase reliability and speed significantly, depending on which configuration is used.

Constantly increasing capacities and decreasing prices for hard disk storage have popularised the 'disk is cheap' myth. There is no question that the cost per gigabyte of hard disk space is incredibly low. However, the cost of backing up the amounts of data commonly available in desktop computer internal hard drives is still conspicuously high. For example, at time of writing, an entry-level DLT (digital linear tape) backup tape drive with a capacity of 80 GB costs about $1800 US dollars, not including the cost of backup software.[7] Doubling the capacity of the tape backup unit to 160 GB more than doubles the purchase cost to over $4200. In addition to the purchase price of tape backup hardware, labour costs add to the total cost of backing up files. The two units described above can use only one tape at a time, which means that a technician must swap tapes manually should the amount of data being backed up exceed the capacity of a single tape. Using the 160-GB tape backup unit, a full backup of 1 terabyte (TB) of data would require eight tapes. This particular unit's data transfer rate is 60 GB/hour, which means that it will take over 16 hours to complete the full backup. Automated tape libraries that can back up more than the capacity of a single tape without manual intervention reduce the amount of manual tape swapping but cost considerably more than the single-tape units. The same vendor's least expensive automated tape backup unit, which has the capacity to perform an unattended backup of 1 TB of data, costs more than $6300.

To put the amounts of disk space used in the above calculations into perspective, the example from Chapter 5 of the 150-page book, scanned as uncompressed, high-quality TIFF files, consumed 2.9 GB of disk space. A terabyte would store approximately 330 such books. However, a terabyte of hard disk space is also a realistic amount to have in a single staff computer and could easily be the size of all the files in a work queue at any given time. The configuration illustrated here is only one possible option for backing up files. Many libraries will already have the necessary backup infrastructure in place (although very few library activities produce as much data as digital content production, so be prepared for a sharp increase in required backup capacity), and others will rely on their parent institution's IT departments for backups. As with the capacities for hard disks, details for tape storage units are given here as an illustration of the additional costs associated with properly managing inexpensive, high-capacity hard disks, and to show that costs rise appreciably as capacity and efficiency increase. Even though hard disks are cheap, they are only half the equation, and can actually account for much *less* than half of the entire disk storage infrastructure required for creating digital content.

General software applications

Software typically used during project operations is a mixture of general-purpose and specialised applications. General-purpose software commonly used during project operations includes:

- *Operating system file management utilities*: Project operations involve frequent copying and deleting of files, creating directories, and other tasks that various operating systems provide utilities for. Microsoft Windows Explorer, Apple Mac OS X Finder, and Linux applications such as GNOME Nautilus and KDE Konqueror all provide basic functionality for managing files.

- *Word processors*: Word processors are used primarily for documentation, but are also used for the creation and maintenance of any other documents required during project operations, such as printed metadata entry forms and problem reporting templates.

- *Spreadsheets and databases*: Using spreadsheet programs such as Microsoft Excel and OpenOffice Calc for some types of metadata management is quite common. Desktop relational databases such as Microsoft Access, FileMaker Pro and OpenOffice Base are also useful, especially as they form the basis of highly functional, locally developed applications.

- *CD and DVD writing software*: The operating system file management utilities mentioned above have the ability to write files to CD-ROMs and DVDs, but if more sophisticated functionality is required (such as burning ISO disk images in Windows XP), specialised burning software may be useful.

- FTP (file transfer protocol) and SCP (secure copy) clients are used for transferring files to web servers.

- *File renaming utilities*: Batch renaming of hundreds of files at once is a routine part of project operations. The file management utilities of operating systems are not capable of performing this type of operation, so utilities such as NameWiz[8] and Bulk Rename Utility[9] for Windows, and A Better Finder Rename[10] and R-Name[11] for Mac are extremely useful. A number of rename utilities exist for Linux as well.

- *Scripting and programming languages*: Languages such as Perl, Python and Java allow the creation of customised command-line and graphical utilities for file management, batch processing, database connectivity and other tasks. Mac OS X's AppleScript is also useful for certain types of scripting, particularly when used with Automator, which provides a graphical user interface to AppleScript.

Capturing and converting printed content

Some of the specialised processes and tools used during the creation and conversion of digital textual resources are described below. This list is not complete but is intended to illustrate useful approaches to completing common tasks.

Processes and software tools

Printed material such as photographs and books is digitised (converted into digital form) using a scanner. The resulting files are then processed in various ways to create the desired master and derivative versions. Best practice favours creating the most accurate images possible at the time of scanning, and saving these images as the master versions. Significant editing or 'correction', such as de-skewing (rotating the image so it is level), tonal and colour correction, or sharpening (improving the focus and clarity) is then performed on derivative versions. High-quality scans require attention to detail and consistency, and in particular to colour management, the set of techniques used to ensure that digital images contain accurate representations of the colours in the source material. Colour management is not covered in detail in this book; useful sources of information on the topic include Anne R. Kenney's 'Digital benchmarking for conversion and access',[12] the US National Archives and Records Administration's *Technical Guidelines for Digitising Archival Materials for Electronic Access*[13] and the Technical Advisory Service for Images' 'Colour management in practice'.[14]

Each scanner model uses a driver, a software utility that allows the computer's operating system to communicate with the scanner. Scanner drivers also include graphical user interfaces that allow the person using the scanner to define the pixel density, colour depth, contrast settings and so on prior to scanning. There are two common types of scanner drivers, TWAIN and ISIS. TWAIN (the word is not an acronym) is considerably slower than ISIS because it usually requires that scan settings such as pixel density, colour depth and image contrast are set for each scan, while ISIS (image and scanner interface specification) drivers are more suited to high-volume scanners as they do not require the same scan-by-scan configuration as TWAIN drivers. Scanning may be initiated from within an image editing program such as Adobe Photoshop[15] or IrfanView,[16] or directly from within the driver's user interface. If image editing software is used, the scanner's driver interface opens and is used to execute the actual scan, but as soon as the scan has been completed the image appears within the image editing software.

Single-image documents such as photographs are usually previewed within the driver interface so that settings can be adjusted before the actual scan is performed. Once the scan is complete, final corrections can be made before the file is saved and assigned a name using documented file naming conventions. Multipage documents such as books can be scanned in a number of ways. If the documents are unbound, each page is scanned as if it were a photograph. If the documents are bound, they must be placed on the scanner such that either single page or two pages (left and right) are scanned at the same time. If the two-page method is used, the resulting image files are usually split down the middle (or 'gutter') to produce separate page images. Splitting can be automated using Adobe Photoshop and other image editing applications.

It is standard practice to include in each image a small border surrounding the document (Figure 9.1). This is done to ensure that the

Figure 9.1   An image with a border around the page edges

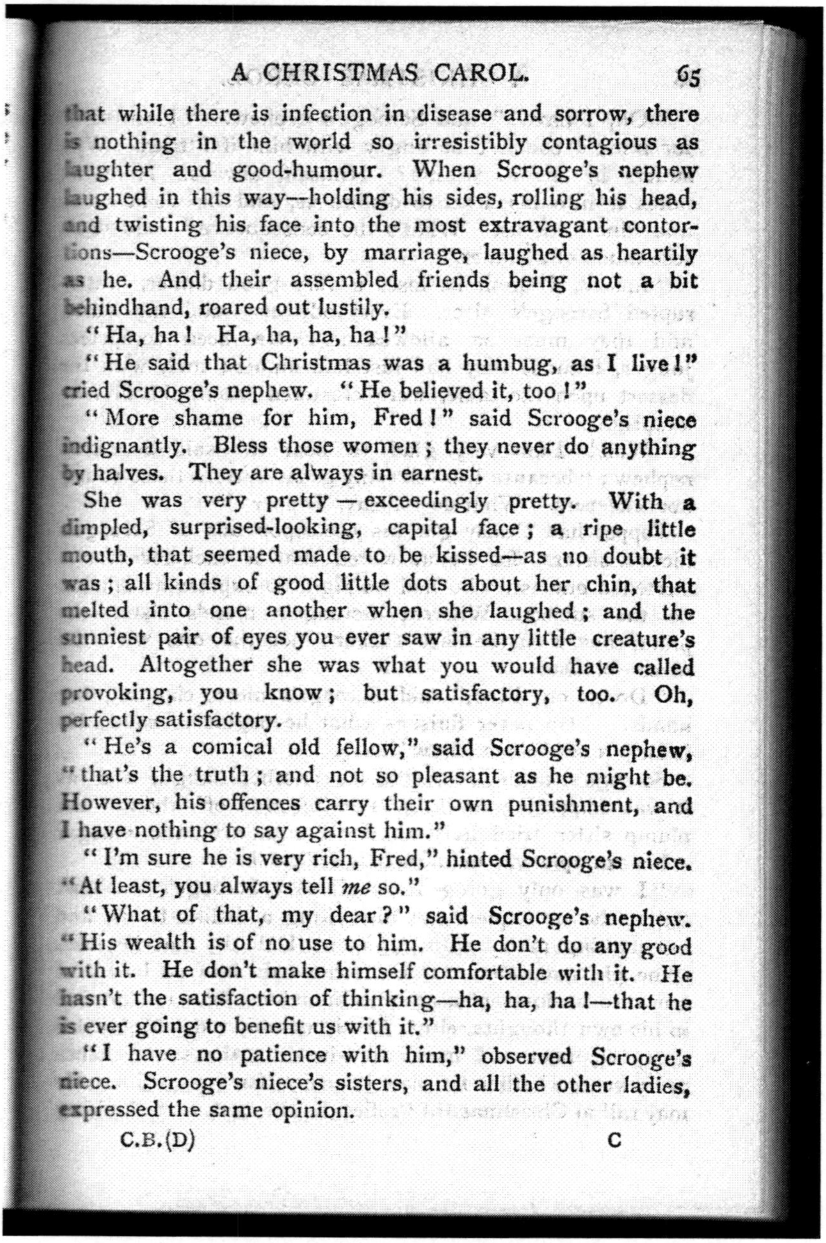

A CHRISTMAS CAROL.   65

that while there is infection in disease and sorrow, there
is nothing in the world so irresistibly contagious as
laughter and good-humour. When Scrooge's nephew
laughed in this way—holding his sides, rolling his head,
and twisting his face into the most extravagant contor-
tions—Scrooge's niece, by marriage, laughed as heartily
as he. And their assembled friends being not a bit
behindhand, roared out lustily.

"Ha, ha! Ha, ha, ha, ha!"

"He said that Christmas was a humbug, as I live!"
cried Scrooge's nephew. "He believed it, too!"

"More shame for him, Fred!" said Scrooge's niece
indignantly. Bless those women; they never do anything
by halves. They are always in earnest.

She was very pretty — exceedingly pretty. With a
dimpled, surprised-looking, capital face; a ripe little
mouth, that seemed made to be kissed—as no doubt it
was; all kinds of good little dots about her chin, that
melted into one another when she laughed; and the
sunniest pair of eyes you ever saw in any little creature's
head. Altogether she was what you would have called
provoking, you know; but satisfactory, too. Oh,
perfectly satisfactory.

"He's a comical old fellow," said Scrooge's nephew,
"that's the truth; and not so pleasant as he might be.
However, his offences carry their own punishment, and
I have nothing to say against him."

"I'm sure he is very rich, Fred," hinted Scrooge's niece.
"At least, you always tell me so."

"What of that, my dear?" said Scrooge's nephew.
"His wealth is of no use to him. He don't do any good
with it. He don't make himself comfortable with it. He
hasn't the satisfaction of thinking—ha, ha, ha!—that he
is ever going to benefit us with it."

"I have no patience with him," observed Scrooge's
niece. Scrooge's niece's sisters, and all the other ladies,
expressed the same opinion.

C.B.(D)   C

entire document is visible, including the edges. The border is usually no more than a centimetre wide around the entire document, and may be even narrower as long as it is consistent between images within the same collection or multipage document. The alternative to including a border is to scan the document as closely as possible along its edges, or to use functions within image editing software to make the border transparent, producing the impression that the image has been cropped along the actual edge of the document.

The specific processes applied to the digitised files and born-digital resources are determined by the nature of the master files, the types of derivative versions required, the type of source material (still image or textual), and the intended search and display architecture of the collection. Table 9.4 provides typical processes performed on still images

Table 9.4 Examples of processes and corresponding software used on still images and textual documents

	Still images		Textual documents	
Process	Example	Typical software	Example	Typical software
Correction	Adjust colour, sharpen, deskew	Adobe Photoshop, IrfanView	Sharpen, deskew page images	Photoshop, IrfanView
Conversion	From TIFF to JPEG	Photoshop, IrfanView, ImageMagick[17]	From TIFF page images to single PDF file; from XML source files to HTML	Adobe Acrobat;[18] Saxon XSLT processor[19]
Renaming	Change filenames from those created by scanner to preferred file name scheme	NameWiz, R-Name	Change file names of extracted text to match corresponding page image file names	NameWiz, R-Name
Extraction	Extract embedded metadata, generate technical metadata	ImageMagick	Extract text from page images using OCR (optical character recognition)	Abbyy FineReader[20]

and textual documents during content production, and examples of software that can be used to perform those processes. The software applications indicated are not necessarily the only ones that can perform the tasks, but they are representative examples.

Born-digital resources are processed in much the same way as digitised ones, although the lack of control over the formats of the master files mentioned in Chapter 5 can make some processes more difficult. For example, if the only version of a still image we have is a low-resolution JPEG file, converting to other formats can be difficult. Similarly, if we only have unstructured word processor files, creating suitable HTML can be challenging.

Hardware

Printed material, whether it is photos, maps, postage stamps, books or individual pages, is digitised using scanners. Listed in Table 9.5 are the most common types of scanners, along with some representative manufacturers, in alphabetical order.

'Document' scanners are a subtype of flatbed scanners. They use an automatic document feeder (ADF), much like the sheet feeder mechanism on a standard photocopier, to allow high-speed scanning without human intervention other than refilling the ADF. Until recently, high-speed document scanners could only output black and white and greyscale images, but models capable of colour scanning are becoming more common. Document scanners provide a highly efficient means of digitising unbound source material.

In general, two factors influence the cost of scanners, maximum document size and speed. The quality of images created using scanners does vary, but virtually all scanners are capable of outputting high-quality images provided that they are calibrated for colour accuracy. Because of these factors, flatbed scanners are the most common type found in libraries. Libraries that do not wish to invest in a planetary scanner, large-format scanner or scanning camera back often outsource the digitisation of oversize documents, or alternatively scan them in sections and assemble (or 'stitch') the images into a single, large image. This technique is useful in some cases but it is always preferable to digitise the entire document at once, as any inconsistencies in the separate images become obvious when the images are assembled.

The speed of scanners is determined by a number of factors, but one that is worth mentioning is the driver software. With TWAIN drivers, the

| Table 9.5 | Types of scanners used in digital library content production |

Type	Description	Typical use	Representative manufacturers
Flatbed	Material to be scanned is placed on a horizontal glass plate (or 'platen'), and the image is captured from below	Still images, single-page and bound documents, books. Maximum size of document typically 28 × 42 cm	Epson,[21] Ricoh,[22] UMAX[23]
Film	Material to be scanned has light passed through it	Photographic film, slides, negatives	Minolta,[24] Nikon[25]
Microfilm and microfiche	Like film scanner but optimised for standard microfilm and fiche material	Microfiche, microfilm	Canon,[26] Minolta, SunRise,[27] Wicks & Wilson[28]
Planetary/ overhead	Scanning head is raised above the document, which lies flat or in a book cradle (defined below)	Maximum size of document typically 60 × 84 cm	BookEye,[29] Minolta, Zeutschel[30]
Large format	Similar configuration as planetary scanners	Blueprints, maps, aerial photos. Maximum size of document typically 100 × 150 cm	Cruse,[31] Lumiere[32]
Scanning camera backs	Used with a standard analog camera body, copy stand, and lighting	Maximum size of document depends on stand, camera field of vision, etc.	BetterLight,[33] PhaseOne[34]

digitisation technician spends considerable time between each scan, even if it is only to click through the buttons on the scanning software. This is not usually the case with ISIS drivers, particularly if each scan can be initiated with a button on the scanner itself, or foot pedal, as is used by many planetary scanners. Scanners that are intended for high-production environments must be able to allow some sort of batch scanning, whether through an ADF or by means of a button or foot pedal on the scanner that allows the technician to avoid using the workstation's mouse and keyboard between scans.

Recently, two companies have developed fully automated book scanners, which use mechanical or pneumatic means to turn the book pages between scans. The Kirtas Technologies[35] APT BookScan 1200 digitises bound documents at a rate of 1200 pages per hour. The 4DigitalBooks[36] Digitising Line is capable of scanning 3000 pages per hour. This type of technology is very expensive (well over $100,000), and only libraries with large-scale and long-term digital content programmes would acquire these products.

Consumer-level and even professional digital cameras are not generally suitable for digitising printed documents for a number of reasons. First, the pixel density of even professional digital SLR cameras is a fraction of the maximum pixel density of high-end planetary and large-format scanners. At the time of writing, the highest count available in a professional-grade digital camera is about 16 megapixels, whereas products like the Cruse CS 155/450 can perform scans containing 150 megapixels, and some models of the Lumiere JumboScan can reach double that figure. Second, digital cameras do not provide the same amount of control over pixel density, colour depth and other settings that are commonplace in the driver software used by most scanners. Finally, achieving high-quality images using cameras requires sophisticated lighting apparatus. In fact, scanning camera backs (which are simply professional-grade cameras using an ultrahigh-density digital capture device instead of film) can only be used in conjunction with expensive lighting equipment. Despite these limitations, some libraries have used digital cameras to create low-resolution images of acceptable quality for some purposes, following guidelines such as those provided by the Technical Advisory Service for Images' 'Getting the best out of low-end digital cameras.'[37] In general, however, digital cameras are not a suitable replacement of the other equipment described above.

Capturing sound and video

Processes and software tools

Analog audio formats and video tapes are digitised (also called 'captured' or 'acquired') by playback on suitable equipment, with the output signal fed to a specialised card called a 'capture card' that fits into an expansion slot in a computer. The capture card contains the electronics that create the digital version of the sound and video. In some cases, an external device called an analog-to-digital converter (ADC) sits between the playback device and the capture card attached to the computer. Video capture cards also digitise the audio signals coming from the source playback equipment. Because analog audio and video are captured in real time (i.e. one hour of video takes one hour to capture), the cost of capture hardware is not determined as much by speed as by the quality of the resulting files, stability and advanced features.

The task of capturing is performed from within audio and video editing software such as Adobe Audition and Adobe Premiere. The drivers for capture cards integrate tightly with sound and video editing applications. As with digitising printed material, audio and video should be captured as accurately as possible given the capabilities of the hardware being used. Copies of the master files can then be edited to remove unwanted sounds such as tape hiss or static from sound, and to correct colour or enhance picture contrast in video. A useful source of detailed information on digitising audio and video for digital library collections is section 7 of *The NINCH Guide to Good Practice in the Digital Representation and Management of Cultural Heritage Materials*.[38] The NINCH Guide also provides advice on digitising 8-, 16- and 35-mm film, which requires specialised equipment such as transfer boxes, multiplexers and chain film scanners.

Born-digital sound and audio are becoming commonplace, mainly because digital audio recorders and video cameras are rapidly replacing their analog predecessors. These devices plug in to either the USB (for audio recorders) or the FireWire (for most video cameras). Files created using these devices are downloaded directly to the computer's hard drive. The files are usually compressed, which means that editing and other processing tasks are not as effective or in some cases not even practical. In addition, conversion of video files from one format (such as Quicktime) to another (such as the higher quality DV format) can lead to picture degradation. Working with born-digital digital audio and video is a typical case of working with what you have – the files will not probably be in formats suitable for master versions.

Typical processes applied to digital audio and video, and representative software applications, are given in Table 9.6.

| Table 9.6 | Examples of processes and corresponding software used on sound and video files |

	Sound			Video	
Process	Example	Typical software		Example	Typical software
Digitisation/ capture	Digitising	Adobe Audition,[39] Audacity[40]		Capturing	Adobe Premiere,[41] Kino,[42] Cinelerra[43]
Editing	Clean background noise	Adobe Audition, Audacity, Cinelarra		Colour correction	Adobe Premiere, MainActor,[44] Cinelarra
Conversion/ encoding	From master format to distribution format	Audacity		From master format to distribution format	Cinelarra

Hardware

Listed here are the most common types of capture cards and external devices, along with some representative manufacturers, in alphabetical order:

- *Audio capture cards and ADCs*: Manufacturers include Apogee,[45] Keywest[46] and Lucid[47]

- *Video capture cards and ADCs*: Manufacturers include Canopus,[48] Matrox[49] and Winnov[50]

Consumer-level (i.e. costing $200 or less) capture cards and external USB/FireWire devices for video and audio capture include products from ADS,[51] Hauppauge[52] and Pinnacle.[53] Products of this type are suitable for creating good quality distribution versions of sound and video files but not master versions.

Evaluating and acquiring specialised hardware and software

Determining which hardware and software to acquire for use in digital library content production is challenging. Few comprehensive or current directories of products exist, and the vendors who supply the products often focus on markets other than libraries, such as photography, document and records management, and commercial publishing and media production. In addition, as the capabilities of scanners, audio and video capture cards, and specialised software increases, their cost rises dramatically, so careful evaluation and purchasing practices (such as negotiating support agreements) become very important. In publicly funded institutions, the costs of some hardware may be high enough to require issuing a formal Request for Information (RFI) or a Request for Proposal (RFP).

Evaluating whether a product is suitable for your application assumes that you have determined the required specifications, in particular specifications describing the resolution, colour depth, bit rate and other technical attributes you have defined for your collection. However, if your library will be undertaking more content production in the future, the evaluation criteria should not focus strictly on the requirements of your current project. In other words, you may want to consider acquiring hardware that has capabilities that exceed those required by your current needs. Not surprisingly, as capabilities increase, so does price. In many cases, acquiring lower-cost hardware that is good enough to meet current needs may be a more attractive option than acquiring hardware that is more flexible, faster and of higher quality and but more expensive.

The products named in the previous two sections are supplied as representative examples and are not necessarily the best product for every project or production environment. Common strategies for finding other products to evaluate include:

- *Contact other libraries*: One of the most effective methods for finding products suitable for use in your own library is to contact staff at other libraries that have undertaken production of content similar to the type you are planning. Project managers and operations supervisors usually enjoy talking about the products they have acquired and use. Be sensitive about asking about costs for higher-end products, however, as many vendor agreements prohibit releasing this information.

- *Research on the web*: As stated above, no useful directories of specialised products for use in digital library content production exist. However, searches for specific product names can often yield useful results, as many reviews mention competing products. If you find some vendor sites, make sure they have distributors in your region, as some vendors may not have a strong presence internationally.

- *Trade shows*: Despite claims above that digitisation vendors do not cater to library markets, some digitisation vendors do attend library conferences and trade shows. Talking to vendor representatives and collecting product information is an important part of the acquisition process. When talking to vendor representatives, try to get a sense of how familiar they are with library digitisation activity.

- Finally, visiting libraries that produce content is extremely useful. Visiting other sites allows you to see the hardware and accompanying software, observe staff in action and ask questions that may not come up during a telephone call. If travel is involved, the cost of visiting other cities may well be worth the investment, particularly when considering purchasing high-end hardware.

The following criteria can be used to evaluate the products found using the strategies described above.

Evaluating hardware

- *Purchase price*: In addition to the initial acquisition cost, a product's purchase price may include annual support fees, delivery and set-up fees, and third-party product or licensing fees. Annual support fees may not be required, but if not paid, may result in loss of vendor support after the initial warranty period. Third-party fees apply to required or optional hardware that accompanies the principal vendor's product (such as lighting apparatus required by scanning camera backs).

- *Price quotes*: As hardware costs increase, vendors frequently require that you contact them for a quote. Specialised hardware is typically not a simple external device or expansion card similar to the ones you might buy for your home computer. Large scanners, equipment for playing analog audio and video formats, and other specialised digitisation hardware can be large and complicated, and can come in a variety of configurations. Vendors will want to work out the best solution to your needs, and may be more willing to negotiate acquisition and other costs for more expensive hardware than they would be for less expensive products where profit margins are lower.

- *Warranties*: Be clear about the length of any warranties that apply to a product and to what is covered by the warranties. Warranties of less than one year should raise suspicion about the overall quality of a product.

- *Consumables and parts*: Many warranties do not include consumables (such as bulbs) or wear and tear on moving parts on scanners, tape players and other hardware. Clarify whether the vendor or the customer is responsible for the costs of consumables and parts that must be replaced frequently.

- *Support options*: Does the vendor offer a variety of support packages? Are annual support packages required, or is the vendor willing to support the product on a 'per incident' basis (i.e. as problems arise) without annual support fees?

- *Repairs*: Are technicians who perform warranty and post-warranty diagnosis and repairs based locally? If the vendor does not have offices in your vicinity, do they contract with a local service bureau to handle support calls? If not, how will diagnosis and repairs be performed? Ask the vendor what the most common problems with the hardware are, and ask for sample costs for common repairs. Also clarify how long replacement parts take to be delivered, and who will perform the repairs (the vendor or local support contractor, or the library).

- *Workstation requirements*: Specialised hardware often requires very specific workstation configurations. For example, scanners may require a specific SCSI (small computer system interface) card. Most types of hardware will have specific operating system requirements, such as Windows XP Professional or Mac OS X.

- *Physical plant requirements*: Some digitisation equipment, such as overhead scanners, requires considerable amounts of space. The power consumption of the lighting systems that accompany some scanners and scanning camera backs is also high. In addition, workstations that are used with some digitisation equipment such as video capture cards can have considerable power requirements, and generate surprising amounts of heat.

- *Software*: Most hardware will come with drivers or capture applications of some sort. Be sure to verify if licence costs for the accompanying software are included in the price of the hardware or if they are charged separately. Also, clarify whether the hardware can be used at all without the accompanying software. Hardware drivers are usually required, but if the accompanying capture software cannot be replaced by standard image, sound and video editing applications, the hardware is only as good as the required software. Unfortunately, if this is the case, it will be impossible to trial the software without having access to the accompanying hardware.

- Most vendors of specialised hardware other than audio and video capture cards will not probably provide a trial unit for testing before purchase.

- During your evaluation, ask vendors for references you can contact. Many libraries develop a standard interview script or list of questions they use when contacting vendor references and some purchasing departments may supply a standard set of questions as part of the formal RFP process.

The cost of hardware increases more or less proportionately with maximum output specifications such as resolution, bit depth and capacity. Capacity is used here to mean physical dimensions of source material (scanners capable of digitising large-format materials generally cost more than scanners that can only digitise smaller originals), speed (the faster the hardware, the more expensive) and scalability (less expensive capture cards and attached workstations may not be able to handle long videos).

Evaluating the operational speed of digitisation hardware is complex, and depends on a number of factors, including the performance of the computer it is attached to. In addition, product brochures, specification sheets and other types of promotional information are notorious for overstating actual tested performance. These figures are often presented out of context without including activity that is essential to digitisation but not included in the actual process of digitisation. Table 9.7 contains examples from two well-known flatbed scanner manufacturers.

The dramatic differences can be explained easily. Scanner 1's specifications only describe the amount of time it takes for the scan head to move from the top to the bottom of the document. However, the actual steps involved in scanning an image with this unit (which only had a TWAIN driver) are (1) preview the image using the driver software, (2) scan the image and (3) wait until the image appears in the image editing application used for correcting the image. The tested scan time shown above is the elapsed time it takes a technician to perform all of these steps (using file format specifications applicable to a particular project).

Table 9.7 **Sample publicised versus tested scan times**

	Scanner 1	Scanner 2
Publicised scan time	'8.5 × 11 colour, 300 dpi in 9.5 seconds'	'simplex mode scanning at 65ppm'
Tested scan time (300 dpi grayscale; includes time for saving files)	1.6 pages per minute	4.4 pages per minute using flatbed platen, not the automatic document feeder

This is the figure that should be used in planning the total number of images that the technician can scan in an hour and is therefore the one that is useful for planning staff levels, timelines, costs and so on. The figures supplied by Scanner 2's vendor describe the use of the scanner's ADF ('simplex' means single sided), which eliminates the need for a technician to handle the source document, other than placing it in the feeder and removing it when scanning is complete. However, the tested scan time describes how long it takes a technician to scan a bound book by putting it face down on the scanner's glass platen. As in the first example, the operational scanning time is considerably longer than the time stated in the product brochure. Vendors should be able to answer questions about the total scans an operator can perform in an hour, at a given combination of pixel density, colour depth and document dimensions. If they cannot, you might suspect that their products are not used in high-production environments.

Evaluating software

Unlike content management systems, specialised software used during project operations is generally not developed locally by libraries, apart from database applications used to manage metadata and problem reporting and utility scripts for file management and other maintenance tasks. However, there is a large amount of high-quality free and open-source software that can be used in digital library content production. The same advantages and disadvantages supplied in Chapter 7 for commercial, open-source and locally developed CMSs apply to software used during project operations.

- *Pricing*: Apart from initial acquisition costs, annual licensing fees and third-party library and utility licensing fees may apply. Be sure to clarify this with the vendor.

- *Support options*: Annual licence fees often entitle libraries to technical support, but this should be clarified with the vendor. Support for open-source software can be provided by vendors (free or for cost) or by the user community, as with support for open-source CMSs.

- *Upgrades*: Are upgrades free, included in annual licensing fees or separately priced? If you do not upgrade, will the vendor support older versions of the software?

- *Hardware and operating system requirements*: Some software used in digital content production may require specific hardware. For example, the system requirements of Adobe Premier indicate that 'For third-party capture cards: Adobe Premiere Pro certified capture card' is required.[54] Unfortunately, deciding which to acquire first, the hardware or the software, is not always straightforward. Many software titles (including Adobe Photoshop and Audacity) are available for multiple operating systems, whereas others (including Adobe Premiere and Cinelerra) have specific operating system requirements.

- *Extended functionality*: In addition to facilitating the creation of individual digital files or objects, software should be able to process multiple files at once (batch processing) where applicable, and should provide tools for managing complex documents where applicable, such as managing audio files associated with video.

- *Standards compliance*: Content creation software should be able to create a wide variety of file formats, and should be able to import and export a wide variety of proprietary and open formats.

File management

Because the fundamental objective of project operations is to produce files, a chapter on project operations would not be complete without a discussion of file management. File management combines conventions for naming files and directories, work queuing, and making best use of available storage and network technologies. In the next chapter I will look at general workflow modelling and the techniques that can be used to determine what tasks must be accomplished in what order, but before moving on to that discussion, it may be helpful to introduce some low-level, hands-on file management issues.

Managing file names

It is good practice to name all the files that make up a resource using the resource's persistent identifier. If you are digitising single-file resources such as photos, file names can be assigned manually as each file is created. However, if you are digitising source material that contains multiple files (such as multipage text), the software used to create the files may not be able to assign filenames that contain the resource's unique identifier. Typically, software that supports batch digitisation will assign filenames incrementally as they are created, often using a meaningless base name like 'image'. A set of files created in this way would have names like image0001, image0002, image0003 and so on. If the resource you are digitising comprises hundreds of files, correcting the name of each one manually is not practical.

Fortunately, dealing with this problem is fairly simple. Using file renaming utilities described earlier, it is possible to change the names of the files from those assigned during digitisation to ones based on the conventions you have defined for resource file names. These utilities allow search and replace and other operations within large batches of file names, and they can modify the incrementing numbers assigned by the creating software to ensure that the new names encode any structural metadata you define within your naming conventions.

After the files that are produced by the digitisation hardware have been converted to the preferred master formats and their names changed to correspond with the resource's persistent identifier, the files are ready for whatever tasks have been defined in your workflow. At this point, another set of naming issues will probably occur: how do you record the various changes that files undergo as they move through the workflow? Additionally, how do you distinguish between various derivative versions of the same master file? File extensions may not suffice as there may be more than one version of the same file that we want to publish in our content management system as JPEGs.

Different versions of the same master file can be distinguished in two ways, either by including characters in the filename that indicate what type of derivative the file is, or by creating a directory for each version. As an illustration of the first strategy, we will use file 001 (identified by the last three digits in the filename) from three of the Daniel Defoe books mentioned earlier in this chapter. In this example, we have two JPEGs for each page image, one that is the same dimensions as the master file (700 pixels wide) and the other that is a thumbnail for use in search results (150 pixels wide). In order to differentiate between these versions of each master image, we also provide all page images in their proper sequence as a single PDF file for printing. We will include an 'm' in the file names for the masters, an 'f' in the file names for the full-sized versions and a 't' in the file names for the corresponding thumbnail images (Table 9.8). Because there is only one PDF file for each book we may choose to omit any version indicator and page image numbering from the file name.

Using this type of file naming convention, each version of each file for each resource has a unique file name. The only problem with the letters we have chosen is that 'f' and 't' are visually very close, which may lead to errors as the files are manipulated by project staff. Choosing more easily discernible version indicators may lessen the likelihood of that problem.

Another approach to managing the file names of all the files that make up a resource is to create directory structures that perform the same function as the single-letter indicators described above. All of the master TIFFs go in one directory, all of the full-sized JPEGs go in another directory, and so on, as in Figure 9.2.

This arrangement is convenient for processing the files, as it allows use of simpler file names and all of the files that are to be converted or

Table 9.8 Sample version file names using single-letter indicators to distinguish versions

Persistent identifier	Filename of master TIFF (file 001)	Filename of full-size JPEG	Filename of thumbnail JPEG	Filename of PDF
dfoe0131	dfoe0131001m .tif	dfoe0131001f .tif	dfoe0131001t .tif	dfoe0131.pdf
dfoe0138	dfoe0138001m .tif	dfoe0138001f .tif	dfoe0138001t .tif	dfoe0138.pdf
dfoe0141	dfoe0141001m .tif	dfoe0141001f .tif	dfoe0141001t .tif	dfoe0141.pdf

Figure 9.2 Example directory structure (in Mac OS X) for managing different versions of the same master files

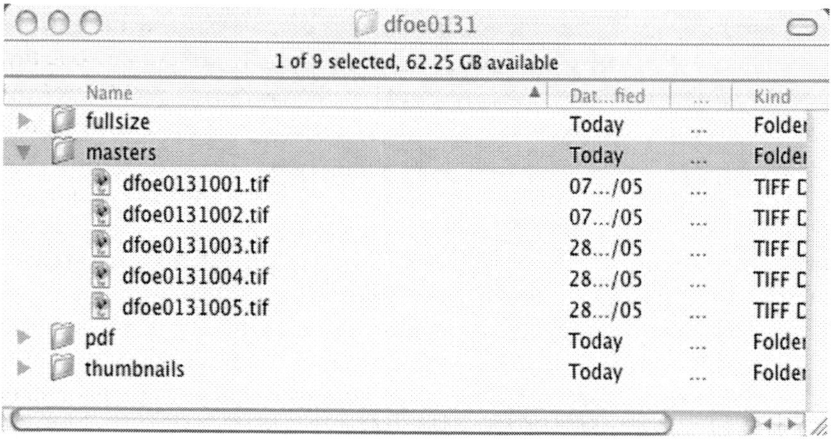

modified as a batch are in one directory. However, this method does not prevent files in different directories from having the same name (e.g. our full-size JPEG and our thumbnail JPEG). Also, because filenames are not necessarily unique, directory structures must be mirrored within the CMS used to present the files on the web so that each file has a unique URL. In our example, the URL for the full-size version of the page image must be different from that of the thumbnail version. The CMS may deal with this problem automatically, or the URLs may need to be disambiguated using explicitly assigned directory or file names.

It is possible to combine the two approaches so that all the files in each directory share a common file name indicator. This approach provides the advantages of both techniques – every file has a unique name, and similar files share the same directory.

Another issue is the maximum length of file and directory names, and the set of characters that can be used in valid file names. The most conservative approach to file names dictates using the ISO 9660 standard,[55] which limits the names of files and directories to eight characters plus a three-character extension. Commonly implemented extensions such as Rock Ridge and Joliet allow for more useful lengths.

Managing disk space

The second aspect of file management is making sure you have somewhere to store your files while they are at every stage of the workflow. This is related to work queuing: files that are in the queue can consume large quantities of disk space, particularly large master files. Allocating sufficient disk space and periodic monitoring of disk usage will help avoid storage crises, as will clear procedures describing where files should be stored while specific tasks are being performed. Usually, it is preferable to copy files to the internal (or 'local') hard drive of the computer where the files are being processed, as this disk is the fastest and most stable. In addition, many software applications read and write files often, particularly when processing large files. Such applications will perform much more slowly if the files they are processing are on central network drives rather than on local drives, and are much more prone to crashes and lockups when used over a network.

The practice of copying files from central networked drives to local drives results in a lot of traffic across the network. In practice, networks are quite slow. The most common network hardware is rated for data transfer of 100 megabits per second, and although this is considerably faster than the next slowest rating (10 megabits per second), large quantities of large files can choke networks of this speed. Network hardware rated at one gigabit (which is ten times faster than 100 megabit hardware) is available, but in general, actual network performance is limited by the slowest piece of network hardware, so network speeds tend to remain low until all of the required hardware is replaced with faster components.

Some libraries use external USB or FireWire drives to alleviate this problem, which are rated at approximately 400 megabits per second (although they rarely achieve that throughput in practice, particularly USB drives). Other libraries use CD-ROMs and DVDs as intermediate file storage. The relatively small capacity of CD-ROMs (about 650 megabytes) has made them all but useless for large quantities of files; DVDs have a much larger capacity (approximately 4.7 gigabytes for a single-sided, single-layer DVD and about 8.5 gigabytes for a single-sided dual-layer DVD) but even these capacities are small compared with the size of inexpensive and much faster external hard drives.

Summary: making decisions about project operations

This chapter has covered a considerable variety of topics: staffing considerations such as work queuing and scheduling, project documentation, strategies for creating metadata, quality control and file management. These topics apply to a wide range of digital library production environments. The remaining topics – the hardware, software and processes required to create digital library content – are somewhat more challenging to describe and deal with on an operational level as the technologies change so rapidly. It is important to keep in mind that project planners should not fixate on particular hardware and software; rather, they should ensure that the criteria for evaluating hardware and software apply to their particular needs and that they make informed decisions about which products to acquire. This is especially important for specialised digitisation hardware, which at the high end can be more expensive than most other types of hardware libraries typically purchase, and yet will become obsolete as the next generation of hardware becomes available.

At this point it might be useful to put this long and detailed chapter in context. Chapters 8, 9 and 10 of this book deal with the practical aspects of creating digital content. Chapter 8, 'Project management', introduced the activities required for successful project planning and execution. The current chapter described the tools and practical techniques involved in creating digital content, and the next focuses on ways of assembling these techniques into effective workflows.

Further reading

Anderson, C. and Maxwell, D.C. (2004) *Starting a Digitisation Centre.* Oxford: Chandos.
A useful source of detailed information on hardware, software, physical space and staffing required for project operations.

Sitts, M.K. (ed.) (2000). 'Developing best practices: developing guidelines from case studies', in *Handbook for Digital Projects: A Management Tool for Preservation and Access.* Andover, MA: Northeast Document Conservation Center. Available at *http://www.nedcc.org/digital/iii.htm*
Presents detailed case studies describing digitising of text, photographs, maps and other oversize documents, and microfilm, plus a case study on OCR and on multi-institution content production. Also includes discussion of strategies that did not work very well.

Hargis, G., *et al.* (2004) *Developing Quality Technical Information: A Handbook for Writers and Editors.* 2nd edn. Upper Saddle River: Prentice Hall.
Even though most of its examples come from software development, this book will be useful to people writing documentation for digital library content production. Particularly useful features include numerous examples showing poor technical documentation and an improved version of it; separate treatments of 'task', 'conceptual' and 'reference' information; and coverage of web-based documentation.

Notes

1. Greenberg, J., Spurgin, K. and Crystal, A. (2005) *Final Report of the AMeGA (Automatic Metadata Generation Applications) Project.* Available at *http://www.loc.gov/catdir/bibcontrol/lc_amega_final_report.pdf*
2. *http://hul.harvard.edu/jhove/*
3. *http://www.niso.org/*. At the time of writing (December 2005), Z39.87 was still in balloting.

4. *http://www.digitalpreservation.gov/formats/content/content_categories.shtml*

5. Lee, S.D. (2001) *Digital Imaging: A Practical Handbook*. London: Library Association Publishing, pp. 83–9.

6. Reiger, O.Y. (2000) 'Establishing a quality control program', in *Moving Theory into Practice: Digital Imaging for Libraries and Archives*. Mountain View, CA: Research Libraries Group, pp. 61–83.

7. Prices and specifications from *http://www.dell.com*, accessed 27 December 2005. The 80-GB capacity unit is a Dell PowerVault 110T VS160 Tape Drive; the 160-GB unit is a PowerVault 110T SDLT 320 Tape Drive; the automated unit is a PowerVault Tape Backup 122T LTO-2.

8. *http://www.softbytelabs.com/NameWiz/index.html*

9. *http://www.bulkrenameutility.co.uk/*

10. *http://www.publicspace.net/ABetterFinderRename/*

11. *http://www.versiontracker.com/dyn/moreinfo/macosx/14404*

12. Kenney, A.R. (2000) 'Digital benchmarking for conversion and access', in *Moving Theory into Practice: Digital Imaging for Libraries and Archives*. Mountain View, CA: Research Libraries Group, pp. 24–60.

13. Puglia, S., Reed, J. and Rhodes, E. (2004) *Technical Guidelines for Digitising Archival Materials for Electronic Access: Creation of Production Master Files – Raster Images*. Washington, DC: U.S. National Archives and Records Administration. Available at *http://www.archives.gov/research/arc/digitising-archival-materials.html*

14. *http://www.tasi.ac.uk/advice/creating/colour2.html*

15. *http://www.adobe.com/*

16. *http://irfanview.com/*

17. *http://www.imagemagick.org/*

18. *http://www.adobe.com/*

19. *http://saxon.sourceforge.net/*

20. *http://www.abbyy.com/*

21. *http://epson.com/*

22. *http://www.ricoh.com/*

23. *http://umax.com/*

24. *http://minolta.com/*

25. *http://www.nikon.com/*

26. *http://www.canon.com/*

27. *http://www.sunriseimaging.com/*

28. *http://www.wwl.co.uk/*

29. *http://www.bookeyeusa.com/*

30. *http://zeutschel.de/*

31. *http://www.crusedigital.com/*

32. *http://www.jumboscan.com/*

33. *http://www.betterlight.com/*

34. *http://www.phaseone.com/*

35. *http://www.kirtas-tech.com/*

36. *http://www.4digitalbooks.com/*

37. *http://www.tasi.ac.uk/advice/creating/bestuse.html*

38. NINCH. (2000) *The NINCH Guide to Good Practice in the Digital Representation and Management of Cultural Heritage Materials.* Available at *http://www.nyu.edu/its/humanities/ninchguide/index.html*
39. *http://www.adobe.com/*
40. *http://audacity.sourceforge.net/*
41. *http://www.adobe.com/*
42. *http://www.kinodv.org/*
43. *http://heroinewarrior.com/cinelerra.php3*
44. *http://www.mainconcept.com/mainactor_v5.shtml*
45. *http://www.apogeedigital.com/*
46. *http://www.keywesttechnology.com/*
47. *http://www.lucidaudio.com/*
48. *http://www.canopus.com/*
49. *http://www.matrox.com/*
50. *http://www.winnov.com/*
51. *http://www.adstech.com/*
52. *http://www.hauppauge.com/*
53. *http://www.pinnaclesys.com/*
54. *http://www.adobe.com/products/premiere/systemreqs.html*
55. *http://en.wikipedia.org/wiki/ISO_9660*

Developing workflows

Effective workflows are vital for the success of digitisation and conversion projects. At the same time, it is difficult to define standardised procedures for most of the tasks typically involved in digitising, converting, describing and making digital content available to end users. Franziska Frey describes this problem very clearly:

> A digital project cannot be looked at as a linear process in which one task follows another. Rather, it must be viewed as a complex structure of interrelated tasks in which each decision has an influence on another one. The first step in penetrating this complex structure is to thoroughly understand each single step and find metrics to quantify it. Once this is done, the separate entities can be put together in context.[1]

Because of this complexity, any library that is undertaking a digitisation or conversion project needs to develop its own workflows. Even if a library is contracting with a vendor for some parts of the work, local procedures of various types will be necessary. Of course, it is possible for one library to adopt the workflows developed by another, and multiple libraries collaborating on a project often share workflows. Even in these cases, however, it is difficult to replicate workflows exactly in different libraries owing to factors such as differences in staffing, technical infrastructure and local competing priorities.

Workflow modelling is the process of analysing the tasks that are required to achieve a specific outcome. This process need not be overly complex – the purpose is simply to determine the tasks required to achieve specific goals, and the order in which those tasks should be performed. The literature of workflow modelling is replete with jargon and abstract methodologies, such as EPC (event-driven process chains), BPM (business process management) and Petri Nets. This chapter presents a simple, practical method for modelling the workflows required for digital collection building, describes several techniques for refining workflows and provides an example illustrating the general method.

Workflow modelling has a number of benefits:

- Assisting in determining the tasks required to achieve a specified outcome and the order in which they must be completed.

- *Costing*: As we saw in Chapter 8, determining the processes and resources required for a project cannot be guessed at. The only sound method of determining the costs for a given set of tasks is to perform a representative set of those tasks and document them carefully. Workflow modelling and evaluation are therefore necessary *prior* to estimation of costs associated with the production of digital content.

- *Improving efficiency*: Workflow modelling can aid in improving the efficiency of individual processes. Efficiencies can also be gained by analysing the movement of data between separate processes.

- *Clarifying duties and responsibilities*: Systematic workflow definitions can help clarify who is responsible for what and can serve as the basis for negotiations between partner libraries, vendors, consultants and other participants in the creation of a digital collection.

- *Promoting workflow re-usability*: In many cases effective workflow 'templates' can be re-used on future projects. A library's repertoire of workflows and procedures is a valuable resource as being able to draw on well-documented, mature workflows can dramatically reduce the amount of effort it takes to start new digitisation and conversion projects.

- *Documentation*: Finally, narrative descriptions of workflow and diagrams depicting workflows serve as the basis for project documentation. This information can serve as the basis for detailed procedural manuals for production staff.

The last point distinguishes between workflow and detailed procedural documentation. Workflow is the high-level definition of tasks required to achieve a specific set of goals, whereas procedural documentation describes specific actions required to complete a task, and treats each task as independent of others in the workflow. They are related, but workflow can be expressed in a few pages (sometimes one) whereas procedural manuals for operationalising the same workflow may be hundreds of pages long. Also, writing detailed procedural documentation should always come after high-level workflows have been finalised, as details that are appropriate for procedural documentation may be determined by their place within the overall workflow.

The workflow development cycle

The general process of workflow modelling can be broken down into the following components. Workflow modelling is a highly iterative process in that workflows need to be tested and refined before they are implemented (and are often improved after being implemented). The initial iteration of a workflow can be created by performing the following tasks:

1. *Identify deliverables*: What are the expected outcomes of the workflow? The answer will depend on the goals of the project and the nature of the material you are digitising or converting. For example, if you are developing workflow for an online collection of rare local historical photos, the deliverables might be defined as high-resolution TIFF files for each photo, plus low-resolution versions of these files for presentation on the web, plus detailed metadata descriptions to accompany the photos. On the other hand, if you are converting a number of old examinations for a college from word processor files to formats more suitable for distribution on the web, you will probably identify Adobe Acrobat versions of the exams and very simple metadata as the deliverables.

2. *Identify tasks*: What are the general tasks required to produce these outcomes? Later in this chapter, I describe some of the tasks typically involved in most digitisation and conversion projects. At early stages in the workflow modelling process, tasks should remain general; subsequent versions of the model will add detail.

3. *Identify solutions*: 'Solutions' in this context are the initial estimations of the resources needed to complete the required tasks, such as major staff roles (technicians, supervisors, vendors), likely hardware requirements (such as a scanner) and software of various kinds. Solutions can also include techniques for using the software and hardware.

4. *Identify sequence*: What is the best sequence in which to arrange the tasks identified above? Defining required inputs and outcomes for tasks can assist in determining potential sequences. The sequence of

tasks in a workflow is determined by how suitable the output from one task is as the input for the next.

All of these tasks are informed by the nature of the content you are putting online, the functionality of the collection and available resources. Your collection's goals define the deliverables, the deliverables define the tasks and the tasks define the solutions.

'Solutions' should be clarified: initially, any staff, hardware and other resources that appear in workflows are strictly *initial estimations* of what will be required. Only after you have completed developing your workflows will you be able to determine with any accuracy the entire set of resources you will need to complete the work. As we saw in Chapter 8, the resources required to execute a project can be determined using a set of simple calculations based on quantity of source material, available time and documented costs of production derived from test runs of your workflows. As used above, 'solutions' are only your first guess at the resources you will need, and function simply as placeholders so you can refine your workflows and move on to the task of calculating the resources you will actually need.

As stated above, workflows require continual refinement during the modelling process. Using two popular techniques, outlining and diagramming, it is possible to create a proposed workflow and to refine each version in various ways, such as asking staff who will be performing the tasks for feedback, asking people not involved in the project for comments, and testing the workflows with hypothetical or actual samples of the material being processed. After multiple iterations of 'paper' testing, if at all possible it is worth validating the workflow by actually performing all of the constituent tasks using representative samples of the material being worked on. Performing this type of 'live' test requires that most of the necessary resources be in place, but it is the best way to validate the workflow model and accompanying procedural documentation. As suggested in Chapter 8, proven and tested workflows are the basis for accurate resource planning and budgeting, so it is important that workflows are tested as early as possible in the project planning process.

The pattern you should keep in mind when developing workflows is model (identify deliverables, tasks, solutions and their most effective sequence), then test, then refine, then remodel until the most effective workflow possible has been defined given the resources available. Once the workflow has been defined and documented in final versions of the outlines and diagrams developed throughout the process, procedural documentation for all of the required tasks can be written.

Outlining techniques

Workflow outlining is the process of creating a hierarchical list of tasks. This activity is similar to the creation of any type of outline, whether it is for a written report, a presentation, a trip or a daily to-do list: create a list of major tasks, then break each of these down into smaller tasks until the desired level of specificity is reached. To illustrate using a simple example, if our goal is to put a collection of photos on the web, with searchable descriptions of each photo, we could start with:

1. Scan photo

2. Put photo online

At this point we can congratulate ourselves – we have completed a very (very) high-level workflow for our project! To make this outline the basis for a more realistic project, we need to add a considerable amount of detail. We can begin by identifying deliverables, tasks, solutions and the order in which the tasks should be performed. For example, we have not included an important deliverable, metadata. Adding it to our outline, we now have

1. Scan photo

2. Metadata

3. Put photos online

We then continue to add additional (or more specific) deliverables, the tasks required to produce them and so on until we have an outline that represents a possible workflow.

As we expand our outline, it is important to pay attention to the language used to express the various components of the workflow. Using verbs in outline items forces us to think in terms of action ('digitise photo'), whereas using nouns identifies deliverables ('digitised photo'); although both are valid components of a workflow model, it is better to use verbs at this stage to help define tasks performed on deliverables. The version of the outline below is more precise than the previous one:

1. Digitise photo

2. Create metadata

3. Verify quality of digitised image

4. Place photo into content management system

Outlining is useful for breaking down complex or general tasks into smaller, more discrete tasks. How 'small' is not easy to define, but in general a workflow outline should only name tasks, not describe how to perform them. In developing a workflow outline, our task is similar to that of 'decomposition', an concept from work breakdown structures in the discipline of project management: '[S]ubdividing the major project deliverables into smaller, more manageable components until the deliverables are defined in sufficient detail to support future project activities (planning, executing, controlling, and closing).'[2] In the context of workflow modelling, this means that tasks should be broken down so that they can be documented clearly and performed efficiently. Specific procedures should be documented separately and will describe significantly more detail than an outline should. A further refinement of our outline, after additional tasks have been broken down and subdivided, could look like this:

1. Digitise photo
   a. Retrieve photo from folder
   b. Scan photo
   c. Check quality of scan
      i. If quality is acceptable, save file
      ii. If quality is not acceptable, rescan photo
   d. Copy TIFF file to archive drive
2. Create metadata
   a. Descriptive metadata
   b. Administrative metadata
3. Create JPEG version for web
4. Upload JPEG file into content management system

Our outline is now approaching a useful representation of a complete and realistic workflow model for a photo digitisation project. The model could be developed even further by adding conditional and parallel activities, which we will add with the aid of diagramming techniques.

Diagramming techniques

Many people think about workflows in visual terms. Workflow diagrams can take a variety of forms, from informal sketches to highly structured representations with codified symbols and nomenclature. In Chapter 6 we encountered another type of diagramming technique, storyboarding, which depicts the search, display and navigational elements of a collection from the user's point of view. By contrast, workflow diagramming depicts the sequence of tasks performed by staff members in the production of the content that makes up a collection. This section presents a selection of diagramming techniques that are commonly used during workflow modelling.

Diagrams produced using these techniques are not an end in themselves (although they do serve as an effective type of documentation). Their purpose is to assist in the workflow modelling process and to validate other representations of a workflow, such as a textual outline. For example, one aspect of workflow modelling that diagramming can clarify is the extent to which processes can be performed concurrently. From this perspective, we can define three types of workflow:

- *Linear*: All the steps in the workflow are performed sequentially (e.g. creating JPEG versions of TIFF files requires that the TIFF files be created first).

- *Parallel*: Interdependent tasks are performed simultaneously (e.g. creating JPEG versions of TIFF files and applying OCR to the same TIFF files can be done independently of one another).

- *Overlapping*: Independent tasks are completed simultaneously and then merged (e.g. the JPEG files and text files are then both added to the search and retrieval system).

These types of workflow are often easier to depict graphically (particularly parallel and overlapping) than they are to represent in an outline. Another example of how diagrams can benefit the workflow modelling process is that some types of diagrams express iterative or conditional processes clearly, such as those used in quality assurance tasks and alternative workflows for problematic material. In addition, some types of diagrams (in particular flowcharts and unified modelling language activity diagrams) use highly formalised sets of symbols that have specific meanings. For example, in a flowchart, a rectangular symbol represents a process and a horizontal cylinder represents data stored on a disk drive. In some cases the formal syntax of diagramming techniques should be adhered to if the diagrams are to be shared with external organisations or if they will be used for communicating with people who are familiar with the formalised notations, such as software application developers. If the formal syntaxes interfere with your ability to visualise the most effective workflows for your desired outcomes, however, they cease to become useful. Relaxing these formalities is acceptable if doing so increases the usefulness of diagramming. You are free to create these diagrams in whatever ways are most comfortable and productive for you. Many people draw preliminary drafts of diagrams on paper and then redo them using applications such as Microsoft Visio and OpenOffice Draw, which provide standardised shape and symbol libraries, connecting lines that automatically 'snap' to symbols, functions for evenly spacing and distributing symbols, and other formatting tools. The proper tools make diagramming quite easy, sometimes to the point at which we can become preoccupied with perfecting our diagrams. Keep in mind that diagrams are tools for developing effective workflows and, apart from their use in project documentation, are not ends in themselves.

Block diagrams

The simplest type of workflow diagram is the block diagram. The symbols used to represent tasks, sequences, conditional decisions and so on take the form of common geometric shapes such as blocks, circles and ovals, or from clipart collections. A basic hand-drawn block diagram depicting a very simple, high-level workflow for digitising some photographs, and a slightly more refined version drawn using Microsoft Visio, are given in Figure 10.1:

The only significant difference between the two other than their appearance is that the one drawn with Visio contains a deviation from a strict linear sequence of tasks: between scanning the photo and saving the resulting TIFF file, the task of checking the quality of the file is represented as a task connected to the otherwise linear workflow by a two-way arrow.

Flowcharts

Flowcharts, which were originally developed to represent algorithms and data flow in computer programming, are useful for modelling workflow because they are familiar to many people and because they provide symbols representing processes, decisions, stored data and documents, and other functional aspects of workflows. Figure 10.2 is an example of a flowchart depicting a slightly more developed version of the workflow that we saw in the block diagram. Note that the flowchart uses symbols signifying 'terminators' (the ovals at the top and bottom of the diagram),

Figure 10.1 A simple, hand-drawn block diagram (left) and a slightly more sophisticated version drawn using Microsoft Visio (right)

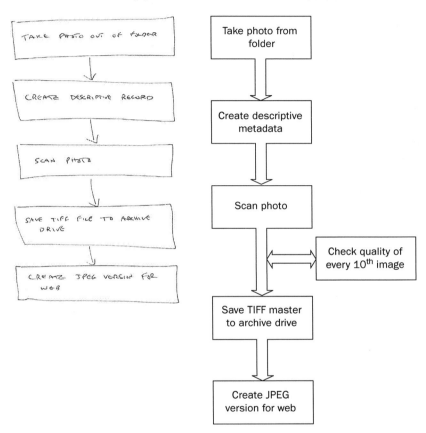

rectangles signifying processes (such as 'Verify descriptive metadata matches photo') and diamond shapes signifying decisions.

This flowchart is also more sophisticated than the block diagram in that it contains explicit references to conditional tasks. Block diagrams can depict conditional tasks as well, but because they lack a formalised set of symbols, they may not be as effective as flowcharts when communicating workflows to staff, partner institutions and vendors. Another advantage of flowcharts is that they are the basis for other types of formalized diagramming techniques, so workflows they depict can be

igure 10.2 A flowchart representing a workflow for scanning still images

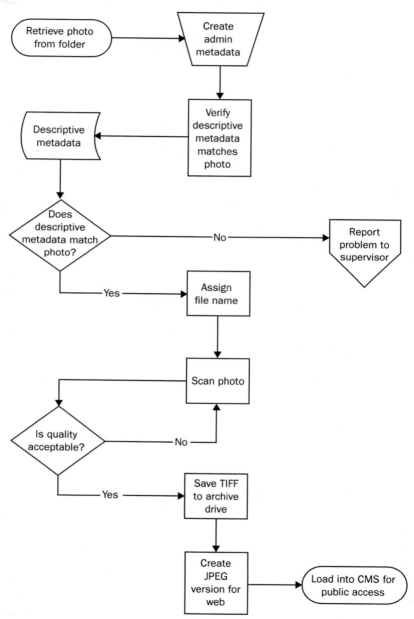

more easily 'mapped' to other types of diagrams than can workflows depicted solely using block diagrams.

Activity diagrams

Activity diagrams are a third type of visualisation technique useful for workflow modelling. They are based on flowcharts, but take into account the vocabulary, methodologies and other aspects of the Unified Modelling Language (UML), a much broader set of concepts originally devised for software development but subsequently used in business process modelling and other fields. UML activity diagrams include notations for depicting concurrent activities, 'agents' (people or organisations) and conditional activities. Figure 10.3 shows an activity diagram for the same workflow depicted in the previous examples. In this diagram, however, the workflow is modelled such that the creation of descriptive and administrative metadata is done as two separate, parallel processes. At the bottom of the diagram, the depiction of saving the TIFF master file to the archive drive and creating the JPEG version for use in the CMS is not entirely accurate (usually, the high-quality TIFF master is created first, and the JPEG derivative version next), and this portion of the diagram should be redone so that the linear sequence of these two tasks is clearer. Activity diagrams are only one type of UML diagram; others, such as package diagrams and class diagrams, are more relevant to software development than to workflow modelling.

A useful feature of activity diagrams is 'swimlanes', horizontal or vertical bands which separate actions performed by different agents (Figure 10.4). Activity diagrams incorporating swimlanes can be particularly useful if the workflow being modelled contains parallel or overlapping tasks.

The examples of block diagrams, flowcharts and activity diagrams are presented to illustrate that the same basic workflow can be depicted in various ways. Factors influencing which diagramming technique is best for a given project include whether the use of a formalised syntax is required (e.g. for communicating with vendors), whether the workflow being modelled will contain parallel or overlapping tasks, and whether the workflow will contain conditional tasks.

Both outlining and diagramming assist in workflow modelling by providing tools for developing, refining and communicating the tasks necessary to produce desired outcomes and the sequences in which those tasks should be performed. Choosing which to use is largely a matter of personal choice, and many people will use both techniques in the process

Figure 10.3 A UML activity diagram illustrating forks and branches

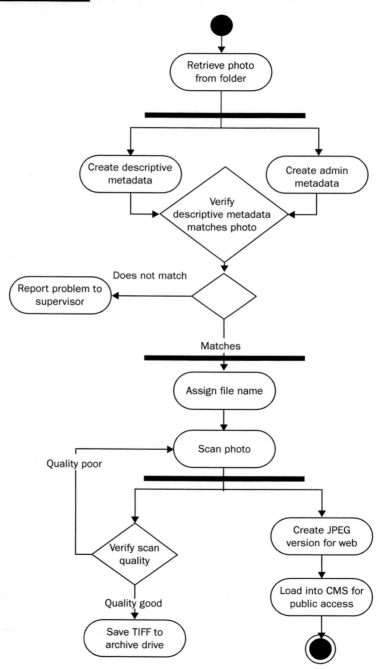

Figure 10.4 A UML activity diagram with swimlanes and agents

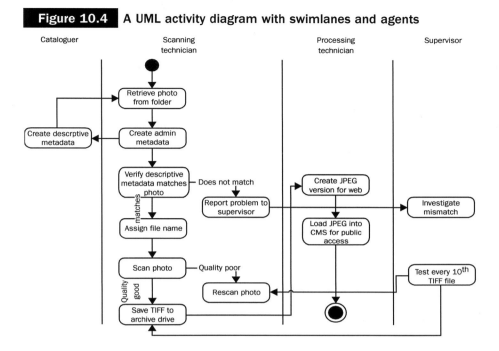

of creating workflows for the same project. Outlines are effective at communicating linear sequences that contain large numbers of tasks and are useful for breaking down general tasks into more specific ones, whereas diagrams are useful for modelling and communicating conditional and parallel tasks. Many people start with outlines and then move to diagrams to integrate non-linear tasks into their workflows. Project managers should be comfortable with both techniques and should not be reluctant to try either one during the workflow modelling process.

Selected workflows from the literature and the field

Workflows for digital library content and metadata production have been discussed by a number of authors, and many libraries and consortia make details about specific workflows available in publications and on project websites. I will take a brief look at a selection of these before moving on to describe a general model for developing digital library content and metadata creation workflows.

For example, Lisa Macklin and Sara Lockmiller provide a detailed sample workflow for photo digitisation in their book *Digital Imaging of Photographs: A Practical Approach to Workflow Design and Project Management*.[3] They enumerate the various stages of the workflow ('Creating negatives', 'Scanning photographs', 'Creating encoded archival description', 'Creating CD ROMs', 'Creating web pages') and within each stage they list the steps, staff, equipment and software. The steps are specific tasks required to complete the workflow stage; for example, within the 'Creating encoded archival description' stage they list two steps, (1) giving the workform for each photo to the cataloguer and (2) the cataloguer completing the description. They preface their sample by saying 'Stages ... do not have to be completed in this order. More than one stage will be in process at any given time.'

Stephen Chapman[4] provides a list of 'typical activities' required in digital conversion projects, including selection, copyright clearance, creation of catalogue records, 'digital image production', creation of structural metadata, creation of full text, and 'advertising, promotion, user evaluation'. Like Macklin and Lockmiller, Chapman acknowledges the non-linear nature of workflows for digital content production: 'Projects will be completed sooner if the tasks are orchestrated in parallel or overlapping rather than linear workflows,' but he does not include any details about how these types of workflows should be planned.

Stuart Lee describes workflow in terms of preparation, benchmarking (the process of setting resolution and colour bit-depth such that the most significant information is captured in the image files), digitisation, quality assurance checks and creating derivatives.[5] Lee provides a useful flowchart containing an overview of the general processes involved in digital imaging projects. A distinctive feature of this flowchart is that it clearly defines the tasks for projects that are completed in-house (i.e. work is performed by library staff) and for projects that are outsourced (i.e. work is performed by vendors and service providers), and the intersections of those tasks. Lee also includes a detailed example from the Celtic and Medieval Manuscripts Imaging Project at the University of Oxford.

Some sample workflows, or workflow documentation, from actual digital collection building projects or from ongoing digital content production services include those from:

- The David Edelberg Handel LP Collection at McGill University documents the hardware, software and detailed procedures, defining (1) digitising the LPs, (2) scanning the album covers, discs and accompanying materials, and (3) creating metadata as the high-level tasks in their workflow.[6]

- The University of Wisconsin Digital Collections Center (UWDCC) provides detailed workflow and procedures for the 'pre-capture', capture, 'post-capture' and metadata stages for digitising audio recordings. The UWDCC also provides some realistic scenarios to illustrate its procedures.[7] Even though it is specific to digitising audio, this document serves as a good model for any type of project.

- The LuEsther T. Mertz Library Rare Book Digitization Project at the New York Botanical Garden does not provide much detail about overall workflow, but it does briefly describe the hardware used in this project and also the standards used to mark up the texts in XML. This site is valuable for its examples of book conservation and preparation as part of the digitisation workflow.[8]

- The New Jersey Digital Highway (NJDH) provides a number of technical documents describing its projects, but the one on creating metadata is particularly useful because it describes the creation of several types of metadata and also provides a brief overview of the general NJDH workflow. The metadata management system is specific to the NJDH but it nicely illustrates the functionality of a comprehensive system.[9]

These examples, and the general descriptions of workflow provided by Macklin and Lockmiller, Chapman, and Lee, are worth investigating closely when you start modelling your own workflows. Seeing how others have operationalised projects is an effective way of getting started with your own. It is also useful to compare the high-level workflow and detailed task documentation from two similar sites (e.g. the David Edelberg Handel LP Collection and the UWDCC cited above) to see how they differ.

A general workflow modelling technique

The general workflow modelling technique presented here is based roughly on the 'stages' defined by Macklin and Lockmiller in their sample workflow and on Chapman's list of 'typical activities'. It is not comprehensive but is intended to assist in the early stages of modelling content and metadata production. Most digitisation or conversion projects involve the same general *types* of tasks, although the details of how those tasks are best accomplished vary widely from project to project, and also vary widely because of local circumstances. The workflow modelling technique described here groups the general types of tasks and presents the most common sequence in which they are performed. The resulting workflow 'template' can then be used as the basis for modelling the workflow for specific projects.

The technique focuses strictly on general types of tasks and assumes the following:

- you have determined the overall goals of your collection (see Chapter 2),
- you have determined the functional requirements for search and retrieval (see Chapter 6),
- you have determined your metadata schemas (see Chapter 4) and
- you have selected and implemented a CMS (see Chapter 7).

In other words, decisions about the goals of your collection, how you envisage users searching for and navigating between items, the structure of your metadata, and the system you are using to present your collection to users all influence workflows and need to be as close to finalised as possible before workflow modelling can begin. The example at the end of this chapter will illustrate how these decisions can have an impact on workflow modelling.

The template defines five stages in the content and metadata production process, identifies the tasks typically performed at each stage, and identifies tasks that are performed at every stage in most workflows (Table 10.1).

The activities in the second column are labelled 'typical' because they are commonly performed in a wide variety of projects. They will not be necessary in every project. For example, 'Conserve/restore item' in the 'Prepare originals' stage will only be necessary if the material being digitised is fragile; for born-digital files, a typical activity at this stage is to ensure that all of the files that make up a document are available.

Activities in the third column are performed at all stages in a workflow. As we saw in Chapter 4, administrative metadata is used to record information such as who worked on the files, and when the work was performed. Work queuing, as we saw in Chapter 9, is the process of ensuring that the material being processed moves between workflow stages and tasks as efficiently as possible. We discussed quality control in Chapter 9, but here it is important to point out that quality control

Table 10.1 The general workflow model template

Workflow stage	Typical activity	Activity at every stage
Create metadata	■ Create admin metadata (including rights management) ■ Create descriptive metadata ■ Determine object filenames	■ Create administrative metadata ■ Perform quality control ■ Queue work for staff
Prepare originals	■ Retrieve item from physical location (or if born-digital, from file system) ■ Conserve/restore item	
Capture/convert	■ Scan/convert/markup in XML ■ Assign filnames ■ Create structural metadata	
Process	■ Create master images (e.g. TIFFs) ■ Create derivative versions (JPEGs for web etc.) ■ Perform OCR	
Store	■ Store masters in long-term space ■ Store derivatives in search and retrieval system	

checks should be built into workflows so that they are performed as files and metadata move from one task to another. Material that contains errors or that is below minimum acceptable quality levels should be corrected as soon as the problems are identified.

To apply the template, use the stages as the basis for an outline or diagram and add the deliverables and tasks that apply to the particular project you are modelling workflow for. It is important to remember that the template is just that – it is not a prepackaged workflow you can apply without modification to a digital library project. Also keep in mind that the sequence of stages presented in the template may not be suitable for every project; for example, it is not uncommon to create descriptive metadata after capturing or converting the originals, to prepare the originals before creating any metadata, or as we have seen in some of the workflow diagrams above, for the creation of descriptive metadata and the digitisation to be performed in parallel. If a sequence different from the one presented in the template suits your particular project, then at least the template has been useful in defining a sequence that does not work for you.

Example workflow

The following example is intended to illustrate how the general workflow model can be applied to a specific project with the goal of digitising 200 handwritten diaries written by 19th century residents of an eastern Canadian province and making them available on the web. The library developing this collection is the public library of the province's capital city, which is partnering with a number of other libraries and the provincial historical association. The diaries are held at various partner libraries but have all been shipped to the lead partner for scanning. Additional information about this project required to plan the workflow:

- *Rights management*: All the diaries are in the public domain.
- *Functional requirements*: The items in this collection are to be represented in both page image and HTML full text. Links will be added from personal names, place names and events to annotations stored in a database. PDF versions of the diaries will also be provided so they can be printed easily.
- *Metadata schemas*: MARC records for these diaries are available from the participating libraries, and are fairly consistent with regard to the level of cataloguing. METS will be used to encode minimal administrative, structural and PREMIS preservation metadata.
- *CMS*: Separate funding has been secured to develop a custom CMS, which will consist of a PHP web interface for staff functions and for presenting the material to end users, and a number of utility scripts for creating metadata files and for miscellaneous file management tasks. The master files are stored on a special directory on the library's main file server (Windows Server 2003).

Based on this information, the deliverables for this project can be defined as:

- digital versions of the 200 diaries (specifically, page images, HTML full text, PDF versions of each diary);

- descriptive metadata based on the existing MARC records in the contributing libraries' catalogues;
- structural and preservation metadata stored in METS files;
- the annotations.

Because the diaries are handwritten, they must be manually typed in order to be searchable as full text. Preliminary investigation has led the library to outsource this work to a vendor, who will deliver the full text of each diary as a basic Text Encoding Initiative (TEI) XML file.

The annotations that are part of this example need to be explained. They are not part of the diaries but are added as part of an 'apparatus providing interpretation' (to use Clifford Lynch's phrase).[10] Links from personal names open a pop-up window that includes a brief biography, links from place names provide a brief explanation of the location and significance of the place, and links from event names provide a brief summary of the event. All of these annotations are stored in a relational database that is part of the CMS. The reason they are introduced in this example is that they are typical of supporting material that libraries frequently add to primary source material, and, more relevant to our current topic, these annotations introduce some interesting workflow issues: in the present example, this supplementary content is not created by library staff, but by subject specialists who are local history experts organised by the historical association and led by a faculty member from one of the local universities who will be acting as an editor. The subject experts will create the annotations using tools provided within the CMS. The library is responsible for the overall project management including establishing the workflows, and for producing the digital versions of the diaries and the website.

To apply the general model to the goals and functional requirements indicated above, we need to enter probable tasks required for achieving the goals identified above in the 'required activity' column of the template, as illustrated in Table 10.2.

At this early stage, we can only make educated guesses at required tasks based on the goals and deliverables. The template is intended to help us move from the general to the specific (at least to the level of specificity appropriate to a useful workflow model), and we will refine the tasks as we move through the process. Simply substituting terms in the template with ones that describe our particular project is one way to start, but tasks that are not represented in the template can be added if they are likely to be part of the workflow.

Table 10.2 General workflow model template with specific activities

Workflow stage	Required activity
Create metadata	■ Convert MARC records into required structure, supplement them if necessary ■ Create administrative metadata ■ Create unique identifiers and filename scheme
Prepare originals	■ Inspect diaries to see whether they are suitable for scanning ■ Have subject experts nominate candidates for annotations ■ Write annotations
Capture/convert	■ Scan diaries ■ Vendor: key texts ■ Create structural metadata
Process	■ Vendor: create basic TEI markup from digital images ■ Apply detailed markup, inc. add element attributes to enable linking to annotations ■ Create web versions from master images
Store	■ Save master images and XML to archive drive ■ Save web images and XML to web server

Next, we should create an outline version of the table above. The goal here is to break down the general tasks into smaller ones and begin reordering them as necessary. Here is the text from the template simply converted into an outline (which I will call version 1):

Create metadata

■ Convert MARC records into required structure, supplement them if necessary

■ Create administrative metadata

■ Create unique identifiers and filename scheme

Prepare originals

■ Inspect diaries to see whether they are suitable for scanning

■ Have subject experts identify candidates for annotations

■ Write annotations

Capture/convert

- Scan diaries
- Vendor: key texts
- Create structural metadata

Process

- Vendor: create basic TEI markup from digital images
- Apply detailed markup, inc. add element attributes to enable linking to annotations
- Create web versions from master images

Store

- Save master images and XML to archive drive
- Save web images and XML to web server

As stated earlier, workflow modelling is iterative, and the pattern of identifying deliverables, then tasks, then solutions, and then their most effective sequence can be applied to creating increasingly refined versions of this outline. A second version of the outline, with the language of the template modified to suit our project better, with larger tasks broken down into smaller ones, and identifying roles other than the digitisation assistant, who performs the majority of the tasks, represented in square brackets, looks like this:

Create metadata

- Convert MARC records into required structure, supplement if necessary
- Create administrative metadata
- Create unique identifier

Prepare diaries

- Inspect diaries to see whether they are suitable for scanning
- [Subject experts] Identify candidates for annotations

Scan images and key full text

- Scan diaries
- [Vendor] Key full text
- [Subject experts] Write annotations
- Create structural metadata for page images

Process files

- [Vendor] Create basic TEI markup
- Apply detailed markup, inc. add element attributes to enable linking to annotations
- Create web versions from master images

Store files

- Save master images and XML to archive drive
- Save web images and XML to web server

In version 2, the significant changes include refinements in the language ('Prepare originals' is now 'Prepare diaries', 'Capture/convert' is now 'Scan images and key full text', and 'Process' is now 'Process files'). 'Create structural metadata' in the first version is now 'Create structural metadata for page images', which limits the scope of this task significantly, as creating structural metadata for the TEI/HTML files is omitted (for the purposes of our example, the managers decided that this information was not worth the cost of creating it – possibly not a wise decision but funding for this project is not unlimited). Also, the task of writing the annotations has moved from the preparation stage to the same stage as scanning the images and keying the texts. However, the outline still needs development in order to represent a complete high-level workflow. For example, so far we have not addressed how the subject experts will access the diaries to identify terms for annotation. Neither have we identified when quality control checks should be performed. Incorporating these tasks and other refinements results in the final version (version 3):

Create administrative metadata

- Create master admin record for diary
- Create unique identifier for diary
- Assign subject expert for this diary

Prepare diary for scanning

- Remove from shipping container
- Inspect diary to see whether it is suitable for scanning
  - If not, make note in admin record and report to supervisor

Scan images and key full text

- Scan diary
  - Ensure filenames follow documented pattern
  - [Supervisor] Perform quality control check on master files
- [Vendor] Key full text
  - Ensure filenames follow documented pattern
- Run structural metadata creation script
- Create printable PDF version of diary for sending to subject expert
- [Subject experts] Write annotations in content management system
- [Editor] Perform quality control on annotations

Process files

- [Vendor] Create basic TEI markup according to documented requirements
- Perform quality control check on returned TEI files
- Apply detailed markup
  - Add element attributes to enable linking to annotations using printed diary returned from subject expert
  - [Supervisor] perform quality control check on TEI markup

Archive master files

- Run archive validation script
  - If problem, report in trouble log
- Run preservation metadata creation script

Prepare presentation files for use in CMS

- Create web versions of page images from master images
- Create HTML files from TEI, and PDF files for public use

- Run web validation script
  - If problem, report in trouble log
- Save web files and XML to CMS

[Supervisor] Perform quality control check of web version

This version of the outline breaks down some of the tasks further, describes significant conditionals and explicitly mentions quality control checks. Also included are several mentions of scripts, such as the one for creating a printable version of the scanned diaries, and the ones for creating structural metadata, for validating archive and presentation files, and for creating XML files containing basic PREMIS preservation metadata. Even though running these scripts is technically a procedure, they are explicitly named because they identify 'solutions' as I defined that word earlier in this chapter – 'resources needed to complete the required tasks' including software. These scripts will need to be developed by the library's IT staff as an existing tool for this specialised purpose probably does not exist. Creation of PDF versions of the diaries appears twice because this process needs to be completed early in the workflow so the subject experts can read the diaries, but in addition, the PDF files intended for public use must be created as late as possible so they incorporate corrections discovered by the quality control checks. Creating an Acrobat PDF file from a group of TIFF or JPEG page images is a simple process that is acceptable to repeat if the workflow justifies doing so.

Version 3 of the outline differs from version 2 in several more ways. First, the creation of the descriptive metadata from the MARC records has been removed, as this process is best completed for all records as a batch, most likely using a custom script or software utility of some sort. The outline now only describes tasks that are performed on individual diaries and not on the group of diaries as a whole. Second, quality control checks on the presentation files for each diary have been added as a top-level task on its own at the very end of the workflow. Third, the creation of preservation metadata has been added. This last task is performed just prior to copying the master copies of the images and TEI files, as the script used to create preservation metadata takes the administrative metadata from the CMS and METS structural metadata that has already been created and converts them into an XML representation of PREMIS elements and their corresponding values.

Now that we have a fairly mature outline of our workflow, we may want to draw a diagram to assist in validating the workflow and for documentation purposes. Because there are a number of roles in our workflow (digitisation assistant, supervisor, keying vendor, subject experts and an annotations editor), a UML activity diagram is suitable because it uses swimlanes to depict agents. To keep the diagram as simple as possible, symbols for activities do not necessarily need to correspond to any particular level in the hierarchical outline. The important thing is that significant tasks from the outline are represented in the diagram so they are placed accurately within the workflow sequence. Also, swimlanes are generally represented as parallel sections of the diagram (imitating lanes in a swimming pool) but to save space in this example we have stacked two lanes on the left of the diagram and two lanes on the right. This stacking does not imply a sequential relationship between the activities included in those swimlanes.

As an example of how diagramming can validate a workflow (Figure 10.5), the process of drawing this particular diagram revealed that we did not include quality control checks on the TEI markup added by the digitisation technician supervisor, which we added to both the diagram and to the outline.

Summary: developing workflows for digital collections

Even though the types of tasks involved in creating content and metadata for digital collections are easy to define, assembling specific tasks into effective sequences – workflow modelling – is not a straightforward process. This chapter has introduced outlining and diagramming as two techniques for assisting in workflow modelling and has also introduced a general workflow modelling technique tailored to digital collection production. The variety of workflows that various institutions have used to operationalise a project illustrates that there are no standardised, turnkey solutions for this type of work and that the work is rarely strictly linear. Thoroughly modelled and tested workflows provide the context for the individual tasks that are required to achieve the goals of a project, and are therefore an essential component in planning and delivering any digital collection.

Figure 10.5 A UML activity diagram representing the workflow for the diary digitisation project

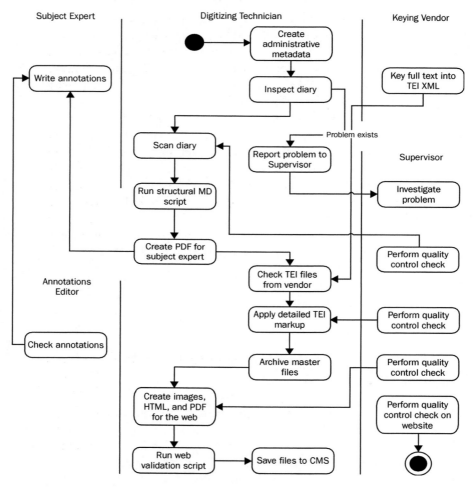

Further reading

Loots, M., Camarzan, D. and Witten, I.H. (2004) *Greenstone from Paper to Collection.*
Available at *http://prdownloads.sourceforge.net/greenstone/Paper-en.pdf*
This 30-page guide is part of the documentation for the popular Greenstone digital library platform. In addition to describing the processes of scanning, OCR and manual typing of texts, the guide also

includes three example projects, plus a Greenstone-specific section entitled 'Getting started in seven steps and 15 minutes'.

Pender, T. (2003) *UML Bible*. Indianapolis: Wiley.
Like many titles in Wiley's Bible series, this one provides both a clear overview of UML diagramming techniques and provides a great level of detail. Although it is written from the perspective of software engineering, the *UML Bible* provides an entire chapter on activity diagrams that is applicable to modelling workflow as well.

Puglia, S., Reed, J. and Rhodes, E. (2004) *Technical Guidelines for Digitising Archival Materials for Electronic Access: Creation of Production Master Files – Raster Images*. Washington, DC: U.S. National Archives and Records Administration. Available at *http://www.archives.gov/research/arc/digitising-archival-materials.html*
This publication, also recommended in Chapter 5 as further reading, is an excellent source of workflows for digitising a wide variety of image-based formats.

Notes

1. Frey, F. (2000) 'Developing best practices: guidelines from case studies', in *Handbook for Digital Projects: A Mangement Tool for Preservation and Access*. Edited by Maxine K. Sitts. Andover, MA: Northeast Document Conservation Center. Available at *http://www.nedcc.org/digital/vii.htm*
2. Project Management Institute. (2001) *Practice Standard for Work Breakdown Structures*. Newton Square, PA: Project Management Institute, p. 75.
3. Macklin, L.L. and Lockmiller, S.L. (1999) *Digital Imaging of Photographs: A Practical Approach to Workflow Design and Project Management*. LITA Guides #4. Chicago: ALA.
4. Chapman, S. (2000) 'Considerations for project management', in *Handbook for Digital Projects: A Mangement Tool for Preservation and Access*. Edited by Maxine K. Sitts. Andover, MA: Northeast Document Conservation Center. Available at *http://www.nedcc.org/digital/vii.htm*
5. Lee, S.D. (2001) *Digital Imaging: A Practical Handbook*. London: Library Association Publishing.
6. 'Digitisation for Preservation of the David Edelberg Handel LP Collection'. Available at *http://coltrane.music.mcgill.ca/mapp/workflow_final.html*
7. Williams, J., Paske, S. and Dast, S. 'Audio Procedures and Workflow for The University of Wisconsin Digital Collections Center (Uwdcc)'. Available at *http://uwdcc.library.wisc.edu/documents/reformatting/AudioWorkflow.pdf*
8. *http://www.nybg.org/bsci/libr/rolen/tech.html*

9. 'Using the NJDH Workflow Management System to Create Metadata'. Available at *http://www.njdigitalhighway.org/documents/wms-guidelines.pdf*

10. Lynch, C. (2002) 'Digital collections, digital libraries and the digitisation of cultural heritage information', *First Monday* 7:5. Available at *http://www.firstmonday.dk/issues/issue7_5/lynch/*

11

Preservation strategies

As mentioned in Chapter 2, the last five years has seen a marked difference in the library and archives communities' attitude toward digital preservation. Significant events since 2000 include the establishment of the National Digital Information Infrastructure and Preservation Program in the US (led by the Library of Congress), publication of Maggie Jones' and Neil Beagrie's *Preservation Management of Digital Materials: A Handbook* (2001), a statement by the Association of Research Libraries' endorsing digitisation as an acceptable preservation method (2004),[1] publication of the PREMIS specification for preservation metadata (2004), and the release of a public draft of a 'Checklist for the Certification of Trusted Digital Repositories' by the Research Libraries Group and the US National Archives and Records Administration (2005). However, strategies for preserving digital materials are still far less mature than those for preserving print and even other non-print analog materials such as film and audio tape. Although the problems surrounding digital preservation are understood fairly well, in general the solutions to those problems have only evolved as far as the pilot, proof of concept, or theoretical stage. The long-term viability of digital preservation strategies has not yet been tested.

Digital preservation has been mentioned in this book a number of times, in conjunction with rationales for digitising, metadata, file formats and project operations. This chapter puts the activities covered earlier into the general context of digital preservation and describes the practical elements of a preservation strategy that is applicable to digital library collections.

The problems

The challenges in preserving digital content have been identified by a number of people, but Howard Besser's articulation neatly summarises the challenges from libraries' perspectives. Besser has formulated five 'problems' with preserving digital resources (which for the most part he calls 'works'):[2]

- *The Viewing Problem*: Unlike analog formats (even formats such as microfiche), digital files are not viewable without computer technology. The short lifespan of the hardware and software technologies required to view specific formats, coupled with the rapid pace of technological change, means that the technology necessary to use digital works will probably not be available in the future.

- *The Scrambling Problem*: Techniques used to compress files and to encrypt them for digital rights management purposes pose serious threats to the files' longevity. As many compression algorithms and rights management technologies are proprietary, they may not be available in the future. Although Besser does not mention that many countries' copyright laws are making circumventing technological protection measures (TPMs) used to enforce digital rights management illegal, even if the technology to unlock files is available in the future, doing so may not be legal.

- *The Inter-Relation Problem*: The integrity of digital works depends on the linkages between individual files that make up a single work. These linkages are fragile – Besser uses the example of a website that is reorganised, leaving behind broken URLs. Addressing the 'inter-relation problem' is one of functions of the structural metadata (although Besser does not use that term) that should accompany preservation metadata.

- *The Custodial Problem*: The custodial roles that libraries and archives have are not as clearly defined for digital works as for analog works. Besser provides the example of a writer's papers: in the past, libraries and archives often took possession of manuscripts, notes, correspondence and other material judged to be of value. If these materials are digital, they are more likely to be lost by the creator (if only because of most peoples' file management practices) or not collected by libraries and archives at all. Besser also points out that the difficulties in determining a digital document's original context and authenticity pose serious challenges to archives, compared with those of print documents.

- *The Translation Problem*: Because the same digital work may look or function (Besser uses the word 'behave') differently in different software environments, it is difficult to ensure that in the future the work will retain its identity to the extent necessary to be considered the same work. Besser provides the example of a video game whose original operating environment was successfully preserved (through emulation, which I will describe below), but when run, the game's pace was much slower than originally intended. The preserved game was considered by its creator to be significantly different from the original. Therefore, when preserving digital works, we need not only to preserve the content but also the 'behaviours' that define how the content was intended to be used.

Two aspects of digital preservation that Besser mentions but does not elaborate on are media obsolescence and media degradation. Obsolescence is a side-effect of the rapid pace at which computer technologies change. The most popular example is that data stored on eight-inch floppy disks is all but irretrievable today. Degradation is the breakdown of the physical carrier that the data is stored on. The most commonly cited example of this problem is that roughly 20% of the data collected during the 1976 Viking Mars landing has been lost due to the condition of the tapes the data was stored on.[3] These two issues also apply to analog information – early films serve as an example of both problems. However, combined with the other problems Besser describes, they illustrate the relative complexities of preserving digital and analog information.

Approaches to digital preservation

The problems defined above can be addressed in a number of ways. Some of the problems require technical solutions, whereas others require organisational solutions. The two types of solutions are not independent of each other: technical solutions alone will prove ineffective without individual and collaborative institutional commitment, and without technical solutions, organisational commitment will be ineffectual. This section deals mainly with technical approaches to digital preservation. Organisational commitment to widely accepted standards such as the OAIS Reference Model and the specifications for Trusted Digital Repositories will be discussed below.

Kenneth Thibodeau's 'Overview of technological approaches to digital preservation and challenges in coming years'[4] provides a useful overview. Thibodeau claims that 'it is impossible to preserve a digital document as a physical object. One can only preserve the ability to reproduce the document.'[5] The physical aspects of a digital document are determined by the medium that the document is stored on. Preserving physical media (which are in general extremely fragile) and the equipment necessary to use them is not considered a viable digital preservation option. Thibodeau's survey of the major approaches to digital preservation, therefore, outlines the options available for preserving documents independent of storage media. Even though preservation of storage media is not feasible, proper management of storage media is extremely important. Two aspects of media management that I will cover later in this chapter are backups and refreshing.

The three general approaches to digital preservation that Thibodeau defines, and the subtypes within each approach, are:

- Preserve technology

  Emulation: Special software can be written to translate instructions used by obsolete software to those that work in current software. In this way, emulation allows old software to run on new platforms.

  Configurable chips: In this approach, old software is run on simulated versions of compatible hardware.

  Recreating software to view old files: File format specifications can be used to create software that will read files complying with that specification. Thibodeau supplies the example of a proof of concept performed by the Victoria, Australia Public Records Office in which they wrote an Adobe PDF viewer only using information available in the published PDF specification.

  Virtual machines: This approach does not apply to retrospective preservation, but new software could be written such that in the future it will execute on any platform, thereby reducing file format obsolescence.

- Migrate

  Version migration: This approach (not considered tenable in the long term) is usually achieved simply by opening old files in new versions of the software used to create the files.

  Format standardisation: Convert variety of formats to a single, standard type. Examples of this preservation approach include converting textual documents in proprietary format to plain ASCII text, and converting image files to TIFF.

  Typed object model (TOM) conversion: In this approach, the essential properties of a document are preserved when converted to newer formats. For example, converting a Microsoft Word document to an

Adobe PDF document preserves the essential visual properties of the original file.

Rosetta Stones translation: This approach compares the digital documents to be preserved with an analog representation of the same documents. In the future, a new version of the documents can be constructed by using the analog version to define equivalent properties in the old and new digital formats.

Object interchange format: Similar to Rosetta Stones but uses a common conceptual model, and not an analog reference model, to allow information exchange between heterogeneous systems.

- Preserve archives

   This approach combines many of the other ones described here but focuses on managing digital documents within the OAIS Reference Model (described in the next section). The technical aspect that differentiates persistent archives from other strategies is that it articulates 'the essential characteristics of the objects to be preserved – collections as well as individual objects – in a manner that is independent of any specific hardware or software.'[6] Significant portions of the data files being preserved are identified with XML tags that encode these essential characteristics to facilitate future preservation activities.

Will individual libraries creating digital collections utilise these approaches? Probably not. However, they may be used by centralised, cooperative preservation repositories, such as a trusted digital repository, described below. Format standardisation is one strategy that might be used widely as it is mature and relatively easy to implement. Version migration is a 'default' for many born-digital documents because of common software upgrade habits, but has the disadvantage of locking the documents into a single vendor's product line. Emulation is finding success in some areas such as video games, and has been used to preserve the BBC Doomsday project (a multimedia resource produced in the mid 1980s that was distributed on proprietary video disks).[7] However, creating the software necessary for emulation will not probably become a routine activity at individual libraries, but they may be done on a cooperative basis to allow viewing of common file formats or obsolete data of particular research value (as is the case in the BBC Doomsday emulation activity). Open formats promote the possibility that in the future, software can be written to view and use compliant files.

The variety of strategies and their respective advantages suggests that no one strategy will emerge as the dominant for a large proportion of digital content. Rather, a number of factors will determine the best preservation strategy used to address a given type of document, format or desired outcome. To represent this view of digital preservation approaches, Thibodeau defines a 'two-way grid' with preservation objectives along the *x*-axis and applicability of approaches along the *y*-axis. Objectives range from 'preserving technology' to 'preserving objects', and applicability ranges from specific to general. Preserving simple textual documents, for instance, can probably rely on general approaches that focus on preserving essential characteristics of the document such as section headings, paragraph formatting, pagination and typographical formatting. Preserving video games, by contrast, will require approaches that focus on preserving the technology (as the game is highly interactive) and will probably need to be specific to the game's original operating environment. Thibodeau's grid provides a useful tool for selecting the most appropriate preservation method for achieving a given set of objectives.

OAIS Reference Model

One of the most influential approaches to digital preservation is the OAIS Reference Model.[8] An OAIS is an open archival information system. The Reference Model has several purposes: to clarify the archival concepts needed for long-term preservation of digital (and to some extent analog material as well), to introduce these concepts to non-archival institutions, to provide a common vocabulary for discussing digital preservation concepts, and to develop consensus on requirements for long-term digital preservation and access. The OAIS Reference Model has been approved as ISO (International Organization for Standardization) standard 14721:2003. The RLG *Trusted Digital Repositories: Attributes and Responsibilities* and the PREMIS preservation metadata data dictionary (described in more detail in the next two sections) both explicitly indicate that they build on the OAIS Reference Model.

One of the most useful aspects of the model is the definition of three types of 'packages' that reflect a document's movement from the producer through the OAIS to the end user. All three packages contain content and 'preservation description information', which is essentially equivalent to what has been described in this book as preservation metadata. These packages are:

- *SIP (Submission Information Package)*: The content as it is sent to an archive by a producer. Details about the content itself and the requirements for the SIP are usually negotiated in advance by the producer and the archive.

- *AIP (Archival Information Package)*: This package consists of SIPs, full preservation description information or other AIPs. The exact nature of AIPs may change over time as they are managed by the archive.

- DIP (Dissemination Information Package): In response to requests for the content, DIPs are delivered to end users and may take a variety of forms, depending on the user's requirements.

From a conceptual point of view, these information packages tie together the roles (producers, management, consumers) and the functions (ingest, archival storage, data management, administration, preservation planning, access) of an archive, each of which are detailed in the Model.

Even though the Reference Model does not specify the design or implementation of an open archival information system, Section 5 of the Model discusses two specific technological approaches to digital preservation, specifically migration (across both media and formats) and 'access service' preservation. Migration activities are applied to the content while it is part of an AIP, since content is managed over time as this type of package. Access service preservation takes two forms, APIs (application programming interfaces) and look and feel preservation. APIs provide documented methods for writing software tools that can access content in AIPs. Look and feel preservation also takes two forms, source code approaches and emulation (as described earlier in this chapter). Source code approaches involve rewriting the software originally used to create or view the content so that it will run in future computing environments, or, in the case of proprietary software, negotiate with the software owner to create a custom viewer so the content can be used.

These SIP, AIP and DIP packages are intended to be specific to a 'designated community' – in other words, the exact form that the packages take and the types of applications built around the packages will vary across intended user groups. Selected implementations of the OAIS Reference Model in libraries include the CEDARS Distributed Archiving Prototype,[9] DSpace's METS SIP Profile[10] and Trusted Digital Repositories.

Readers seeking more information on the OAIS Reference Model should consult Brian Lavoie's introductory guide,[11] which is a lucid 19-page distillation of the 148-page original document.

Trusted digital repositories

In 2002 the Research Libraries Group and OCLC published a report defining the attributes and responsibilities of trusted digital repositories (TDRs),[12] 'whose mission is to provide reliable, long-term access to managed digital resources to its designated community, now and in the future.'[13] The OAIS Reference Model is the basis for many TDR attributes and responsibilities, and Appendix A of the report identifies a number of specific activities required to fulfil the functions of an OAIS as enumerated above. In August 2005, RLG and the US National Archives and Records Administration published a public comment draft of *An Audit Checklist for the Certification of Trusted Digital Repositories*,[14] which, as the title suggests, sets out clear metrics (or criteria) for certifying institutions managing TDRs as 'trusted'. Preliminary repositories that have agreed to be audited include the National Library of the Netherlands, the Inter-University Consortium for Political and Social Research (ICPSR) and the Portico electronic journals archive.[15] Ronald Jantz and Michael J. Giarlo have analysed some of the technical aspects of TDRs in a recent article in *D-Lib Magazine*.[16]

Individual libraries are not likely to establish TDRs because the resources required to become and remain certified are significant enough that TDRs will probably only be possible on national or even international levels. In this model, individual libraries or even groups of libraries collaborating on a digital collection would not become fully certified TDRs but would become clients of centralised repositories. However, as the *Audit Checklist* points out, libraries that do not intend to establish certified repositories will benefit from developing policies and practices that are consistent with those required of TDRs, as depositing digital assets will require adherence to minimum requirements. Deposits to TDRs will be OAIS SIPs, and basing local specifications and practices on the requirements defined for a TDR will facilitate the submission of SIPs if a library chooses to deposit with a TDR in the future.

Preservation metadata

Chapter 4 introduced the functions of preservation metadata. As indicated there, the two most fully developed preservation metadata specifications are PREMIS and the New Zealand National Library's specification. In this section I will focus on PREMIS because it is the more recent of the two, and because it is documented more thoroughly than the New Zealand specification. The PREMIS Data Dictionary also provides several useful examples of how preservation metadata might be applied, as well as a discussion of some of the implementation issues libraries will encounter. I will take a closer look at one of the examples provided in the PREMIS specification, discuss implementation and conformance, and discuss some reasons why preservation metadata is so important.

An example from PREMIS

The sixth PREMIS example discusses a TIFF file and an accompanying descriptive metadata record contained in an XML file. The example provides preservation metadata values for both the TIFF and the XML files. Each file has its own Object, Event, Agent and Rights metadata. Rather than itemise all of the elements used in the example (the Object section for the TIFF file alone contains 45 elements, the Event section contains ten), I will summarise the metadata in Table 11.1.

While Object and Agent metadata for both files are similar, the differences in Event and Rights metadata illustrate some of the variations in preservation metadata that can exist within a single resource (in this case, consisting of two files). To extend the example, if at a later time it is necessary to move the TIFF file, performing a fixity check (running a checksum generator against the file and comparing the results with earlier checksum to test whether the file has been altered), or migrating the TIFF file to a new master file format, Event metadata (including associated Agent metadata) would have to be created and added to the metadata management system. Likewise, if the library wanted to change the descriptive metadata, it would need to get permission to do so as described in the XML file's Rights metadata, and the corresponding Event metadata would need to be generated as well.

PREMIS implementation and conformance

The PREMIS Working Group surveyed 70 libraries in November 2003 and found that relational databases were the most common tool for storing metadata, but that XML files are also commonly used.[17] Although respondents' database models are not described, the PREMIS

	TIFF image file	XML descriptive metadata file
Object preservation metadata	Includes characteristics such the file's persistent identifier, a checksum value, file format, file size and details about the software applications used to create the file	Similar to elements used for TIFF files
Event preservation metadata	Describes ingestion into the preservation repository	Describes 'modification of display' by applying an XSLT stylesheet to the XML file
Agent preservation metadata	Describes the person performing the ingestion event	Describes the person performing the transformation event
Rights preservation metadata	Indicates that the image is in the public domain	Indicates that the granting agent is the Getty Research Library, Special Collections Cataloging department; also describes the following restriction: 'Core descriptive metadata not to be changed without referral to Special Collections Cataloging'

Table 11.1 Summary of metadata from PREMIS Data Dictionary example 6

Data Dictionary does provide some examples of standard relational database models (one-to-many, for example) and one example of an object-relational model. Despite these examples, the Data Dictionary does not recommend any specific data models and makes it clear that it does not prescribe specific data management implementations.

With regard to conformance to the PREMIS element set, the Data Dictionary stresses that libraries must not alter the meaning of individual elements. Libraries may add elements, but their names should not conflict with existing PREMIS elements. Also, libraries may restrict the use of repeatable PREMIS elements so that they are not repeatable in local usage, but the reverse is not true – elements that are defined as non-repeatable cannot be implemented as repeatable. Finally, some elements are mandatory, and because these elements 'represent the minimum amount of information 1) necessary to support the long-term preservation of digital objects, and 2) that must accompany a digital object as it is transferred from the custody of one preservation repository to another',[18] their inclusion is required for PREMIS conformance.

Justification for managing preservation metadata

Why is it important that we create and maintain preservation metadata? As Howard Besser says, 'Various types of metadata that appear unimportant today may prove critical for viewing [...] files in the future.'[19] In Chapter 4 we saw several of Maggie Jones and Neal Beagrie's rationales for creating preservation metadata: to document the technology required for the object, to document the changes the object has undergone over time, to document rights information and to facilitate future use of the object. Additional justifications they provide include:

- *Continuity*: Because digital preservation requires repeated actions such as periodic refreshing and migration, it is important that these actions are documented consistently and thoroughly so that successive generations of managers and technicians have a longitudinal view of the actions already taken.

- *Accountability*: Preservation metadata provides an effective audit trail.

- *Authenticity*: Metadata may be an important means of reliably establishing the authenticity of material as it passes through the various changes required to preserve it.

- *Cost*: Effective metadata can lower the overall cost of digital preservation activities, as 'it will be more complex and therefore more costly to maintain access to digital materials without documentation describing its technical characteristics.'

- *Feasibility*: Without effective preservation metadata, it may not be possible to provide access to digital content in the future.[20]

Preservation policies

Libraries that are committed to preserving the digital content they create must develop a digital preservation policy. The preceding discussion of the challenges in preserving digital content, the variety of approaches that are available, and the role of organisational and technical standards illustrates the complexities that individual libraries must sort through when articulating how they intend to ensure that that their digital content is available and accessible in the future. A written preservation policy is the embodiment of a comprehensive, sustainable approach to digital preservation.

The most succinct guide for developing digital preservation policies is provided as part of Cornell University Library's online tutorial on digital preservation, 'Digital preservation management: implementing short-term strategies for long-term problems.'[21] Cornell recommends developing a policy framework that includes a 'set of explicit statements that defines the organization's level and nature of commitment and responsibility.' This framework should include the following:

- an explicit statement of the institution's compliance with the OAIS Reference Model;

- a statement demonstrating that the institution is committed to complying with current and emerging preservation standards;

- a 'mission statement and comprehensive policies that document and authorize the steps an organization undertakes to receive, store, preserve, and provide access to digital materials under its care, encompassing legal, fiscal, and ethical considerations and requirements.';

- business plans necessary to fulfil the stated commitments to digital preservation;

- details on the institution's technical infrastructure supporting digital preservation;

- a statement of the institution's protocols and safeguards for maintaining the security and integrity of its digital assets;

- a statement of procedural accountability ensuring that preservation policies and activities are documented, shared and applied.

Writing four years before the Cornell tutorial was published, Oya Y. Rieger[22] defined the components of a digital preservation policy as (1) organisational infrastructure, (2) policies for selection, conversion and reselection, (3) preservation actions, and (4) technology forecasting. Two of these components are worth highlighting as supplements to Cornell's more current definition. (Actually, Rieger was the Coordinator of the Digital Imaging and Preservation Research Unit at Cornell when she wrote the chapter cited here.) First, Rieger's description of policies for selection builds on what I have covered in Chapter 2 by adding the notion of 'reselection' of analog resources for redigitisation in the event that previously created digital versions become unavailable. The criterion for reselection is the relative costs and benefits of redigitising the material versus preserving the initial digital versions. The second of Rieger's components is 'technology forecasting', or monitoring developments in technology with respect to how they will impact digital preservation.

Although Rieger does not present these components as parts of a written, public policy statement (she is not explicit about the creation of such a document), these two components are important for internal planning purposes and should be included in public digital preservation policies. The option of redigitising is significant because it runs counter to the accepted best practice of digitising content once, at the highest possible quality. As we saw in Chapter 5, the long-term costs of preserving digital content can be substantial. A preservation policy should therefore address reselection as an option. Inclusion of Rieger's second component in a digital preservation policy, technology forecasting, demonstrates that the library is taking a proactive approach to determining what the long-term impact of new technologies is on its digital preservation efforts.

Relatively few institutions have formal digital preservation policies. A survey performed in 2005 by the Northeast Document Conservation Center found that only 29% of the responding libraries, archives and museums that create digital content have written preservation policies;[23] a recent Cornell survey of participants in their preservation management training programme indicated that even though over 50% of respondents said their library had a digital preservation policy, just over 30% had actually implemented it.[24] Finding preservation policies on library websites (a reasonable place to look for public versions of such policies) is not as easy as these survey results suggest. However, policies from the National Library of Australia,[25] Columbia University Libraries,[26] the Florida Center for Library Automation[27] and OCLC's Digital Archive[28] are publicly available and can serve as models for developing preservation policies for your own library.

Practical technologies

A number of useful, practical technologies that specifically target digital preservation are available. The Digital Curation Centre maintains a list of digital preservation tools[29] that should be consulted. The three technologies described below are intended to provide examples of tools that can be implemented fairly easily and inexpensively (they are all open source and freely available). However, it is important to put 'fairly easily and inexpensively' into the proper perspective: technological solutions alone will not ensure long-term access to digital content, as they can be effective only if appropriate policies to support their use have been developed and implemented.

JHOVE

We have seen JHOVE (the JSTOR/Harvard Object Validation Environment)[30] already in Chapters 4 and 9. JHOVE is used to identify a file's format (PDF, XML, etc.), to validate a file's format (in other words, to verify that a file ending in .jpg is a standard JPEG file), and to characterize a file (for example, to determine the pixel density of a TIFF file). JHOVE can also generate checksums in a number of formats (checksums are numbers generated by standardised algorithms that can be created at various points in time and compared to detect whether the file has been modified since the last check). All three of these functions are necessary prerequisites to a number of preservation activities, such as the creation of preservation metadata, integrity auditing and format migration.

DSpace

The popular DSpace institutional repository management software incorporates a number of features relevant to digital preservation. This is not surprising, as one of the commonly stated functions of an institutional repository is to preserve material created by the members of a university community (although equivalents are being established outside of universities as well).

DSpace was designed to accommodate the OAIS Reference Model.[31] Future versions of DSpace will use a data storage model based on OAIS Archvial Information Packages, and MIT is currently developing a specification for an OAIS Submission Information Package based on METS (cited above).

DSpace allows end users (typically faculty, graduate students and so on) to submit their own works into the repository. Two preservation features built into the software are employed in the submission process.

First, the format of the file that is being submitted is detected by DSpace and it is checked against a list of 'supported' formats, configurable by the DSpace admin. This list contains only formats that the local library has committed to preserving. Second, the submitter is asked to accept a licence agreement that specifically includes references to preservation activities such as format migration. The purpose of these two features is to assist in the enforcement of the preservation policy established for the repository, not to apply automated preservation processes to the submitted files.

Another preservation feature worth mentioning is that DSpace automatically generates checksums on submitted files. Although the use of checksums is fairly widespread, DSpace's submission process provides a convenient opportunity for their creation, and because DSpace also creates other administrative metadata upon document submission, the checksum can be stored along with the other metadata. A member of the DSpace user community has created a utility that periodically regenerates checksums for all items in a DSpace repository and reports any anomalies to the repository administrator.

Finally, the DSpace@Cambridge Digital Preservation Tools and Strategies Project[32] is undertaking a number of activities to extend DSpace's preservation capabilities, such as using JHOVE (described below) to validate submitted files, developing policy and practice for preserving Geographic Information Systems data, and developing DSpace-specific format migration strategies.

LOCKSS

As its name suggests, LOCKSS (Lots of Copies Keep Stuff Safe)[33] is used to create redundant copies of digital content to ensure their ongoing preservation. This open-source software uses a peer-to-peer network architecture to maintain redundant copies of content on inexpensive computers. In the event that a problem occurs with the original copy (e.g. an electronic journal publisher's site), users are automatically routed to a redundant copy. LOCKSS respects copyright – the content producer must authorise the copying, and the use of the software is often written into the licence agreements between libraries and publishers.

LOCKSS is used mainly for mirroring electronic journals (Oxford University Press, Johns Hopkins University Press and Project Muse are among the publishers participating in the LOCKSS program), but some non-commercial digital library applications are beginning to appear.

For example, the MetaArchive of Southern Digital Culture[34] is using LOCKSS within its membership to mirror locally created content, and The Association of Southeastern Research Libraries[35] is using LOCKSS to preserve electronic theses and dissertations.

Practical things you can do

Many libraries do little to preserve high-risk or unique print material, so why should they treat digital material differently? As Maggie Jones and Neil Beagrie point out, preserving digital resources requires active management, not passive reactions to crises:

> The major implications for life-cycle management of digital resources, whatever their form or function, is the need actively to manage the resource at each stage of its life-cycle and to recognise the inter-dependencies between each stage and commence preservation activities as early as practicable. This represents a major difference with most traditional preservation, where management is largely passive until detailed conservation work is required, typically, many years after creation and rarely, if ever, involving the creator.[36]

The following list of action items is applicable to digital library collections, and may not be applicable to general digital preservation (i.e. content outside digital collections building). It is not intended to be a comprehensive digital records management or archiving strategy (although some of the items can form part of such a strategy). Some of the suggestions here will facilitate cooperative, multi-institution preservation efforts, while some will help reduce the risk to individual libraries who are currently managing their own digital assets.

Develop a policy

As stated above, a published preservation policy requires a library to focus attention on digital preservation issues and to state its commitment to addressing those issues. In addition to the guidelines and policies cited above, libraries should consult the PREMIS Working Group's report on the survey they implemented in late 2003[37] (for an overview of other institutions' preservation activities) and the RLG *Audit Checklist for the*

Certification of Trusted Digital Repositories (for a comprehensive benchmark against which to define local policies and practices).

Create and maintain the required metadata

Preservation metadata is key to all other accompanying digital preservation activities. The use of checksums for validating the integrity of files considered valuable enough to preserve is an effective and simple preservation activity that libraries should be implementing as a matter of course.

In some respects structural metadata is as important as preservation metadata, given that both are required to ensure the integrity of complex digital objects over time. METS, which provides a framework for combining descriptive, administrative, preservation and structural metadata, and even for encoding the digital resource itself, is probably the most robust vehicle for managing digital resources, particularly given its use by a number of OAIS-compliant preservation initiatives.

Use open formats

Chapter 5 (File Formats) and to a certain extent Chapter 3 (Copyright) dealt with the reasons why open file formats are desirable for master copies. Readers interested in additional perspectives on various file formats for preservation should consult the proceedings of the ERPANET Seminar on File Formats for Preservation (May 2004).[38] As suggested in Chapter 5, the US National Digital Information Infrastructure and Preservation Program's 'Sustainability of Digital Formats Planning for Library of Congress Collections' website[39] is an excellent resource on the preservation aspects of a very wide range of file formats.

Include master copies and metadata in regular backup/restore procedures

It should go without saying that an essential aspect of digital preservation is a robust data backup programme. Libraries that maintain their own servers will presumably have such a programme in place already, which should also include rigorously tested restore procedures and redundant, off-site copies.

Given the size of master files, it is often desirable to separate them from the backups of a library's other data backups. Master files that are not accessed regularly can be excluded from normal backup and restore procedures if special copies have been created for long-term storage; however, these copies should not be placed on a shelf and forgotten under the assumption that they will be useable when they are needed. If they are not tested for media degradation and integrity and moved to fresh media on a regular basis, they are being neglected and will eventually become inaccessible. It is also important to ensure that proprietary backup software is not used to create these copies, and that the backup software does not use any encryption or compression algorithms.

Refresh storage media regularly

Physical media, whether they are magnetic hard drives, magnetic tapes or optical disks, have limited lifespans. Therefore, to ensure that the files on the media remain accessible, the files should be copied to new media on a routine basis. This process is known as 'refreshing' the media.

It is difficult to determine the validity of claims by media manufacturers regarding their products' life expectancy. A comparison of recent attempts to estimate the life expectancies of magnetic tapes and various optical media by the US National Archives, the Library of Congress and the US National Institute of Standards and Technology concluded that life expectancy predictions 'serve only as a measure of general trends for media types'[40] and that in most cases environmental conditions can have a dramatic effect on the life expectancy of the media.

Periodic checks of file integrity (using checksums, for example, managed as part of preservation metadata), combined with frequent media refreshing, will lessen the likelihood of losing files due to media degradation.

Document and test disaster recovery procedures

The *Audit Checklist for the Certification of Trusted Digital Repositories* requires certified repositories to have a written disaster preparedness and recovery plan, and to test those plans regularly (metrics D3.4 and D3.5). Libraries that are not seeking certification as TDRs need to formulate disaster recovery plans (and regular testing procedures) as well. Recovery plans will vary across institutions as they should take into account the likelihood of local risks; for example, some sites are more prone to flooding, and others to earthquakes. Such plans and testing procedures are not specific to libraries that create digital collections – any library that manages its own operational records will presumably have a disaster preparedness and recovery plan in place.

Summary: making decisions about digital preservation

Preserving digital content presents problems that cannot be addressed casually or passively. Therefore, it is essential that libraries develop a comprehensive preservation policy that addresses institutional responsibilities, compliance with the OAIS Reference Model and other open preservation standards, and disaster recovery protocols. This institutional-level commitment must be demonstrated with practical actions such as the use of open file formats, the use and maintenance of effective preservation metadata, and rigorous media refreshing routines. Planning documents for each new collection should explicitly reference the library's digital preservation policy, both to create measurable outcomes for project evaluation and also to reinforce the notion that digital preservation must take place within the content's overall life cycle, not as an afterthought.

Further reading

Alemneh, D.G., Hastings, S.K. and Hartman, C.N. (2002) 'A Metadata approach to preservation of digital resources: the University of North Texas Libraries' experience' *First Monday* 7:8. Available at *http://firstmonday.org/issues/issue7_8/alemneh/*
Even though this article pre-dates both the National Library of New Zealand and PREMIS preservation metadata specifications, this case study at the University of North Texas illustrates many of the issues that any library undertaking a digital preservation programme will face. Of particular interest is the brief description of the metadata creation workflow for the government information web pages being preserved at the University of North Texas.

Cornell University Library. 'Digital preservation management: implementing short-term strategies for long-term problems'. Available at *http://www.library.cornell.edu/iris/tutorial/dpm/*

This tutorial (winner of the 2004 Society of American Archivists' Preservation Publication Award) contains an informative (and fairly sophisticated) timeline, section quizzes, a 'Chamber of horrors' illustrating obsolete media, 'Did you know?' sidebars that incorporate unusual examples, resource lists, exercises and a glossary. Overall, this tutorial is very engaging and thorough.

Hixson, C. (2005) 'When just doing it isn't enough: the University of Oregon takes stock', *RLG DigiNews* 9:6. Available at *http://www.rlg. org/en/page.php?Page_ID=20865#article1*

This reassessment of the University of Oregon Libraries' digital collection building programme should serve as a frank reality check for libraries starting out or still early on in their own programmes. The author even includes URLs to archived e-mail messages to her colleagues describing a 'statement of need' to fill important gaps in their digital preservation policies. A pull-quote used in the article is a blunt warning to other libraries: 'The Oregon model of "just do it" is about to do us in.'

Jones, M. and Beagrie, N. (2003) *Preservation Management of Digital Materials: A Handbook*. London: The British Library. Digital version available at *http://www.dpconline.org/graphics/handbook/*

Practical and comprehensive, this handbook defines the technical and legal issues that surround preserving digital content, and provides guidance at the institutional level (i.e. at the level of policies and strategies) and organisational level (i.e. at the level of creating and managing digital materials) for developing effective, sustainable preservation strategies.

Lavoie, B. and Dempsey. L. (2004) 'Thirteen ways of looking at ... digital preservation', *D-Lib Magazine* 10:7/8. *http://www.dlib.org/dlib/july04/ lavoie/07lavoie.html*

The authors provide 13 aspects of digital preservation supporting their thesis that digital preservation is moving from predominantly technical concerns toward 'a process operating in concert with the full range of services supporting digital information environments, as well as the overarching economic, legal, and social contexts.' Noteworthy are 'Digital preservation as ... an understood responsibility', 'Digital preservation as a set of agreed outcomes' and 'Digital preservation as a complement to other library services'.

National Library of Australia. PADI: Preserving Access to Digital Information. Available at *http://www.nla.gov.au/padi/*
This directory of digital preservation resources is probably the most comprehensive single site of its kind. Updated frequently, it can be searched or browsed by resource types (e.g. events, projects and discussion lists) or topics (including digitisation, national approaches and strategies). An e-mail list, padiforum-l, and a quarterly digest newsletter are also available.

Notes

1. *http://www.arl.org/preserv/digit_final.html*
2. Besser, H. (2000) 'Digital longevity', in *Handbook for Digital Projects: A Management Tool for Preservation and Access*. Edited by M. Sitts. Andover, MA: Northeast Document Conservation Center, pp. 156–62. Available at *http://www.nedcc.org/digital/ix.htm*
3. Cedars Project. *Cedars Guide to Intellectual Property Rights*, p. 5. Available at *http://www.leeds.ac.uk/cedars/guideto/ipr/guidetoipr.pdf*
4. Thibodeau, K. (2002) 'Overview of technological approaches to digital preservation and challenges in coming years', in *The State of Digital Preservation: An International Perspective*. Washington, DC: Council on Library and Information Resources, pp. 4–31. Available at *http://www.clir. org/PUBS/reports/pub107/thibodeau.html*
5. *ibid.*, p. 13.
6. *ibid.*, p. 27.
7. *http://www.si.umich.edu/CAMILEON/domesday/domesday.html*
8. Consultative Committee for Space Data Systems. (2002) *Reference Model for an Open Archival Information System (OAIS)*. Washington, DC: National Aeronautics and Space Administration. Available at *http://ssdoo.gsfc.nasa.gov/nost/wwwclassic/documents/pdf/CCSDS-650.0-B-1.pdf*
9. *http://www.leeds.ac.uk/cedars/guideto/cdap/guidetocdap.pdf*
10. *http://cwspace.mit.edu/docs/xsd/METS/SIP/profilev0p9p1/metssipv0p9p1.pdf*
11. Lavoie, B.F. (2004) 'The Open Archival Information System Reference Model: Introductory Guide'. *Digital Preservation Coalition Technology Watch Series Report 04-01*. Available at *http://www.dpconline. org/docs/lavoie_OAIS.pdf*
12. RLG. (2002) *Trusted Digital Repositories: Attributes and Responsibilities*. Mountain View, CA: RLG. Available at *http://www.rlg.org/en/pdfs/ repositories.pdf*
13. *ibid.*, p. i.
14. RLG. (2005) *An Audit Checklist for the Certification of Trusted Digital Repositories: Draft for Public Comment*. Mountain View, CA: RLG. Available at *http://www.rlg.org/en/pdfs/rlgnara-repositorieschecklist.pdf*
15. *http://www.rlg.org/en/page.php?Page_ID=20647*

16. Jantz, R. and Giarlo, M.J. (2005) 'Digital preservation: architecture and technology for trusted digital repositories', *D-Lib Magazine*, 11:6. Available at *http://www.dlib.org/dlib/june05/jantz/06jantz.html*

17. *Data Dictionary for Preservation Metadata*. Final Report of the PREMIS Working Group. Dublin and Mountain View, CA: OCLC and RLG, 2005, page 6-2.

18. *ibid.*, page 6-1.

19. Besser, H. (2000) *op. cit.*, p. 165. Available at *http://www.nedcc.org/digital/ix.htm*

20. Jones, M. and Beagrie, N. (2001) *Preservation Management of Digital Materials: A Handbook*. London: The British Library, pp. 115–16. Available at *http://www.dpconline.org/graphics/handbook/*

21. *http://www.library.cornell.edu/iris/tutorial/dpm/program/orginf.html*

22. Rieger, O.Y. (2000) 'Projects to programs: developing a digital preservation policy', in *Moving Theory into Practice: Digital Imaging for Libraries and Archives*. Edited by Anne R. Kenney and Oya Y. Rieger. Mountain View, CA: Research Libraries Group, pp. 135–52.

23. Clareson, T. (2006) 'NEDCC Survey and Colloquium explore digitization and digital preservation policies and practices', *RLG DigiNews* 10:1. Available at *http://www.rlg.org/en/page.php?Page_ID=20894#article1*

24. Kenney , A.R. and Buckley, E. (2005) 'Developing digital preservation programs: the Cornell Survey of institutional readiness, 2003-2005', *RLG DigiNews* 9:4. Available at *http://www.rlg.org/en/page.php?Page_ID=20744#article0*

25. *http://www.nla.gov.au/policy/digpres.html*

26. *http://www.columbia.edu/cu/lweb/services/preservation/dlpolicy.html*

27. *http://www.fcla.edu/digitalArchive/daInfo.htm*

28. *http://www.oclc.org/support/documentation/digitalarchive/preservationpolicy.pdf*

29. *http://www.dcc.ac.uk/tools/digital-curation-tools/*

30. *http://hul.harvard.edu/jhove/*

31. Tansley, R., Bass, M. and Smith, M. 'DSpace as an Open Archival Information System: Current Status and Future Directions'. Paper presented at the 7th European Conference on Research and Advanced Technology for Digital Libraries, Trondheim, Norway, 17–22 August 2003. Available at *http://www.ecdl2003.org/presentations/papers/session11b/Tansley/dspace-ecdl2003.ppt*

32. *http://wiki.dspace.org/DigitalPreservationToolsAndStrategies*

33. *http://lockss.stanford.edu/*

34. *http://www.metaarchive.org/index.html*

35. *http://www.solinet.net/resources/resources_templ.cfm?doc_id=3680*

36. Jones and Beagrie (2001) *op. cit.*, p. 11.

37. *http://www.oclc.org/research/projects/pmwg/surveyreport.pdf*

38. *http://www.erpanet.org/events/2004/vienna/index.php*

39. *http://www.digitalpreservation.gov/formats/*

40. Navale, V. (2005) 'Predicting the life expectancy of modern tape and optical media', *RLG DigiNews* 9:4. Available at *http://www.rlg.org/en/page.php?Page_ID=20744#article3*

12

A case study

This chapter brings together some of the most important ideas covered in *Putting Content Online* by applying them to a fictional but realistic collection of documents. The case study presented avoids questions of digital preservation and of promoting and evaluating the collection so that it may focus on the planning and technical aspects of producing a collection of digital documents. In addition, even though a large portion of the funding comes from sources external to the library, the case study does not include development of a formal funding proposal. Most of the detail presented in the book so far clusters around planning and technical issues, and the case study is intended to illustrate how those details can fit together in one particular instance. That said, some readers may be tempted to jump to this chapter in the hope that reading it will allow them to accelerate their knowledge of the process of developing a digital collection. It might have that effect as the chapter is basically an extended example, but it is not intended to be read without knowledge of the topics and issues covered in depth in the previous chapters.

As a review of the overall collection and project planning process, I will revisit the list of large-scale phases first identified in Chapter 2 and discussed again in Chapter 8. I will also expand that list by itemising the technical specifications that must be finalised, the tasks involved in planning the content production (also introduced in Chapter 8), and finally, two items under 'Execute the project' that up until this point have been conspicuously absent, creating the content and making it available to end users:

1. Define goals and scope of the collection

2. Evaluate and select source material

3. Clear permission to use the source material

4. Define project objectives and preliminary milestones

5. Determine technical specifications

    a. Metadata

    b. Search and display

    c. File formats

    d. Content management system

6. Develop workflows

7. Determine preliminary procedures based on workflows; begin project documentation

8. Determine what resources you need (hardware, software, staff)

9. Decide if you will outsource

10. Develop budget

11. Identify and acquire necessary resources

12. Finalise milestones

13. Finish project documentation

14. Hire and train staff, if necessary

15. Execute the project

    a. Create the content and metadata

    b. Add content and metadata to CMS

16. Evaluate the project

17. Evaluate the collection

This outline also acts as a checklist for the case study, as it is the closest we can get to a complete checklist for developing a digital collection and making it available to users.

Description of the collection and the project

Our fictional collection is the personal archive of a well-known Canadian environmentalist named Allen Holder. He is retiring and has decided to donate his collection to a local university, which has an Environmental Studies programme. Because the University is a charitable organisation, he will receive a tax credit based on the assessed value of his material.

The collection contains:

- 90 notebooks used on fieldtrips and site visits. These notebooks contain handwritten text and a large number of diagrams and rough sketches. Each notebook contains an average of 800 pages. The collection also contains 57 articles published in academic journals, newsletters and newspapers.
- 570 printed photographs of landscapes, shorelines, plant specimens, and
- 76 video segments making up approximately 26 hours of footage. The video is mostly on VHS tape, but some early material is on Super8 film and about 4 hours is on MiniDV tapes.

The University Library has never undertaken a digitisation project before. Therefore, it must build all of the infrastructure required to develop this online collection. Because of the importance of this donation and the donor's wishes to make the collection available online, the Library's administration has placed a high priority on this project and has committed to sharing the costs of the project. They have assembled a project team consisting of the Environmental Studies Librarian (who will chair the committee), the Systems Librarian, the Special Collections Librarian and a Cataloguer.

Two local and one national environmental organisations have formed a partnership to fund staffing for up to two summer students to do the work. To be eligible, the students must be studying Environmental Studies or related fields. The Library has agreed to contribute the project team's time, to pay for hardware for the project, and to host a CMS, preferably an open-source one. This loose partnership was formed before any of the real costs of the project were known, and was arranged with the assistance of Holder himself.

Defining the collection's goals

The first step in planning this collection is to define its goals and scope. As we saw in Chapter 2, the goals should describe the content, the intended audiences and the general ways that the planners envisage users accessing the content. The project team believes that the intended audiences would find searching or limiting by date, geographical area and subject useful, as the material spans a number of years and describes specific geographical areas. I will discuss selection of metadata schemas later. At this point the goals describe what the project team has in mind, not necessarily what the final product will be:

> The Allen Holder Archive makes available the personal papers and selected publications of Allen Holder, an environmentalist active from the early 1970s who performed research across Canada but primarily on Canada's west coast. Material in the collection includes field notebooks, photos and video footage, and also a selection of Holder's published articles. The Archive will be of interest to researchers and environmental advocates and will be searchable by date, geographical coverage and subject.

There are no plans at this point to add more content to the collection, so the team does not include in the statement of goals any indication of how the collection will grow over time.

Evaluating the content and clearing permissions

As stated above, Allen Holder donated his personal archive in the hope that it would be digitised and made broadly available. In addition, a number of partners have come together to assemble a good deal of resources in order to develop the online collection. At this point, however, the project team does not yet know if the resources that have been assembled will be sufficient to put the entire collection online. They will not know how much it will cost to complete the project until after they develop a workflow and perform tests to determine how long the project will take and how many staff will be needed. If their calculations show that they will not be able to digitise all of the source material (as is the donor's wish), they need to be prepared to establish criteria by which they can evaluate the material they will spend money on and the material they will not. Of course, because the donor has some authority over the material and the project, any criteria that the Library develops will have to meet his approval. The Library can develop its own evaluation criteria, but using criteria that have been developed and used by other libraries can be a useful method for lending some objectivity to determining which material gets digitised and which does not, if that decision has to be made.

Given the size and nature of the Holder material, the Columbia University Library evaluation criteria mentioned in Chapter 2 are appropriate:

- rareness or uniqueness
- artefactual or associational value
- importance for the understanding of the relevant subject area
- broad or deep coverage of the relevant subject area
- useful and accurate content
- information on subjects or groups that are otherwise poorly documented
- enhancement of historical strengths of the institution
- potential for enduring value in digital form[1]

Most of the material in the collection meets these criteria, but if the project team finds that limited resources require them to choose a subset of the collection for digitisation, they have a predefined set of criteria that will allow them to rank individual items.

The copyright status of material provides an important selection criterion. Brief research into the status of items in the collection shows that the donor is the copyright holder on all but 17 of the published journal articles. Permission will be sought from the copyright holders and these articles will be added later if permission is granted. The Environmental Studies Librarian and Special Collections Librarian have convinced Holder to make his material available under a Creative Commons Attribution-NonCommercial licence.

Another evaluation criterion that the project team considers is the ease with which the material can be digitised. The team and the donor decide that digitising the Super8 film is not necessary: the project team identifies the potential technical challenges involved in digitising what is now an uncommon format, and the donor supports that decision by indicating that the content of these early film segments is probably of little value compared with the other material.

After some of the material has been disqualified from the digital collection based on copyright and technical criteria, the following material remains:

- *Writings*: 90 notebooks, 40 articles
- *Photos*: 570 photographs

- *Videos*: Approximately 19 hours of video footage on VHS and 4 hours MiniDV tapes (in total, 62 separate video segments)

The project team verifies that the reduced set of source material is consistent with the collection's goals as previously defined and is satisfied that they can go ahead with the next planning phase.

The copyright status of items in this particular collection is fairly straightforward: Holder created all of the material and is the copyright owner. The only exception is the group of articles whose copyright is owned by the publishers. In projects where the copyright status of the content is more complex, it is at this stage that the work of obtaining permission to digitise and use the content takes place.

Planning the project

Once the source material has been evaluated and the Library has resolved any copyright issues, the team can move on to the next phase in planning the project.

Project objectives and milestones

At this point the team needs to define the project's objectives. To do this, they to assemble an inventory of the source material broken down by format:

Type of document	No. of documents	Total no. of items to be digitised
Notebooks	90	7860 pages
Articles	40	240 pages
(Total amount of text to be digitised)	(130)	(8100 pages)
Photos	570	570 photos
Videos	62	62 video segments, comprising 19 hours of footage including 4 hours MiniDV

This inventory is similar to the one used in Chapter 8, in which we determined the approximate number of newspaper pages to be scanned by multiplying the number of issues for each of two newspapers by the average number of pages per issue. The source material in the Allen Holder collection is in a variety of formats (text, images and video), so it is useful to group the material in terms of those types of documents, as each will probably require a different workflow. Digitising the texts will fall within one workflow, digitising the images will fall within another, and digitising the videos will fall within a third. Even though the two types of text, notebooks and articles, can be digitised using the same workflow, entering them on separate lines in this inventory assists in the team's calculations because of the differing number of pages in the two types of document. The photos are straightforward, but the 62 video segments should be described in hours of footage as the elapsed time it will take to process each one will be an important determinant of the overall cost of the project.

Using the scope of the collection, and the amount of time known to be available (4 months, i.e. the amount of time the summer students will be available), the project team has defined the following preliminary milestones:

End of month	Texts	Photos	Videos
1	33 (2025 pages)	145	16 (5 hours)
2	66 (4050 pages)	290	32 (10 hours)
3	99 (6075 pages)	435	48 (15 hours)
4	130 (8100 pages)	570	62 (19 hours)

Texts are counted in both documents and pages, and videos are counted in both segments and hours, because each of those units is useful for planning purposes. The function of this inventory is to determine the amount of work that will need to be completed during the project, and as we will see when the project team develops their workflows, describing each format in terms of the basic components that tasks are applied to is the most reliable method for determining how long the work will take.

Descriptive metadata

The first set of technical specifications that need to be finalised deals with the types and nature of the metadata that will be used in the collection.

In order to assist in determining the nature of the descriptive metadata that will be used, the project team has created simple use cases representing what it feels will be typical tasks users will want to perform. This set of use cases has identified the following tasks:

- Search and browse by author and co-author (even though virtually all works are by Allen Holder alone, some of the articles are co-authored).
- Search and browse by title of document.
- Browse and limit by date of publication or creation.
- Read a summary or abstract of the works, and search this using keywords.
- Search and browse by subject headings or descriptors.
- Search and limit by geographical location.
- Browse and limit by document genre (article, landscape photo, etc.).
- Browse and limit by document type (text, image, video).
- Search other common bibliographical elements such as journal title and publisher using keywords.

The team also feels that users would benefit from knowing the file format of the digital item before opening it, and that there is a statement indicating that Allen Holder owns the copyright to the material and that it may be used under a Creative Commons Attribution-NonCommercial licence. In addition, there is consensus that subject headings should be drawn from a suitable controlled vocabulary, and based on the recommendation of the Environmental Studies Librarian, they have chosen to use terms from three vocabularies, the Australian Department of the Environment and Heritage thesaurus,[2] Library of Congress Subject Headings, and for Canadian personal and place names, the name headings maintained by Library and Archives Canada.

All of these functional requirements can be met by a subset of elements from the unqualified Dublin Core element set. The project team selects the elements described in the table on the next page, defines local labels for use in end user and staff interfaces, and stipulates some usage notes for each element based on usage conventions as defined in the Dublin Core Library Application Profile.

The 'relation' and 'coverage' elements can be qualified when this collection's metadata is exported for use in another system if that system can support Qualified Dublin Core, such as a central database containing metadata from a group of collections, or via Open Archives Initiative Protocol for Metadata Harvesting. The qualifiers as described in the table above can be added to the metadata at time of export as all of the instances of the elements use the same qualifier.

In order for the 'date' element to be qualified for use in other systems, each instance of that element needs to be qualified because there are two possible qualifiers that can apply to each document. In order to perform this

Unqualified Dublin element	Local label	Usage notes	Repeatable
Creator	Author	See DC-LAP	Yes
Title	Title	See DC-LAP	No
Contributor	Contributor	See DC-LAP	Yes
Date	Date created	See DC-LAP: use date 'created' for unpublished material	No
Date	Date issued	See DC-LAP: use date 'issued' for published material	No
Publisher	Publisher	See DC-LAP	Yes
Relation	Source	For journal articles. See DC-LAP: all instances of this element can be qualified with 'isFormatOf' when sharing data with external systems.	No
Description	Abstract	See DC-LAP. Use only if abstract already exists.	No
Subject	Subject	Assign 1–5 subject headings/descriptors to each item; use EHT, LCSH and LAC personal and place names.	Yes
Type	DCMI Type	Use DCMI Type Vocabulary	No
Type	Genre	Use values from list of local genre categories	Yes
Format	Format	Use DCMI Internet Media Types	No
Coverage	Location	Use place names here (not in subject) from LAC name authorities. All instances of this element can be qualified with 'spatial' when sharing data with external systems.	Yes
Rights	Rights	Use value 'Copyright Allen Holder and distributed under a Creative Commons by-nc 2.5 license.'	No

per-instance qualification, the CMS will need to be configured to distinguish between the two types of date elements. The same applies to the 'type' element, which can be qualified in two different ways, one with values from the Dublin Core Metadata Initiative Type Vocabulary[3] and the other with values from a locally maintained list of document genres. The project team would like to allow users to browse and limit searches using this element and also another list of genres selected from a locally maintained list that will be meaningful to the anticipated users of the Allen Holder Archive. This list need not be comprehensive before the creation of descriptive metadata begins. Entries can be added as needed, but granularity should not be any more specific than the ones in this preliminary list:

- Article
- Field notes
- Interview
- Landscape
- Shoreline

Descriptive metadata will be created on printed worksheets, as doing so will allow staff to make notes, changes and so on easier than if they were creating the metadata directly within the CMS. They then add descriptive metadata to the CMS when they add the PDFs, JPEGs and video files.

Administrative metadata

The administrative metadata will take the form of an Excel spreadsheet that has fields for the following information:

- Unique identifier for resource
- Copyright status of the resource
- Date(s) of digitisation
- Date(s) the resource passed final quality control
- Date(s) of creation of derivative files for use in the CMS
- Date(s) of creation of the descriptive metadata
- Date the master files making up the resource were archived, and location of the files
- A checksum for each master file, generated by a Perl script written by the Systems Libarian; in the case of the texts, for which there is one master file per page, a single comma-separated-value file is created for each text containing the checksums for all page images (with date of checksum generation, file path and checksum in each record), named after the text's identifier.

- Date the resource was made available to users

- Problems discovered through initial inspection of source document and through normal quality control checks on the files and metadata generated during project operations, including the actions taken to resolve the problems

In addition to the dates of the tasks, the initials of the person performing the tasks is to be recorded. This spreadsheet will act as a master list during content production, and the supervisor will ensure that all values are complete as part of the quality control process.

The unique identifier for each item in the collection will be used both to identify items in the master list and to serve as the basis of the filenames. The identifiers will be formed by concatenating the prefix 'holder' (to identify which collection the item belongs to) to a four-digit number that will be sequentially assigned to each item in the master list. For example, 'holder0079' identifies the 79th item in the list. The use of four positions for the serial number assumes that the collection will hold no more than 9999 items, which in this case is a safe assumption. Because the Allen Holder Archive is the first digital collection that the Library has undertaken, it does not yet have a comprehensive system for assigning identifiers that will take into account multiple collections. However, the conventions used in the Holder project are fairly simple and consistent, so creating new unique identifiers for items in this collection in the future may not be terribly difficult if it is felt that doing so is necessary. One factor that may influence any decision in the future is whether the metadata for the Holder Archive has been disseminated outside the CMS and the other locations that it is maintained in; if it has been disseminated, changing the unique identifiers may cause more problems than leaving them as they were created. The project team notes this lack of Library-wide standards as an area that they will want to explore before creating their second digital collection.

Structural metadata

Because structural metadata is related to the search and display requirements of the collection and to the master file types selected, the project team cannot finalise the structural metadata until after those requirements have been finalised. At this point they can assume that the unique identifiers will form the basis of filenames generated during the production of the content, probably using a convention such as appending indicators describing the function of the named file to the unique identifier (as illustrated in Table 9.8). The team will revisit structural metadata for this collection after it has made some decisions about the CMS and just prior to commencing work on developing the workflows.

Preservation metadata

As noted in the section on administrative metadata, staff will generate a checksum for each master file and store it in the record for each resource. These checksums will be used to verify the integrity of the master file when they are moved to new locations, migrated to new preservation formats, restored from backups, or as part of normal periodic integrity audits.

Search and display

The project team wants the collection to be simple and easy to use. Therefore, they have decided that texts will be presented as single-file PDFs, and the images will be displayed in a simple, conventional way. To make the videos easier to use, they will add simple credits to the beginning of each clip based on the author, title, date and geographical location from the metadata. As two formats for the video files will be available (QuickTime and Windows Media), the project team would like links to both to be positioned near each other on the item display page.

File formats

In accordance with best practices for the various types of documents that are in the collection, and the search and display requirements defined above, the following file formats are selected:

Document type	Master formats	Delivery formats
Text	TIFF greyscale images scanned at 300 dpi, with LZW compression	Single Adobe PDF for each document, optimised for delivery over the web
Images	TIFF 24-bit colour or greyscale images scanned at 300 dpi	JPEG images downsampled to 100 dpi
Video	MPEG-2 (4:2:2 Profile[4]); in all cases, one MPEG file is to be created, not separate video and audio files.	QuickTime and Windows Media file optimised for delivery over the web

The team has chosen 300 dpi as the resolution of the text and still images because very high quality in master files is not required – the Library intends to keep the printed documents and images in their Special Collections division and to preserve them in that format. Three hundred dots per inch greyscale provides clear representation of images in the texts and also allows for efficient use of Adobe Acrobat's OCR functions, and still images scanned at that resolution are of fairly good quality (both greyscale and colour). For the videos, digitisation is considered to be a form of preservation, as VHS tape is not generally believed to be as stable or as easy to preserve as printed documents (even photographs). Therefore, the Library has decided to digitise the videos at as high as quality as possible using open file formats. Accordingly, the team has chosen to follow the lead of the Library of Congress by using the same format stated as the preference for video at the Library of Congress's NDIPP website.[5]

Content management system

After evaluating several open-source CMSs, the project team selected Streetprint Engine[6] to host their collection. Local systems staff installed and configured a copy, and were eager to take advantage of modifying the application slightly to suit the project team's requirements. Streetprint Engine handles multiple document types, has metadata handling capabilities sufficiently flexible for this particular collection, has an OAI-PMH (Open Archives Initiative Protocol for Metadata Harvesting) data provider, and allows end users to add comments to individual items in the collection.

In total, it took local staff two days to install and configure Streetprint and to modify its default display to the specifications consistent with the project team's requirements. Streetprint's default display behaviour is to treat PDFs and videos as being 'attached' to page-image-based texts and to provide separate links to these files. The Systems Librarian, who knows how to program using the language that Streetprint is written in, modified the source code so that it displayed PDFs and video files in the same way as it displayed still images, using a generic text and movie icon, respectively, instead of a thumbnail image in browse, search results and full record web pages.

Streetprint's OAI-PMH functionality is highly desirable to the project team because they want to distribute their collection's descriptive metadata as widely as possible. OAI-PMH, combined with use of the unqualified Dublin Core element set (and optionally qualifying some elements), is a standards-based, effective mechanism for increasing access to metadata. Streetprint's user commenting features are seen as a way of both encouraging user interaction with the collection and as a tool for gauging the impact of the collection as expressed in users' comments.

Structural metadata revisited

Before moving on to workflows, the project team needs to finalise the conventions for structural metadata. The ways in which the files that make up the digital versions of the item in the collection fit together are determined by the file formats selected for master and distribution copies of those resources. In the case of the Allen Holder Archive, the project team has chosen to digitise the texts as individual page images and then combine them to form PDFs for distribution over the web. Therefore, structural metadata will be required to indicate the order in which the page images need to be ordered to reflect the structure of the original document. Because each page image is a separate file, we can use simple file naming techniques to represent that order. Each photograph and each video segment will consist of single files, so although there is no need to incorporate structural metadata into the names of files for these documents, the filenames should act as unique identifiers relating the documents to the collection as a whole.

The filenaming conventions used in this project are as documented below:

Component	Base name	Sequence number	File type indicator	Structural segment	Extension
Values	holder	0000–9999	m = master p = presentation t = thumbnail	000–999	.tif .pdf .jpg .mpg .mov .wmv
Function	Indicates collection that file belongs to; in all cases, the basename is 'holder'	Indicates the serial number of the document	Indicates whether the file is a master version, a presentation version (i.e. for use in the CMS), or a thumbnail (for use in search results, browse lists, and record displays for images)	For textual documents, indicates the position of the page image in the text. Used only in page image masters (for use in the CMS, all page images are assembled into a single PDF file)	The file's extension

Some examples of filenames that illustrate the filenaming conventions include:

	Texts	Images	Videos
Examples with sequence number	holder0348p.pdf	holder0521m.tif holder0521t.jpg holder0521p.jpg	Holder0024m.mpg Holder0024p.mov
Examples with structural indicator	holder0348m125.tif holder0348m126.tif holder0348m127.tif	n/a (image documents use only one file)	n/a (video documents use only one file)

Note that the combination of file type indicator (m, p or t) and the file's extension ensure a unique filename for each master and presentation version (and in the case of images, of the thumbnail version) of each file. Also, the structural segment is only used for master versions of the textual documents' page images, and is not used in versions that are presented to the end user in the CMS.

Another method for managing structural metadata for the texts would be to store the sequence order in a database rather than encoding it in the filenames. This method would be suitable if individual page images were to be presented within the CMS using a page turner. In that case, the filenames of individual page images would not determine the order that the pages should be assembled in, and the CMS would access the database to determine which image would be 'next' or 'previous' relative to the current page. For page images that are going to be assembled into a single file as is the case with the texts in the Allen Holder Archive, embedding the sequence of the page images in the filenames, as illustrated above, is a better approach because the software that will be used to combine them into a single file, Adobe Acrobat, uses filenames to determine the order the images are supposed to be assembled in.

Developing the workflows

Now that the technical specifications have been established, the project team is ready to start developing workflows for the texts, images and videos in the collection. This is an important phase in planning the project as comprehensive workflows are essential for accurate estimates of how long it will take to create the content and metadata, and for determining the resources that will be required to complete the project on schedule.

The project team applies the general workflow modelling technique introduced in Chapter 10 to each of the types of source material. Using this technique, they begin with a template that groups the tasks necessary to achieve the desired deliverables into five basic stages, and then identify specific tasks within each stage. The completed template then forms the basis for a more detailed outline of the proposed workflow.

In order to save space and keep the examples focused, the development of the workflows below moves directly from the general workflow templates to the completed outlines. In practice, each workflow would be refined by using several intermediate versions of an outline or workflow diagram (examples of refining the general template into a fully developed workflow outline are provided in Chapter 10) as it moves through the standard workflow development cycle:

1. Identify deliverables (i.e. the documents described in your project objectives, plus the various types of metadata that you have defined).

2. Identify the tasks required to produce the deliverables.

3. Identify solutions (staff roles, likely hardware and software, techniques for using the software and hardware) to operationalise the necessary tasks.

4. Identify the sequence that most efficiently implements the identified solutions.

Finally, creating a separate workflow for each type of source material requires considerable effort and may appear repetitive, but the team is aware of the risks in creating a generic workflow and adopting it for each format. Although the latter approach may prove to be satisfactory, it will probably lead to inaccurate resourcing and costing. After all, this is the Library's first digital collection, and the project team has not completed a similar project that it can use as the basis for estimating costs.

Workflow for the writings

The general workflow model for the notebooks and articles, as with the other material, begins with the 'prepare originals' stage because the collection was delivered to the Library in a set of document boxes.

Therefore, the items must be handled by the staff prior to any metadata creation:

Workflow stage	Required activity
Prepare originals	■ Remove original from document box ■ Inspect original document to see whether it will pose any problems while scanning
Create metadata	■ Create unique identifier ■ Create administrative metadata, including base filename for master version ■ Create descriptive metadata
Capture/convert	■ Scan document one page at a time and assign page-level filename to each image
Process	■ Perform quality control ■ Ensure that page images are named sequentially ■ Convert page images into Adobe PDF
Store	■ Run script to create checksums ■ Copy masters to archive drive ■ Add PDF to CMS

After developing several intermediate versions of the outline, the project team has arrived at the following version of the workflow:

- Remove original from document box
    - Create unique identifier and add to administrative metadata
    - Inspect original document to see whether it will pose any problems while scanning
    - If found, make note in administrative metadata
- Create descriptive metadata on worksheets
- Scan document
    - Perform test scan
    - After scanner settings have been established, scan documents one page at a time in to TIFF files and assign page-level filename to each image
- Perform quality control
    - (Supervisor) Inspect sample of TIFF files

- – Ensure that page images are named sequentially
- – If they are not, note problem in log
- ■ Convert page images into Adobe PDF
- ■ Run script to create checksums on master images, producing delimited file named after the unique identifier for the document
- ■ Copy masters to archive drive
- ■ Copy checksum file to project folder
- ■ Add descriptive metadata and PDF to CMS
  - – (Supervisor) Perform quality control on item in CMS
  - – If no problems, approve for viewing by end users

Notice that in the fully developed outline, the creation of administrative metadata is represented as a subtask of 'Remove original from document box'. This is legitimate: the purpose of the template is to identify the most common tasks that typically need to be performed in most digitisation projects, while the fully developed outline is a sequential representation of the tasks the project team has identified as being necessary to produce the deliverables. Development of a practical, efficient workflow is the goal, not preserving integrity of the initial template.

This workflow defines two roles, technician and supervisor. As stated in Chapter 10, identifying roles at this point is done merely to define the staff who are likely to be required to perform the work. Precise estimations of required staff resources will be completed later. Separate scanning staff and metadata creation staff are not identified at this point because the project team feels that there is no need to separate these roles. The staff doing all of the work will be Environmental Studies students who will both perform the digitisation and create the metadata.

Workflow for the photos

The general workflow model template for the photos differs from the template for the writings in that each image document consists of only one file. Consequently, there is no need to assign page-level filenames incorporating the structural segment (the three-digit number indicating the position of the page image in the text). In addition, the processing stage for the photos differs from the processing stage for the texts in that each photo only has one corresponding image file:

Workflow stage	Required activity
Prepare originals	■ Remove original from document box ■ Inspect original document to see whether it will pose any problems while scanning
Create metadata	■ Create unique identifier ■ Create administrative metadata, including filename for master version ■ Create descriptive metadata
Capture/convert	■ Scan photo and assign filename to master copy of image
Process	■ Perform quality control ■ Create thumbnail and JPEG versions
Store	■ Save masters to archive drive ■ Run script to create checksum, and add to admin metadata ■ Copy masters to archive drive ■ Add images to CMS

A refined version of the workflow is:

- Remove original from document box
    - Create unique identifier and add to administrative metadata
    - Inspect original document to see whether it will pose any problems while scanning
    - If found, make note in administrative metadata
- Create descriptive metadata on worksheets
- Scan photo
    - Perform preview of image
    - After scanner settings have been established, scan image and assign filename to master copy
- Perform quality control
    - (Supervisor) Inspect TIFF file
    - Ensure that file is named properly
    - Note any problems in log

- Create thumbnail and JPEG versions, ensuring that they are named properly
- Save masters to archive drive
- Run script to create checksum, and add to admin metadata
- Copy master to archive drive
- Add descriptive metadata and presentation mages to CMS
  - (Supervisor) Perform quality control on item in CMS
  - If no problems, approve for viewing by end users

The tasks required to digitise the photos and create the required metadata are fairly straight forward. Two significant differences between this workflow and the one for the writings are (1) that each photo requires only one image file, so verifying the sequence of the page images is eliminated, and (2) the checksum value for the master TIFF file is recorded in the administrative metadata, not the name of the file produced by the checksum script (this file is only created for the writings).

Workflow for the VHS videos

The videos pose several challenges. First, the project team has realised that the VHS videos and MiniDV videos will require different workflows. The team did not break out the two formats in their initial inventory of source material, but while thinking about the workflow for the videos came to the conclusion that processing the two formats will involve enough differences that each format needs it own workflow.

Second, the project team, in consultation with the Library administration, decides that they do not want to digitise the VHS videos themselves because they do not want to invest in the hardware necessary to create high-quality master video formats. They are willing to buy some software and do the processing, however, because local staff will be creating the descriptive metadata and adding some of this metadata to the beginning of each video segment. Consequently, the team has developed the following workflow template for VHS videos:

Workflow stage	Required activity
Prepare originals	■ Remove original from document box ■ Inspect original document to see whether it will pose any problems while being played

Workflow stage	Required activity
Create metadata	<ul><li>Create unique identifier</li><li>Create administrative metadata, including filename for master version</li><li>Create descriptive metadata</li></ul>
Capture/convert	<ul><li>Send to vendor</li></ul>
Process	<ul><li>Obtain digital versions from vendor</li><li>Perform quality control</li><li>Create descriptive metadata by skimming video</li><li>Add credits to start of segment</li><li>Create web versions</li></ul>
Store	<ul><li>Save masters to archive drive</li><li>Run script to create checksum, and add to admin metadata</li><li>Copy masters to archive drive</li><li>Add web versions to CMS</li></ul>

The refined version is:

- Remove VHS tape from document box
  - Create unique identifier
  - Inspect tape to see whether it will pose any problems while being played
  - If found, make note in administrative metadata
- Prepare tapes for shipping to vendor
  - Print admin metadata on sheet
  - Put sheet in envelope with tape
- Send all tapes to vendor
- (Vendor) Digitise the video
- Get tapes and digital versions from vendor
- (Supervisor) Perform quality control on digital versions
  - Ensure that file is named properly
  - Ensure master video is of acceptable quality
- Create descriptive metadata by skimming video
- Add credits to start of segment
- Create web versions
  - Perform quality check on web versions

- Save masters to archive drive
- Run script to create checksum, and add to admin metadata
- Copy master to archive drive
- Add descriptive metadata and presentations versions to CMS
    - (Supervisor) Perform quality control on item in CMS
    - If no problems, approve for viewing by end users

The project team has decided that the best way to ship basic information about each tape to the vendor is to print it out and package it with each tape. The most important piece of information that the library staff need to supply for each tape is the filename that is to be used for the digital version of each video segment. Defining this as part of administrative metadata will ensure that files coming back from the vendor will be easy to reintegrate into the Library's workflow and will reduce the likelihood of errors resulting from inaccurate unique identifiers.

Quality control inspections of the master files are done as soon as they come back from the vendor, so that any problems can be addressed before additional work is performed. One unusual aspect of this workflow is that it applies to both individual video tapes and to the entire group of VHS tapes: the 'Send all tapes to vendor' task applies to all of the tapes, not to an individual tape. Tasks leading up to that point apply to individual tapes, and tasks following the return of the tapes and digital files to the Library apply to individual files. The Library and vendor have agreed that it would be best for all of the tapes to be digitised at the same time instead of over a period of time. The implications of this decision for project planning are that the tasks that precede sending the tapes to the vendor need to be performed on all tapes early in the project, and the tasks that apply to the digital versions of the tapes need to be performed after the files are delivered by the vendor. These requirements are not consistent with the milestones defined earlier, but as long as the project staff are aware of this exception, they will be able to plan around it. For example, production of the writings, images and MiniDV material can move ahead of schedule while the videos are being digitised by the vendor.

Workflow for the digital videos

As stated above, the MiniDV video segments need their own workflow, primarily because they are not being processed by a vendor but are being processed locally. The template for this material is:

Workflow stage	Required activity
Prepare originals	■ Remove tape from document box ■ Copy original from tape to hard drive
Create metadata	■ Create unique identifier ■ Create administrative metadata, including filename for master version
Capture/convert	■ Create master copy by converting to MPEG-2
Process	■ Perform quality control ■ Create descriptive metadata by skimming video ■ Add crerdits to start of segment ■ Create web versions
Store	■ Save masters to archive drive ■ Run script to create checksum, and add to admin metadata ■ Copy master to archive drive ■ Add web vresions to CMS

The refined workflow outline is:

■ Remove MiniDV tape from document box
 – Create unique identifier
 – Inspect tape to see whether it will pose any problems while being played
 – If found, make note in administrative metadata
■ Copy contents of tape to directory named after unique identifier on hard drive of video workstation
■ Convert files to MPEG-2 masters
■ Perform quality control on digital versions
 – Ensure that file is named properly
 – (Supervisor) Ensure master video is of acceptable quality
■ Create descriptive metadata by skimming video
■ Add credits to start of segment
■ Create web versions
 – Perform quality check on web versions

- Save masters to archive drive
- Run script to create checksum, and add to admin metadata
- Copy master to archive drive
- Add descriptive metadata and presentations versions to CMS
  - (Supervisor) Perform quality control on item in CMS
  - If no problems, approve for viewing by end users

The conversion from MiniDV tape to the master format is done by plugging a MiniDV camera into a computer and using software to save the video into MPEG-2, so no specialised hardware is required.

A high-level view of the workflows

Having four separate workflows suggests that the project will be fairly complex to plan and manage. Therefore, the project team decides to draw a simple, high-level diagram that will (1) assist them in determining what tasks can be shared across workflows and therefore documented accordingly, (2) highlight important differences in the workflows and (3) show where the quality control activity occurs across the four workflows:

Writings	Photos	MiniDV Videos	VHS Videos
Prepare document and create administrative metadata	Prepare document and create administrative metadata	Prepare document and create administrative metadata	Prepare document and create administrative metadata
Create descriptive metadata	Create descriptive metadata	Convert MiniDV to master file format	Send tapes to vendor
Scan	Scan	Perform quality checks on masters	Perform quality checks on masters
Perform quality checks on masters	Perform quality checks on masters	Create descriptive metadata	Create descriptive metadata
Process	Process	Process	Process
Store	Store	Store	Store
Perform quality checks on distribution copies in CMS			
Make available to users			

The project team identifies this third goal because the team suspects that quality control may prove to be a bottleneck in the production process, as there will only be one person, the Environmental Studies librarian, performing that task. Below is a version of the drawing that represents quality control checks performed by the supervisor differently than the other tasks (with the checks shown as ovals instead of rectangles):

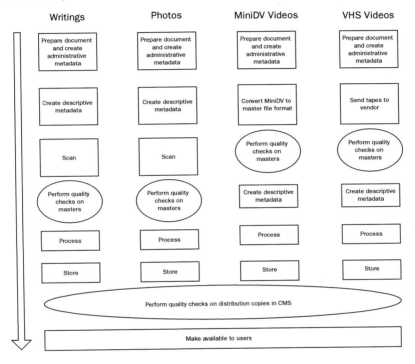

The isolation of the suspected bottleneck is an example of how a workflow diagram can be created to emphasise particular aspects of a project in ways that textual outlines may not highlight. Although the textual outlines indicate that there are two sets of quality control inspections in each workflow (of the masters and of the versions created for the web), diagramming all of the workflows together highlights the bottlenecks in a way that could be used to lobby for additional staff to assist with the inspections, for example. As stated in Chapter 10, diagrams are intended to assist in the workflow modelling process. The project team could develop additional diagrams to serve other purposes if the need arose, or simply if they wanted to experiment with other ways of representing the workflows as defined in the textual outlines. If some of those experiments provided insights into how to improve the workflows, the team would modify their outlines accordingly.

In addition to showing where the quality control checks form potential bottlenecks, the diagram illustrates how the first set of tasks (preparing the source material and creating an administrative metadata record) is common to all four workflows, and how the last two sets of tasks (processing the files and storing them in the archive drive and the CMS) are also common. Although the processing set of tasks appears across all four workflows in the diagram, in practice there will be a considerable difference in how each source material type is processed, so the diagram is misleading in that particular instance. If the project team wanted to improve this diagram, in order to use it in a presentation to library administration for example, they would do well to add some detail to the processing set of tasks to clarify this aspect of the workflows.

Note that the diagram does not correspond to every task in the workflow outlines; rather, it illustrates major groups of tasks in much the same way that the initial workflow templates did. The groups of tasks it uses, however, are derived from the fully developed workflow outlines, not the preliminary templates.

Staffing

As stated in Chapter 8, staff roles are defined by grouping similar tasks in the workflow together so that job descriptions can be developed and eventually people hired.

During development of the workflow outlines, the project team explicitly identified the roles of supervisor and vendor. All other tasks will be performed by the summer students they will be hiring for the project. There is no need to distinguish between 'metadata creator' and 'digitisation technician' roles in this case because the project team has already decided that the same people will perform all the work. Of course, the 'vendor' role will not be developed into a job description, but it is important to identify all agents or parties who are part of the project, and in particular, who will be performing specific tasks identified in the workflow.

Documentation and procedures

Now that workflows have been developed, the project team needs to move on to developing detailed procedures for performing the tasks identified in the workflows. All four members take part in the documentation effort – the Environmental Studies Librarian is responsible for documenting the use of the CMS, the Cataloguer for documenting the creation of descriptive metadata, and the Systems Librarian for documenting the digitisation activities (including converting the MiniDV video to MPEG), for creating the administrative metadata and filenames, and for moving the master files to the archive drive. The Special Collections Librarian is responsible for documenting the inspection and handling of the source material and for overall coordination of the documentation.

The project team has chosen to use a wiki for the procedural documentation, primarily because a wiki will allow all staff to update the documentation when necessary. The particular wiki platform they choose has a discussion forum and 'printer-friendly' link on each page, and also has an updating feature that e-mails staff when a page has been added or modified. A staff member who is not part of the project team has volunteered to assist with adding the documentation to the wiki before the students start their jobs.

One logistical problem must be overcome first, however: the team does not have access to the digitisation hardware and software that will be used during the project. To overcome this obstacle, the team performs its scanning trials on a flatbed scanner that the Library already owns. This machine is a general-purpose scanner but is suitable for scanning photographs and for performing face-down scanning of Holder's notebooks. The Library also has a copy of Adobe Acrobat that is used to prepare PDF versions of documents for the Library's website. The only software that they do not have access to at this point is the video editing application, but after some research and phone calls to various people on campus who have experience editing digital video, they assemble enough information on how long their tasks should take to make them confident that their figures are as sound as they can be at this point.

Budgeting

After developing reasonably detailed procedural documentation based on the workflows, the project team starts to plan the trial runs that will allow them to determine how long it takes to do the work, and therefore what the staff costs are likely to be.

The team has assembled the following spreadsheet documenting how long it takes to perform the required tasks. The figures show how long it takes, on average, to perform the tasks on each document. The spreadsheet includes the technician's time only (i.e. not the vendor's or the supervisor's):

	Texts	Photos	VHS videos	MiniDV videos
Digitisation	60 min	5 min	n/a (done by vendor)	n/a (conversion is performed in during processing)
Processing	15 min	5 min	20 min (does not include time to create descriptive metadata)	40 min (includes conversion time but not time to create descriptive metadata)
Creating descriptive metadata	10 min	7 min	20 min	20 min
Creating other metadata	5 min	5 min	5 min	5 min
Adding documents and descriptive metadata to CMS	10 min	10 min	10 min	10 min
Total time	100 min	32 min	55 min	75 min

Using the average times to complete each task, the project team calculates the total number of hours of work that will be required to complete the entire project, and, knowing the wage the University pays for the type of work the students will be doing, the total cost for their work. Times (per document and totals) are rounded up to one decimal place:

	Texts	Photos	VHS videos	MiniDV videos
Student assistant time required	100 min	32 min	55 min	75 min
No. of documents	130	570	52	10
Number of hours to complete all documents	1.7 h × 130 documents = 221 h	0.6 h × 570 documents = 342 h	1 h × 52 documents = 52 h	1.3 h × 10 documents = 13 h
Student assistant wage (inc. benefits)	$18.36 × 221 h = $4057.56	$18.36 × 342 h = $6279.12	$18.36 × 52 h = $954.72	$18.36 × 13 h = $238.68

The total number of hours required to perform the work is 628, and the total amount required to pay the student technicians' wages at the standard rate the University pays for the type of work involved is $11,530.08. These calculations only show the students' time and costs – they do not include the supervisor's time or the time that other members of the project team have devoted to the project. These other staff costs are legitimate expenses even if they are 'in kind'; for the current project, the project team does not account for them, but they may need to if the Library administration required tracking project costs in more detail, or if the funders required evidence of how much money the Library was contributing to the project.

Defining required resources

With estimates of how much work will be necessary to complete the project and how much that work will cost, the project team now has to itemise what resources it will need. In addition to staff, these resources include funds to have the VHS tapes digitised, and funds for hardware and software. The project team will also have to estimate how much physical space will be required to perform the work.

First, the project team calculates the number of work hours per day required to complete the project by using the following formula: the number of hours per day required to complete all work equals the total number of hours required to complete all work divided by the number of days available. Represented in a spreadsheet, the calculations are:

Position title	Hours required to complete all work	Days available	Hours per day required to complete all work
Technician	628	15 weeks – 1 statutory holiday = 74 days	8.5
Supervisor (at 50% of technicians' time)	314	74	4.3

Then, they determine the number of positions needed to complete work within the given timelines, using this formula: the number of positions required to complete all work equals the number of hours per day required to complete all work divided by the number of hours in a standard work day.

Position title	Hours in standard work day (1 FTE)	Hours per day required to complete all work	Full-time positions required to complete all work in days available (FTE)
Technician	7	8.5	1.3

As the number of full-time positions required is less than the number of students the funders are willing to pay for, the project team can decrease the number of work days and finish the project ahead of schedule. If two students work fulltime (7 hours per day, 5 days per week), they could complete the work in just under 9 weeks (628 hours of work/2 students = 314 hours of work per student; if each one can do 35 hours of work per week, they will each complete 314 hours in just under 9 weeks). The project team decides that they will plan on completing the project 12 weeks after the students begin work, in order to provide time for training and also in case unexpected delays arise. The Environmental Studies librarian has received permission to spend her entire summer on this project, but the other team members must integrate the Holder Archive activity into their regular work schedules throughout the summer.

In order to make this example complete, it is worth pointing out that if the number of full-time technician positions required exceeded the number the Library had funding for, the project team would have to find additional staff resources, either by asking for more money or by reallocating existing staff from within the Library.

Knowing that two student positions are sufficient to complete the work, work space and two computers already owned by the Library are set aside for the students. The Library is willing to purchase two flatbed scanners to use on this project (and for use on future digitisation projects). The following software will also need to be purchased in order for the students to perform their jobs:

- Adobe Acrobat (one copy for each student)
- Image editing software (one copy for each student)
- Video editing software (one copy)

The Systems Librarian calculates that the following amounts of disk space will need to be reserved for the master versions of the files produced during this project:

Document type	Master formats	Amount of content	Estimated file space necessary for masters (uncompressed)	Estimated file space necessary for masters (compressed)
Text	TIFF page greyscale images scanned at 300 dpi	8100 pages	8 MB/page = 65 GB	1.5 MB/page = 12.2 GB
Images	TIFF 24-bit colour or greyscale images scanned at 300 dpi	570 images	8 MB/image = 4.6 GB	2 MB/image = 1.2 GB
Video	MPEG-2, 4:2:2 Profile	19 h @ 2 GB/h	n/a	2 GB/h = 38 GB

The images will probably take up less space than predicted in this table as many of the photos are black and white, and these will be scanned into greyscale images, not full colour, which produces smaller image files. The total estimated disk space adds up to less than 55 GB, which is well within the amount of space available on the Library's file server. The Systems Librarian confirms that there is sufficient space on the web server running the CMS to store the distribution versions of the master files.

The Library does not issue a Request for Proposal for the digitisation of the VHS videos because the University's Financial Services department does not require them to do so if the total cost of the service will be below $50,000 (which will certainly be the case as they do not have that much money to spend anyway). Instead, they find several local digital video production services and send each one a list of requirements for the work, including the number of tapes, the number of segments, the duration of all of the videos, the file naming requirements (based on the segment's unique identifier as defined in the administrative metadata specification), the file format requirements, the preferred delivery mechanism (on an external hard drive that the Library will provide), and the contact information of three clients the Library can contact. The project team sends quotation requests to four companies, and after evaluating the responses of the three that met the requirements, selected the company that indicated it could deliver the digitised video within two weeks for a cost of $3,260. The Library has agreed to cover this cost.

Acquiring hardware and software

The Library procures a general-purpose flatbed scanner and a high-speed document scanner with an automatic document feeder. The total cost for this hardware is approximately $4,700. Software for the project cost just over $600.

Estimated project budget

Before commencing with hiring the students, the Library's administration asks the project team to prepare a brief budget, which is shown below:

Cost	Source of funds	Amount
Student technicians	Funders (cash)	$11,530.08
VHS digitisation	Funders (cash)	$3,260.87
Hardware and software	Library (cash)	$5,340.12
Library staff (Environmental Studies librarian)	Library (in kind)	$23,304.26
Total cash costs		$20131.07
Total in kind costs		$23,304.26
Total		$43,435.33

Library staff other than the Environmental Studies librarian are not included, as the other members of the project team have not been granted any relief time to work on the project. In addition, computers used by the student are not included, although they could be declared as in-kind contributions if the funders wanted a more complete accounting of the resources the Library is committing to the project.

At the request of the Library's administration, the project team prepares a presentation that is delivered at a meeting of the donor, the funders, a member of the University's Environmental Studies Programme and relevant Library staff. At this meeting, the team receives approval to start spending funds.

Final preparations

Several outstanding tasks remain before work can start. First, the project team finalises the production milestones, based on 12 weeks of work:

End of month	Texts	Photos	Videos
1	45 (2,700 pages)	190	21 (7 h)
2	90 (5,400 pages)	380	42 (14 h)
3	130 (8,100 pages)	570	62 (19 h)

Next, the team must finish the project documentation. This is not a huge task because the team developed detailed procedural documentation during their workflow trials. The team works on completing the documentation while they perform the final task in preparation for starting work, hiring students.

Executing the project: doing the work

The first week of the project is taken up with refining the procedures and documentation, arranging the physical work space, and training the students in scanning and creating the various types of metadata. During this week the supervisor works through all of the tasks with the two students, adjusting the procedures and, with the assistance of Library Systems staff, troubleshooting a small number of technical glitches that occur. An area that needs improvement is the way in which entries were recorded in the problem logs, which the supervisor and students resolve after a short period of trying different methods.

One issue that the supervisor pays close attention to as the staff moves into production is performing quality control checks promptly. In order to address earlier concerns that she would not be able to keep up with the students' output, she devotes the first hour of each day to inspecting the previous day's output. This routine works well in general, apart from the occasional need to spend more than an hour each day documenting unanticipated quality control issues.

Overall, the project unfolds more or less as planned. Work on the texts and images matches the defined milestones with reasonable exceptions. The work required on the VHS videos to prepare them for shipping to the vendor is performed as early as possible to ensure that the files are delivered to the Library with plenty of time to process them before the end of the summer. Careful monitoring of progress, regular staff meetings and prompt attention to issues as they come up keep the project on track. Several problems identified during the project are worth mentioning:

- The digital movie camera that the students were using to transfer the MiniDV content from the tapes suffered a serious malfunction. It was replaced with another camera borrowed from a Library staff member and all of the videos were transferred successfully.

- Several of the MPEG files delivered by the company digitising the VHS videos could not be opened by the student technicians. The company resolved the problem and sent new files to the Library.

- One student had to take four consecutive days off. To compensate for this, the other student performed eight hours of overtime work during that week, but losing three days' worth of work did not adversely impact the project's milestones.

- After three weeks into the project, the students and supervisor agreed that using a spreadsheet to record problems was not working well, mainly due to the spreadsheet program's inability to allow more than one person to modify the file simultaneously. To address this issue, the Systems Librarian created a simple database using an open-source CMS that allowed multiple staff to create and update problem log entries efficiently, and that incorporated better mechanisms for creating reports of open and resolved entries.

Evaluating the project

During the project, the supervisor, with the support of the rest of the project team, ensures that defined milestones are met, that the quality of the digital content and metadata remains consistent, and that staff and vendor costs remain within expected limits. Keeping on top of these aspects of the project helps the team prepare a positive interim report for the Library's administration, the donor and the funders. The report they deliver after the project is completed is also positive, and includes a number of recommendations for planning and executing future digitisation projects. The most substantial is that the Library strike a working group to develop descriptive, administrative, structural and preservation metadata standards, and to provide guidance when planning new collections and to promote awareness within the Library of important metadata standards being developed and used nationally and internationally.

Notes

1. *http://www.columbia.edu/cu/libraries/digital/criteria.html*
2. *http://www.deh.gov.au/about/deh-thesaurus.html*
3. *http://www.dublincore.org/documents/dcmi-type-vocabulary/*
4. *http://www.digitalpreservation.gov/formats/fdd/fdd000034.shtml*
5. *http://www.digitalpreservation.gov/formats/fdd/fdd000028.shtml*
6. *http://streetprint.org*

Index